Data Structures & Algorithms

in Swift

By Kelvin Lau & Vincent Ngo

Data Structures & Algorithms in Swift

Kelvin Lau & Vincent Ngo

Notice of Rights

Notice of Liability

Trademarks

ISBN: 978-1-950325-40-5

Table of Contents

Book License

By purchasing *Data Structures & Algorithms in Swift*, you have the following license:

- You are allowed to use and/or modify the source code in *Data Structures & Algorithms in Swift* in as many apps as you want, with no attribution required.
- You are allowed to use and/or modify all art, images and designs that are included in *Data Structures & Algorithms in Swift* in as many apps as you want, but must include this attribution line somewhere inside your app: "Artwork/images/designs: from *Data Structures & Algorithms in Swift*, available at www.raywenderlich.com".
- The source code included in *Data Structures & Algorithms in Swift* is for your personal use only. You are NOT allowed to distribute or sell the source code in *Data Structures & Algorithms in Swift* without prior authorization.
- This book is for your personal use only. You are NOT allowed to sell this book without prior authorization, or distribute it to friends, coworkers or students; they would need to purchase their own copies.

All materials provided with this book are provided on an "as is" basis, without warranty of any kind, express or implied, including but not limited to the warranties of merchantability, fitness for a particular purpose and noninfringement. In no event shall the authors or copyright holders be liable for any claim, damages or other liability, whether in an action of contract, tort or otherwise, arising from, out of or in connection with the software or the use or other dealings in the software.

All trademarks and registered trademarks appearing in this guide are the properties of their respective owners.

Before You Begin

This section tells you a few things you need to know before starting, such as what you'll need for hardware and software, where to find the project files for this book and more.

To follow along with this book, you'll need the following:

- **A Mac running the latest macOS**. This is so you can install the latest version of the required development tool: Xcode.
- **Xcode 13 or later** Xcode is the main development tool for writing code in Swift. You need Xcode 13 at a minimum, since that version includes Swift 5.5. You can download the latest version of Xcode for free from the Mac App Store, here: apple.co/1FLn51R.

If you haven't installed the latest version of Xcode, be sure to do that before continuing with the book. The code covered in this book depends on Swift 5.5 and Xcode 13 — you may get lost if you try to work with an older version.

Book Source Code & Forums

Where to download the materials for this book

The materials for this book can be cloned or downloaded from the GitHub book materials repository:

- https://github.com/raywenderlich/alg-materials/tree/editions/4.0

Forums

We've also set up an official forum for the book at https://forums.raywenderlich.com/c/books/data-structures-algorithms-swift. This is a great place to ask questions about the book or to submit any errors you may find.

"To my team, family, and friends."

— *Kelvin Lau*

"To my friends and family who I know will never read this book."

— *Vincent Ngo*

About the Authors

Kelvin Lau is an author of this book. Kelvin is a physicist turned Swift iOS Developer. While he's currently entrenched with iOS development, he often reminisces of his aspirations to be part of the efforts in space exploration. Outside of programming work, he's an aspiring entrepreneur and musician. You can find him on Twitter: @kelvinlauKL (https://twitter.com/kelvinlauKL)

Vincent Ngo is an author of this book. A software developer by day at a growing startup, and an iOS/Flutter enthusiast by night, he believes that sharing knowledge is the best way to learn and grow as a techie. Vincent starts every morning with a Cà phê sữa đá (Vietnamese coffee) to fuel his day. He enjoys playing golf, meditating, and watching animated movies. You can find him on Twitter: @vincentngo2 (https://twitter.com/vincentngo2)

About the Editors

Steven Van Impe is the technical editor of this book. Steven is a computer science author and lecturer at the University College of Ghent, Belgium. You can find Steven on Twitter as @pwsbooks (https://twitter.com/pwsbooks).

Ray Fix is the final pass editor of this book. During the day, Ray works on next-generation microscopes made for iPad at Discover Echo Inc. in San Diego, California. He enjoys learning new things and is excited about math, data, visualization, machine learning and computer vision. Swift is his problem-solving language of choice and he has been using it and teaching others about it since its 2014 public release. Twitter: @rayfix (https://twitter.com/rayfix).

Acknowledgments

We'd like to acknowledge the efforts of the following contributors to the Swift Algorithm Club GitHub repo (https://github.com/raywenderlich/swift-algorithm-club), upon whose work portions of this book are based.

Matthijs Hollemans, the original creator of the Swift Algorithm Club. Matthijs contributed many of the implementations and corresponding explanations for the various data structures and algorithms in the Swift Algorithm Club that were used in this book, in particular: Graph, Heap, AVL Tree, BST, Breadth First Search, Depth First Search, Linked List, Stack & Queue, Tree, Selection Sort, Bubble Sort, Insertion Sort, Quick Sort, Merge Sort, and Heap Sort. Matthijs spends much of his time now in machine learning. Learn more at http://machinethink.net.

We'd also like to thank the following for their contributions to the repo:

- **Donald Pinckney**, Graph https://github.com/donald-pinckney
- **Christian Encarnacion**, Trie and Radix Sort https://github.com/Thukor
- **Kevin Randrup**, Heap https://github.com/kevinrandrup
- **Paulo Tanaka**, Depth First Search https://github.com/paulot
- **Nicolas Ameghino**, BST https://github.com/nameghino
- **Mike Taghavi**, AVL Tree
- **Chris Pilcher**, Breadth First Search

"As an iOS developer, should I learn about algorithms and data structures?" This question comes up a lot in the online discussion groups that I hang out in. Let me attempt to answer that question by sharing some of my own experiences as a professional developer.

Like many people who got into programming as a hobby, I am mostly self-taught and don't have a formal computer science background. Over the years, I may have picked up the occasional tidbit of knowledge, but I never had a solid foundation in the theory behind algorithms and data structures.

Was this a problem? Nope, most of the time I was just fine. As modern day developers, using the data structures provided by the standard library is more than enough for much of the software we write. Swift's arrays and dictionaries go a long way.

However... there have been times when I was not able to write the software I wanted to, either because I did not understand how to approach the problem or because I did not understand how to make a solution that was fast enough.

Whenever I ran into such a programming roadblock, I felt that maybe I wasn't smart enough to be a software developer after all — but really, I just lacked the tools needed to solve these problems. With a better vocabulary of algorithms and data structures, I would have been able to write all the software I wanted.

Usually, my first attempt to solve an unknown problem was to use an "obvious" brute-force algorithm that tried all possible combinations. Sometimes that works well enough, but more often than not, a naïve solution like this takes days to compute and is just not feasible. (I had never heard of Big-O notation, either!)

But in most cases, there's no need to derive a solution by yourself from first principles! Often, these problems have already been solved many times before by other people, and they have well-known solutions. The trick is to understand what sort of problem you're dealing with — and that's where learning about algorithms and data structures pays off. Once you know what a problem is called, it's easy to find a solution for it.

So then, do you *need* to learn about algorithms and data structures as an iOS developer? I'd say no; you can probably solve 95% of all your programming needs without them. But at some point, you're going to get stuck on a problem where the naïve brute-force solution is not feasible. In situations like that, it's good to have an algorithms and data structures toolbox.

A few years ago, I wanted to fill this gap in my knowledge. I bought a number of algorithms books and started implementing the algorithms in Swift. Because I believe that teaching is the best way to learn, I decided to create a repo on GitHub with my own descriptions of the things I was learning about. And so the Swift Algorithm Club was born. It started receiving contributions from others almost right away, and together we've built a cool community of algorithms enthusiasts with descriptions for 100 algorithms and data structures... and counting.

Because handling the number of pull requests became too much for me to handle as a side project, I donated the code to raywenderlich.com and it found a great home there. The new maintainers of the repo, Kelvin and Vincent, have done a great job of making it the awesome resource that it is today — and now they've taken that knowledge and made it even better by turning it into this book!

If you're interested in leveling up on your algorithms and data structures, you've come to the right place. And when you're done reading this book, head on over to The Swift Algorithm Club on GitHub for even more A&DS goodness!

—Matthijs Hollemans

Section I: Introduction

The chapters in this short but essential section will motivate the study of data structures and algorithms and give you a quick rundown of the Swift standard library, whose facilities you can use as a basis for creating your own data structures and algorithms.

Chapter 1: Why Learn Data Structures & Algorithms?

By Kelvin Lau

The study of data structures is one of efficiency. Given a particular amount of data, what is the best way to store it to achieve a particular goal?

As a programmer, you regularly use various collection types, such as arrays, dictionaries and sets. These are data structures that hold a collection of data, each structure having its own performance characteristics.

As an example, consider the difference between an array and a set. Both are meant to hold a collection of elements, but searching for an element in an array takes far longer than searching for an element in a set. On the other hand, you can order the elements of an array but you can't order the elements of a set.

Data structures are a well-studied discipline, and the concepts are *language agnostic*; A data structure from C is functionally and conceptually identical to the same data structure in any other language, such as Swift. At the same time, the high-level expressiveness of Swift makes it an ideal choice for learning these core concepts without sacrificing too much performance.

Algorithms, on the other hand, are a set of operations that complete a task. This can be a sorting algorithm that moves data around to put it in order. Or it can be an algorithm that compresses an 8K picture to a manageable size. Algorithms are essential to software and many have been created to act as building blocks for useful programs.

So why should you learn data structures and algorithms?

Interviews

An important reason to keep your algorithmic skills up to par is to prepare for interviews. Most companies have at least one or two algorithmic questions to test your abilities as an engineer. A strong foundation in data structures and algorithms is the "bar" for many software engineering positions.

Work

Using an appropriate data structure is crucial when working with lots of data. Using the right algorithm plays a significant role in the performance and scalability of your software. Your mobile apps will be more responsive and have better battery life. Your server apps will be able to handle more concurrent requests and use less energy. Algorithms often include proofs of correctness that you can leverage to build better software.

Using the correct data structure also helps to provide context to the reader. As an example, you might come across a `Set` in your codebase. Immediately, you can deduce:

1. Consumers of the `Set` don't care about the order of the elements since `Set` is an **unordered** collection
2. `Set` also ensures that there are no duplicate values. You can assume consumers are working with **unique** data
3. `Set` is great for checking for value membership, so it's likely the engineer introduced a `Set` for this purpose

Once familiar with various data structures, you can extract additional context from code using data structures as "cues". This is a powerful skill that will help you understand how a piece of software works.

Self-Improvement

Knowing the strategies used by algorithms to solve tricky problems gives you ideas for improvements that you can make to your code. The Swift standard library has a small set of general-purpose collection types; they don't cover every case. And, yet, as you will see, these primitives can be used as a great starting point for building more complex and special-purpose abstractions. Knowing more data structures than just the standard array and dictionary gives you a bigger collection of tools that you can use to build your apps.

> A wise man once said: The practice of algorithms is akin to how musicians practice their scales. The more polished your foundations are, the better you will become in working with more complex pieces of software.

The goal of this book

This book is meant to be both a reference and an exercise book. If you're familiar with other books from raywenderlich.com, you'll feel right at home. Each chapter is followed by a short chapter with some challenges. The solutions to these challenges appear at the end of each of these chapters. **Do yourself a favor and make a serious attempt at solving each challenge before peeking at the solution.**

This book is divided into five sections, each covering a specific theme:

1. Introduction
2. Elementary data structures
3. Trees
4. Sorting
5. Graphs

This book is best read in chronological order, but it also works well as a reference if you want to skip around.

If you're new to the study of algorithms and data structures, you may find some of the material challenging. But, if you stick with it to the end, you will be well on the way to becoming a Swift data structures and algorithms master. Let's get started!

Chapter 2: Complexity

By Kelvin Lau

Will it scale?

This age-old question is always asked during the design phase of software development and comes in several flavors. From an architectural standpoint, scalability is how easy it is to make changes to your app. From a database standpoint, scalability is about how long it takes to save or retrieve data in the database.

For algorithms, scalability refers to how the algorithm performs in terms of execution time and memory usage as the input size increases.

When you're working with a small amount of data, an expensive algorithm may still feel fast. However, as the amount of data increases, an expensive algorithm becomes crippling. So how bad can it get? Understanding how to quantify this is an important skill for you to know.

In this chapter, you'll take a look at the Big O notation for the different levels of scalability in two dimensions–execution time and memory usage.

Time complexity

For small amounts of data, even the most expensive algorithm can seem fast due to the speed of modern hardware. However, as data increases, cost of an expensive algorithm becomes increasingly apparent. **Time complexity** is a measure of the time required to run an algorithm as the input size increases. In this section, you'll go through the most common time complexities and learn how to identify them.

Constant time

A constant time algorithm is one that has the same running time regardless of the size of the input. Consider the following:

```
func checkFirst(names: [String]) {
  if let first = names.first {
    print(first)
  } else {
    print("no names")
  }
}
```

The size of the `names` array has no effect on the running time of this function. Whether the input has ten items or 10 million items, this function only checks the first element of the array. Here's a visualization of this time complexity in a plot between time versus data size:

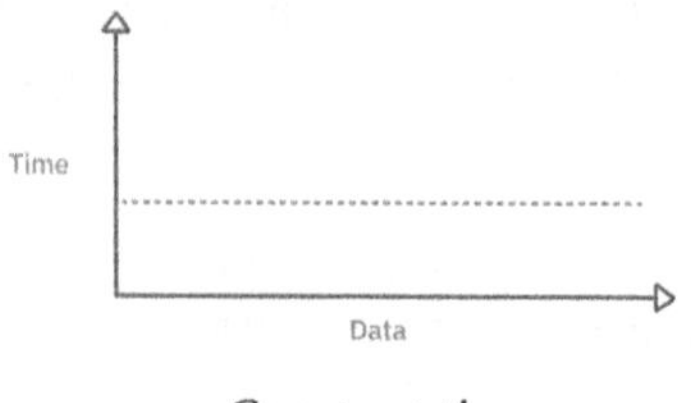

Constant time

As input data increases, the amount of time the algorithm takes does not change.

For brevity, programmers use a notation known as **Big O notation** to represent various magnitudes of time complexity. The Big O notation for constant time is $O(1)$.

Linear time

Consider the following snippet of code:

```
func printNames(names: [String]) {
  for name in names {
    print(name)
  }
}
```

This function prints out all the names in a `String` array. As the input array increases in size, the number of iterations that the `for` loop makes increases by the same amount.

This behavior is known as **linear time** complexity:

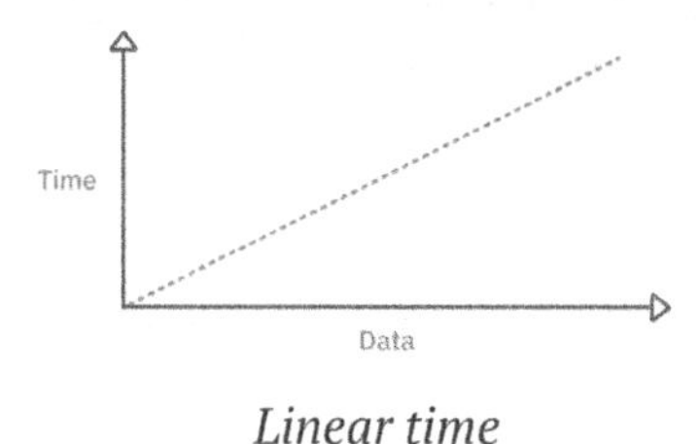

Linear time

Linear time complexity is usually the easiest to understand. As the amount of data increases, the running time increases by the same amount. That's why you have the straight linear graph illustrated above. The Big O notation for linear time is $O(n)$.

> What about a function that has two loops over all the data and calls six $O(1)$ methods? Is it $O(2n + 6)$?
>
> Time complexity only gives a high-level shape of the performance, so loops that happen a set number of times are not part of the calculation. All constants are dropped in the final Big O notation. In other words, $O(2n + 6)$ is surprisingly equal to $O(n)$.
>
> Although not a central concern of this book, optimizing for absolute efficiency can be important. Companies put millions of dollars of R&D into reducing the slope of those constants that Big O notation ignores. For example, a GPU-optimized version of an algorithm might run 100x faster than the naive CPU version while remaining $O(n)$. Although we will ignore this kind of optimization, speedups like this matter.

Quadratic time

More commonly referred to as ***n* squared**, this time complexity refers to an algorithm that takes time proportional to the square of the input size. Consider the following code:

```
func printNames(names: [String]) {
  for _ in names {
    for name in names {
      print(name)
    }
  }
}
```

This time, the function prints out all the names in the array for every name in the array. If you have an array with ten pieces of data, it will print the full list of ten names ten times. That's 100 print statements.

If you increase the input size by one, it will print the full list of 11 names 11 times, resulting in 121 print statements. Unlike the previous function, which operates in linear time, the *n* squared algorithm can quickly run out of control as the data size increases.

Here's a graph illustrating this behavior:

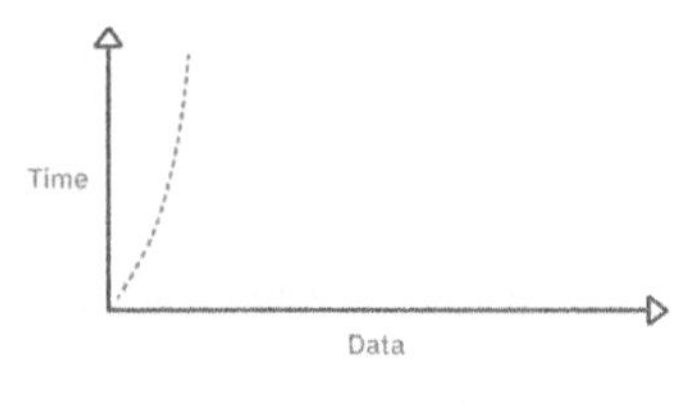

Quadratic time

As the size of the input data increases, the amount of time it takes for the algorithm to run increases drastically. Thus, n squared algorithms don't perform well at scale.

The Big O notation for quadratic time is $O(n^2)$.

> No matter how inefficiently a linear time $O(n)$ algorithm is written (multiple passes etc), for a sufficiently large n, the linear time algorithm will execute faster than a super optimized quadratic algorithm. Always. Every time.

Logarithmic time

So far, you've learned about the linear and quadratic time complexities wherein each element of the input is inspected at least once. However, there are scenarios in which only a subset of the input needs to be inspected, leading to a faster runtime.

Algorithms that belong to this category of time complexity are ones that can leverage some shortcuts by making some assumptions about the input data. For instance, if you had a **sorted** array of integers, what is the quickest way to find if a particular value exists?

A naive solution would be to inspect the array from start to finish to check every element before reaching a conclusion. Since you're inspecting each of the elements once, that would be a $O(n)$ algorithm. Linear time is fairly good, but you can do better. Since the input array is sorted, there is an optimization that you can make. Consider the following code:

```
let numbers = [1, 3, 56, 66, 68, 80, 99, 105, 450]

func naiveContains(_ value: Int, in array: [Int]) -> Bool {
  for element in array {
    if element == value {
      return true
    }
  }

  return false
}
```

If you were checking if the number 451 existed in the array, the naive algorithm would have to iterate from the beginning to end, making a total of nine inspections for the nine values in the array. However, since the array is sorted, you can, right off the bat, drop half of the comparisons necessary by checking the middle value:

```
func naiveContains(_ value: Int, in array: [Int]) -> Bool {
  guard !array.isEmpty else { return false }
  let middleIndex = array.count / 2

  if value <= array[middleIndex] {
    for index in 0...middleIndex {
      if array[index] == value {
        return true
      }
    }
  } else {
    for index in middleIndex..<array.count {
      if array[index] == value {
```

```
            return true
          }
        }
      }
      return false
    }
```

The above function makes a small but meaningful optimization wherein it only checks half of the array to come up with a conclusion.

The algorithm first checks the middle value to see how it compares with the desired value. If the middle value is bigger than the desired value, the algorithm won't bother looking at the values on the right half of the array; since the array is sorted, values to the right of the middle value can only get bigger.

In the other case, if the middle value is smaller than the desired value, the algorithm won't look at the left side of the array. This is a small but meaningful optimization that cuts the number of comparisons by half.

What if you could do this optimization repeatedly throughout this method? You'll find out in Chapter 20, "Binary Search."

An algorithm that can repeatedly drop half of the required comparisons will have logarithmic time complexity. Here's a graph depicting how a logarithmic time algorithm would behave as input data increases:

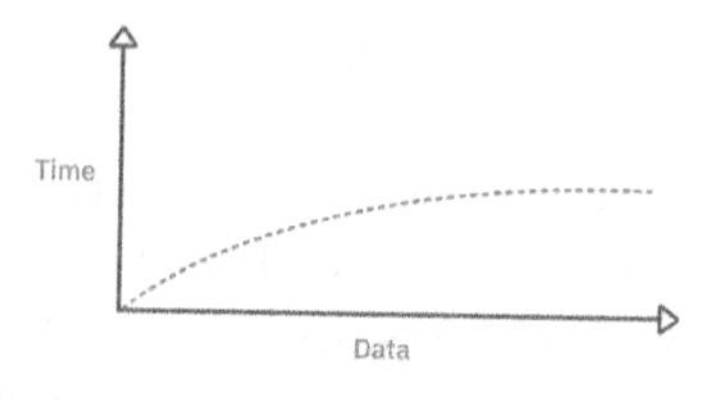

Logarithmic time

As input data increases, the time it takes to execute the algorithm increases at a slow rate. If you look closely, you may notice that the graph seems to exhibit asymptotic behavior. This can be explained by considering the impact of halving the number of comparisons you need to do.

When you have an input size of 100, halving the comparisons means you save 50 comparisons. If input size was 100,000, halving the comparisons means you save 50,000 comparisons. The more data you have, the more the halving effect scales. Thus, you can see that the graph appears to approach horizontal.

Algorithms in this category are few but extremely powerful in situations that allow for it. The Big O notation for logarithmic time complexity is *O(log n)*.

> Is it log base 2, log base 10, or the natural log?
>
> In the above example, log base 2 applies. However, since Big O notation only concerns itself with the shape of the performance, the actual base doesn't matter.

Quasilinear time

Another common time complexity you'll encounter is quasilinear time. Quasilinear time algorithms perform worse than linear time but dramatically better than quadratic time. They are among the most common algorithms you'll deal with. An example of a quasilinear time algorithm is Swift's `sort` method.

The Big-O notation for quasilinear time complexity is *O(n log n)* which is a multiplication of linear and logarithmic time. So quasilinear fits between logarithmic and linear time; it is worse than linear time but still better than many of the other complexities that you'll see next. Here's the graph:

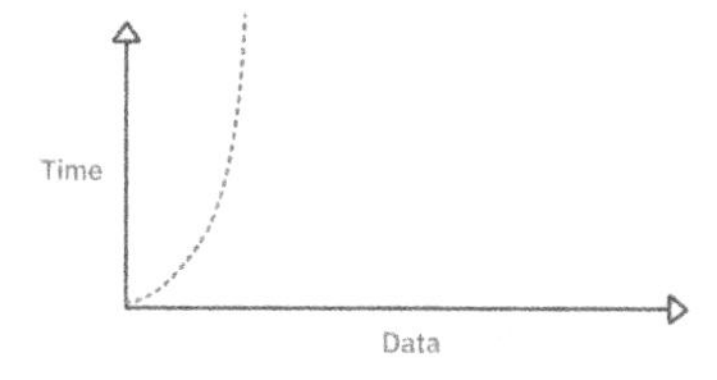

Quasilinear time

The quasilinear time complexity shares a similar curve with quadratic time but doesn't go up quite as fast so is more resilient to large data sets.

Other time complexities

The five time complexities you've encountered so far are the ones you'll encounter in this book. Other time complexities do exist but are far less common and tackle more complex problems that are not discussed in this book. These time complexities include polynomial time, exponential time, factorial time and more.

It is important to note that time complexity is a high-level overview of performance, and it doesn't judge the speed of the algorithm beyond the general ranking scheme. This means that two algorithms can have the same time complexity, but one may still be much faster than the other. For small data sets, time complexity may not be an accurate measure of actual speed.

For instance, quadratic algorithms such as insertion sort can be faster than quasilinear algorithms, such as mergesort, if the data set is small. This is because insertion sort does not need to allocate extra memory to perform the algorithm, while mergesort needs to allocate multiple arrays. For small data sets, the memory allocation can be expensive relative to the number of elements the algorithm needs to touch.

Comparing time complexity

Suppose you wrote the following code that finds the sum of numbers from 1 to *n*.

```
func sumFromOne(upto n: Int) -> Int {
  var result = 0
  for i in 1...n {
    result += i
  }
  return result
}

sumFromOne(upto: 10000)
```

The code loops 10000 times and returns `50005000`. It is $O(n)$ and will take a moment to run in a playground as it counts through the loop and prints results.

You can write another version:

```
func sumFromOne(upto n: Int) -> Int {
  (1...n).reduce(0, +)
}
sumFromOne(upto: 10000)
```

In a playground, this will run faster because it calls compiled code from the standard library. However, if you look up the time complexity for `reduce`, you'll discover that it is also $O(n)$ as it calls the + method `n` times. It is the same Big O, but has smaller constants because it is compiled code.

Finally, you can write:

```
func sumFromOne(upto n: Int) -> Int {
  (n + 1) * n / 2
}
sumFromOne(upto: 10000)
```

This version of the function uses a trick that Fredrick Gauss noticed in elementary school. Namely, you can compute the sum using simple arithmetic. This final version of the algorithm is *O(1)* and tough to beat. A constant time algorithm is always preferred. If you put this version in a loop you still end up with linear time. The previous *O(n)* versions are just one outer loop away from slow, quadratic time.

Space complexity

The time complexity of an algorithm can help predict scalability, but it isn't the only metric. Space complexity is a measure of the resources required for the algorithm to run. For computers, the resources for algorithms is memory. Consider the following code:

```
func printSorted(_ array: [Int]) {
  let sorted = array.sorted()
  for element in sorted {
    print(element)
  }
}
```

The above function will create a sorted copy of the array and print the array. To calculate the space complexity, you analyze the memory allocations for the function.

Since `array.sorted()` will produce a brand new array with the same size of `array`, the space complexity of `printSorted` is *O(n)*. While this function is simple and elegant, there may be some situations in which you want to allocate as little memory as possible.

You could revise the above function to the following:

```
func printSorted(_ array: [Int]) {
  // 1
  guard !array.isEmpty else { return }

  // 2
  var currentCount = 0
  var minValue = Int.min

  // 3
  for value in array {
    if value == minValue {
      print(value)
      currentCount += 1
    }
  }

  while currentCount < array.count {

    // 4
    var currentValue = array.max()!

    for value in array {
      if value < currentValue && value > minValue {
        currentValue = value
      }
    }

    // 5
    for value in array {
      if value == currentValue {
        print(value)
        currentCount += 1
      }
    }

    // 6
    minValue = currentValue
  }
}
```

This implementation respects space constraints. The overall goal is to iterate through the array multiple times, printing the next smallest value for each iteration.

Here's what this algorithm is doing:

1. Check for the case if the array is empty. If it is, there's nothing to print.
2. `currentCount` keeps track of the number of print statements made. `minValue` stores the last printed value.

3. The algorithm begins by printing out all values matching the `minValue`, and updates the `currentCount` according to the number of print statements made.
4. Using the `while` loop, the algorithm finds the lowest value bigger than `minValue` and stores it in `currentValue`.
5. The algorithm then prints all values of `currentValue` inside the array while updating `currentCount`.
6. `minValue` is set to `currentValue` so the next iteration will try to find the next minimum value.

The above algorithm only allocates memory to keep track of a few variables, so the space complexity is *O(1)*. This is in contrast with the previous function, which allocates an entire array to create the sorted representation of the source array.

Other notations

So far, you've evaluated algorithms using Big O notation. This is by far the most common measurement that programmers evaluate with. However, there exist other notations as well.

Big Omega notation is used to measure the best-case runtime for an algorithm. This isn't as useful as Big O because getting the best case is often untenable.

Big Theta notation is used to measure the runtime for an algorithm that has the same best and worse case.

Playground line-based execution bug

This book uses playgrounds extensively. Under certain conditions, you may find Xcode 13 incorrectly disables line-based execution. In these cases, just use the execution control button at the bottom of the playground window to run the entire playground.

Key points

- **Time complexity** is a measure on the time required to run an algorithm as the input size increases.
- You should know about constant time, logarithmic time, linear time, quasilinear time and quadratic time and be able to order them by cost.
- **Space complexity** is a measure of the resources required for the algorithm to run.
- **Big O** notation is used to represent the general form of time and space complexity.
- Time and space complexity are high-level measures of scalability; they do not measure the actual speed of the algorithm itself.
- For small data sets, time complexity is usually irrelevant. For example, a quasilinear algorithm can be slower than a quadratic algorithm when *n* is small.

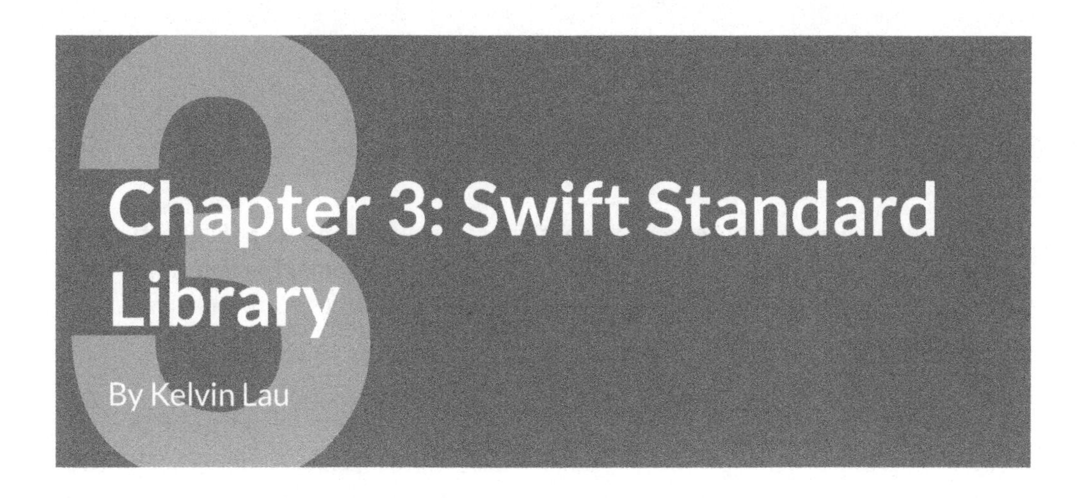

Chapter 3: Swift Standard Library

By Kelvin Lau

The **Swift standard library** is the framework that contains the core components of the Swift language. Inside, you'll find a variety of tools and types to help build your Swift apps. Before you start building your own custom data structures, it is important to understand the primary data structures that the Swift standard library already provides.

In this chapter, you'll focus on the three main data structures that the standard library provides right out of the box: `Array`, `Dictionary`, and `Set`.

Array

An array is a general-purpose, generic container for storing an ordered collection of elements, and it is used commonly in all sorts of Swift programs. You can create an array by using an *array literal*, a comma-separated list of values surrounded by square brackets. For example:

```
let people = ["Brian", "Stanley", "Ringo"]
```

Swift defines arrays using protocols. Each of these protocols layers more capabilities on the array. For example, an `Array` is a `Sequence`, which means that you can iterate through it **at least** once. It is also a `Collection`, which means it can be traversed multiple times, non-destructively, and accessed using a subscript operator. An array is also a `RandomAccessCollection`, which makes guarantees about efficiency.

The Swift `Array` is known as a *generic collection*, because it can work with any type. In fact, most of the Swift standard library is built with generic code.

As with any data structure, there are certain notable traits that you should be aware of. The first of these is the notion of **order**.

Order

Elements in an array are explicitly *ordered*. Using the above `people` array as an example, `"Brian"` comes before `"Stanley"`.

All elements in an array have a corresponding zero-based integer index. For example, the `people` array from the above example has three indices, one corresponding to each element. You can retrieve the value of an element in the array by writing the following:

```
people[0] // "Brian"
people[1] // "Stanley"
people[2] // "Ringo"
```

Order is defined by the array data structure and should not be taken for granted. Some data structures, such as `Dictionary`, have a weaker concept of order.

Random-access

Random-access is a trait that data structures can claim if they can handle element retrieval in a constant amount of time. For example, getting "Ringo" from the people array takes constant time. Again, this performance should not be taken for granted. Other data structures such as linked lists and trees do not have constant time access.

Array performance

Aside from being a random-access collection, other performance areas are of interest to you as a developer, particularly, how well or poorly does the data structure fare when the amount of data it contains needs to grow? For arrays, this varies on two factors.

Insertion location

The first factor is one in which you choose to insert the new element inside the array. The most efficient scenario for adding an element to an array is to append it at the end of the array:

```
people.append("Charles")
print(people) // prints ["Brian", "Stanley", "Ringo", "Charles"]
```

Inserting "Charles" using the append method will place the string at the end of the array. This is a *constant-time* operation, meaning the time it takes to perform this operation stays the same no matter how large the array becomes. However, there may come a time that you need to insert an element in a particular location, such as in the very middle of the array.

To help illustrate why that is the case, consider the following analogy. You're standing in line for the theater. Someone new comes along to join the lineup. What's the easiest place to add people to the lineup? At the end, of course!

If the newcomer tried to insert himself into the middle of the line, he would have to convince half the lineup to shuffle back to make room.

And if he were *terribly* rude, he'd try to insert himself at the head of the line. This is the worst-case scenario because every person in the lineup would need to shuffle back to make room for this new person in front!

This is exactly how the array works. Inserting new elements from anywhere aside from the end of the array will force elements to shuffle backward to make room for the new element:

```
people.insert("Andy", at: 0)
// ["Andy", "Brian", "Stanley", "Ringo", "Charles"]
```

To be precise, *every* element must shift backward by one index, which takes *n* steps. If the number of elements in the array doubles, the time required for this `insert` operation will also double.

If inserting elements in front of a collection is a common operation for your program, you may want to consider a different data structure to hold your data.

The second factor that determines the speed of insertion is the array's **capacity**. Underneath the hood, Swift arrays are allocated with a predetermined amount of space for its elements. If you try to add new elements to an array that is already at maximum capacity, the Array must restructure itself to make more room for more elements. This is done by copying all the current elements of the array in a new and bigger container in memory. However, this comes at a cost; Each element of the array has to be visited and copied.

This means that any insertion, even at the end, could take *n* steps to complete if a copy is made. However, the standard library employs a strategy that minimizes the times this copying needs to occur. Each time it runs out of storage and needs to copy, it doubles the capacity.

Dictionary

A dictionary is another generic collection that holds **key-value** pairs. For example, here's a dictionary containing a user's name and a score:

```
var scores: [String: Int] = ["Eric": 9, "Mark": 12, "Wayne": 1]
```

Dictionaries don't have any guarantees of order, nor can you insert at a specific index. They also put a requirement on the `Key` type that it be `Hashable`. Fortunately, almost all of the standard types are already `Hashable` and in the more recent versions of Swift, adopting the `Hashable` protocol is now trivial. You can add a new entry to the dictionary with the following syntax:

```
scores["Andrew"] = 0
```

This creates a new key-value pair in the dictionary:

```
["Eric": 9, "Mark": 12, "Andrew": 0, "Wayne": 1]
```

The "Andrew" key is inserted somewhere into the dictionary. Dictionaries are unordered, so you can't guarantee where new entries will be put.

It is possible to traverse through the key-values of a dictionary multiple times as the `Collection` protocol affords. This order, while not defined, will be the same every time it is traversed until the collection is changed (mutated).

The lack of explicit ordering disadvantage comes with some redeeming traits.

Unlike the array, dictionaries don't need to worry about elements shifting around. Inserting into a dictionary always takes a constant amount of time.

Lookup operations also take a constant amount of time, which is significantly faster than finding a particular element in an array that requires a walk from the beginning of the array to the insertion point.

Set

A set is a container that holds unique values. Imagine it being a bag that allows you to insert items into it, but rejects items that have already been inserted:

```
var bag: Set<String> = ["Candy", "Juice", "Gummy"]
bag.insert("Candy")
print(bag) // prints ["Candy", "Juice", "Gummy"]
```

Since sets enforce uniqueness, they lend themselves to a variety of interesting applications, such as finding duplicate elements in a collection of values:

```
let values: [String] = [...]
var bag: Set<String> = []
for value in values {
  if bag.contains(value) {
    // bag already has it, therefore it is a duplicate
  }
  bag.insert(value)
}
```

You won't use sets nearly as much as arrays and dictionaries, but it is still common enough to be an important data structure to keep in your toolbelt. There is one caveat, though. Similar to dictionaries, values in a set have no notion of order. Keep that in mind when you use a set to aggregate data.

The Swift Collections package

The Swift standard library only implements the three most important data structures: `Array`, `Set`, and `Dictionary`. For additional data structures, you can check out the **Swift Collections** package. This package allows new collection types to be developed and tested by the community before they become part of the official standard library.

In the next section, you'll take a deeper look at one of the data structures from this package.

Deque

Earlier, you learned that inserting elements in the front of an `Array` causes a shuffle of all the elements.

At first glance, the `Deque` (pronounced "deck") data structure seems to serve the same purpose as the `Array`. You can use it as a general-purpose container that holds values in order. Just like the `Array`, you can call `append` to add elements to the `Deque`, or `remote(at:)` to remove a specific element at some index.

In fact, the interface is nearly identical since both `Array` and `Deque` implement the same collection protocols. So why use a `Deque` over an `Array`? The tradeoffs are hard to see until you consider time complexity.

A `Deque` is a double-ended queue. Therefore, `Deque` optimizes for modifications from both the front and the back of the collection. Unlike `Array`, inserting or removing an element from the front of a `Deque` is a cheap $O(1)$ operation.

Great - so what are the downsides? In programming, everything is about tradeoffs. For `Deque`, it's about improving modifications in the front for the cost of slightly degraded performance on everything else. As a programmer, it's your job to weigh the options and pick the best tool for the job. If your app requires frequent modifications to the front of a collection, a `Deque` will perform much better than an `Array`. That could translate to a better user experience - one that could make the difference between a snappy and sluggish app.

The Swift Collections package contains additional data structures, such as `OrderedDictionary` and `OrderedSet`. As the prefix suggests, these are variants of `Dictionary` and `Set` that retain the order of the elements. Like `Deque`, these data structures have some performance tradeoffs. You can learn more about them at https://swift.org/blog/swift-collections/.

Key points

- Every data structure has advantages and disadvantages. Knowing them is key to writing performant software.
- Functions such as `insert(at:)` for `Array` have performance characteristics that can cripple performance when used haphazardly. If you find yourself needing to use `insert(at:)` frequently with indices near the beginning of the array, you may want to consider a different data structure such as the linked list.
- `Dictionary` trades away the ability to maintain the order of its elements for fast insertion and searching.
- `Set` guarantees uniqueness in a collection of values. `Set` is optimized for speed and abandons the ability to retain the order of the elements.
- The Swift Collections package contains specialized data structures that perform better in certain scenarios.

Section II: Elementary Data Structures

This section looks at a few important data structures that are not found in the Swift standard library but form the basis of more advanced algorithms covered in future sections. All of them are collections optimized for (and enforce) a particular access pattern. You will also get a glimpse of how protocols in Swift can be used to build up these useful primitives.

Each concept chapter is followed by a Challenge chapter where you will be asked to answer something about the data structure, write a utility function, or use it directly to solve a common problem. Worked solutions to the Challenge chapters are located at the end of the book. We encourage you not to peek at our solution until you have given the challenge a shot yourself.

Chapter 4: Stacks

By Kelvin Lau

Stacks are everywhere. Here are some common examples of things you would stack:

- pancakes
- books
- paper
- cash

The **stack** data structure is identical, in concept, to a physical stack of objects. When you add an item to a stack, you place it on top of the stack. When you remove an item from a stack, you always remove the top-most item.

Good news: a stack of pancakes. Bad news: you may only eat the top-most pancake.

Stack operations

Stacks are useful and also exceedingly simple. The main goal of building a stack is to enforce how you access your data.

There are only two essential operations for a stack:

- **push**: Adding an element to the top of the stack.
- **pop**: Removing the top element of the stack.

Limiting the interface to these two operations means that you can only add or remove elements from one side of the data structure. In computer science, a stack is known as a **LIFO** (last-in-first-out) data structure. Elements that are pushed in last are the first ones to be popped out.

Stacks are used prominently in all disciplines of programming. To list a few:

- iOS uses the *navigation stack* to push and pop view controllers into and out of view.
- Memory allocation uses stacks at the architectural level. Memory for local variables is also managed using a stack.
- *Search and conquer* algorithms, such as finding a path out of a maze, use stacks to facilitate backtracking.

Implementation

Open up the starter playground for this chapter. In the **Sources** folder of your playground, create a file named **Stack.swift**. Inside the file, write the following:

```
public struct Stack<Element> {

  private var storage: [Element] = []

  public init() { }
}

extension Stack: CustomDebugStringConvertible {

  public var debugDescription: String {
    """
    ----top----
    \(storage.map { "\($0)" }.reversed().joined(separator:
"\n"))
    -----------
```

```
    """
  }
}
```

Here, you've defined the backing storage of your `Stack`. Choosing the right storage type for your stack is important. The array is an obvious choice since it offers constant time insertions and deletions at one end via `append` and `popLast`. Usage of these two operations will facilitate the **LIFO** nature of stacks.

For the fancy chain of function calls in `debugDescription`, required by the `CustomDebugStringConvertible` protocol, you are doing three things:

1. Creating an array that maps the elements to `String` via `storage.map { "\($0)" }`.
2. Creating a new array that reverses the previous array using `reversed()`.
3. Flattening out the array into a string by using `joined(separator:)`. You separate the elements of the array using the newline character `"\n"`.

This creates a printable representation of `Stack` types you can use for debugging.

push and pop operations

Add the following two operations to your `Stack`:

```
public mutating func push(_ element: Element) {
  storage.append(element)
}

@discardableResult
public mutating func pop() -> Element? {
  storage.popLast()
}
```

Fairly straightforward! In the playground page, write the following:

```
example(of: "using a stack") {
  var stack = Stack<Int>()
  stack.push(1)
  stack.push(2)
  stack.push(3)
  stack.push(4)

  print(stack)
```

```
    if let poppedElement = stack.pop() {
      assert(4 == poppedElement)
      print("Popped: \(poppedElement)")
    }
  }
```

You should see the following output:

```
---Example of using a stack---
----top----
4
3
2
1
-----------
Popped: 4
```

`push` and `pop` both have a $O(1)$ time complexity.

Non-essential operations

There are a couple of nice-to-have operations that make a stack easier to use. In **Stack.swift**, add the following to `Stack`:

```
public func peek() -> Element? {
 storage.last
}

public var isEmpty: Bool {
  peek() == nil
}
```

A stack interface often includes a `peek` operation. The idea of `peek` is to look at the top element of the stack without mutating its contents.

Less is more

You may have wondered if you could adopt the Swift collection protocols for the stack. A stack's purpose is to limit the number of ways to access your data. Adopting protocols such as `Collection` would go against this goal by exposing all the elements via iterators and the subscript. In this case, less is more!

You might want to take an existing array and convert it to a stack to guarantee the access order. Of course it would be possible to loop through the array elements and `push` each element.

However, since you can write an initializer that sets the underlying private storage. Add the following to your stack implementation:

```
public init(_ elements: [Element]) {
  storage = elements
}
```

Now, add this example to the main playground:

```
example(of: "initializing a stack from an array") {
  let array = ["A", "B", "C", "D"]
  var stack = Stack(array)
  print(stack)
  stack.pop()
}
```

This code creates a stack of strings and pops the top element "D." Notice that the Swift compiler can type infer the element type from the array so you can use `Stack` instead of the more verbose `Stack<String>`.

You can go a step further and make your stack initializable from an array literal. Add this to your stack implementation:

```
extension Stack: ExpressibleByArrayLiteral {
  public init(arrayLiteral elements: Element...) {
    storage = elements
  }
}
```

Now go back to the main playground page and add:

```
example(of: "initializing a stack from an array literal") {
  var stack: Stack = [1.0, 2.0, 3.0, 4.0]
  print(stack)
  stack.pop()
}
```

This creates a stack of `Doubles` and pops the top value 4.0. Again, type inference saves you from having to type the more verbose `Stack<Double>`.

Stacks are crucial to problems that *search* trees and graphs. Imagine finding your way through a maze. Each time you come to a decision point of left, right or straight, you can push all possible decisions onto your stack. When you hit a dead end, simply backtrack by popping from the stack and continuing until you escape or hit another dead end.

Key points

- A stack is a **LIFO**, last-in first-out, data structure.
- Despite being so simple, the stack is a key data structure for many problems.
- The only two essential operations for the stack are the **push** method for adding elements and the **pop** method for removing elements.

Chapter 5: Stack Challenges

By Kelvin Lau

A stack is a simple data structure with a surprisingly large amount of applications. Open the starter project to begin. In it, you'll find the following challenges.

Challenge 1: Reverse an Array

Create a function that uses a stack to print the contents of an array in reversed order.

Challenge 2: Balance the parentheses

Check for balanced parentheses. Given a string, check if there are `(` and `)` characters, and return `true` if the parentheses in the string are balanced. For example:

```
// 1
h((e))llo(world)() // balanced parentheses

// 2
(hello world // unbalanced parentheses
```

Solutions

Solution to Challenge 1

One of the prime use cases for stacks is to facilitate backtracking. If you push a sequence of values into the stack, sequentially popping the stack will give you the values in reverse order.

```
func printInReverse<T>(_ array: [T]) {
  var stack = Stack<T>()

  for value in array {
    stack.push(value)
  }

  while let value = stack.pop() {
    print(value)
  }
}
```

The time complexity of pushing the nodes into the stack is **$O(n)$**. The time complexity of popping the stack to print the values is also **$O(n)$**. Overall, the time complexity of this algorithm is **$O(n)$**.

Since you're allocating a container (the stack) inside the function, you also incur a **$O(n)$** space complexity cost.

> **Note**: The way you should reverse an array in production code is to call the `reversed()` method that the standard library provides. For `Array`, this method is **$O(1)$** in time and space. This is because it is **lazy** and only creates a reversed view into the original collection. If you traverse the items and print out all of the elements, it predictably makes it **$O(n)$** in time while remaining **$O(1)$** in space.

Solution to Challenge 2

To check if there are balanced parentheses in the string, you need to go through each character of the string. When you encounter an opening parentheses, you will push that into a stack. Vice-versa, if you encounter a closing parentheses, you should pop the stack.

Here's what the code looks like:

```
func checkParentheses(_ string: String) -> Bool {
  var stack = Stack<Character>()

  for character in string {
    if character == "(" {
      stack.push(character)
    } else if character == ")" {
      if stack.isEmpty {
        return false
      } else {
        stack.pop()
      }
    }
  }
  return stack.isEmpty
}
```

The time complexity of this algorithm is ***O(n)***, where *n* is the number of characters in the string. This algorithm also incurs an ***O(n)*** space complexity cost due to the usage of the `Stack` data structure.

Chapter 6: Linked Lists

By Kelvin Lau

A linked list is a collection of values arranged in a linear, unidirectional sequence. A linked list has some theoretical advantages over contiguous storage options such as the Swift Array:

- Constant time insertion and removal from the front of the list.
- Reliable performance characteristics.

A linked list

As the diagram suggests, a linked list is a chain of **nodes**. Nodes have two responsibilities:

1. Hold a value.
2. Hold a reference to the next node. A `nil` value represents the end of the list.

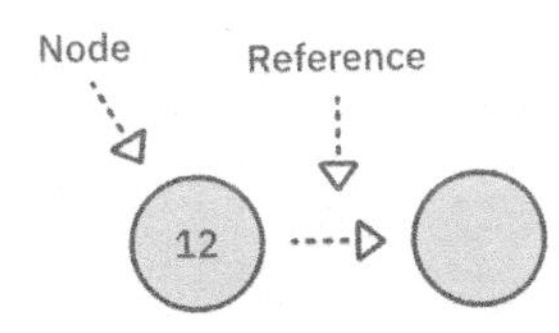

A node holding the value 12

In this chapter, you'll implement a linked list and learn about the common operations associated with it. You'll learn about the time complexity of each operation, and you'll implement a neat little Swift feature known as copy-on-write.

Open up the starter playground for this chapter so that you can dive right into the code.

Node

Create a new Swift file in the **Sources** directory and name it **Node.swift**. Add the following to the file:

```
public class Node<Value> {

  public var value: Value
  public var next: Node?

  public init(value: Value, next: Node? = nil) {
    self.value = value
    self.next = next
  }
}

extension Node: CustomStringConvertible {

  public var description: String {
    guard let next = next else {
      return "\(value)"
    }
    return "\(value) -> " + String(describing: next) + " "
  }
}
```

Navigate to the playground page and add the following:

```
example(of: "creating and linking nodes") {
  let node1 = Node(value: 1)
  let node2 = Node(value: 2)
  let node3 = Node(value: 3)

  node1.next = node2
  node2.next = node3

  print(node1)
}
```

You've just created three nodes and connected them:

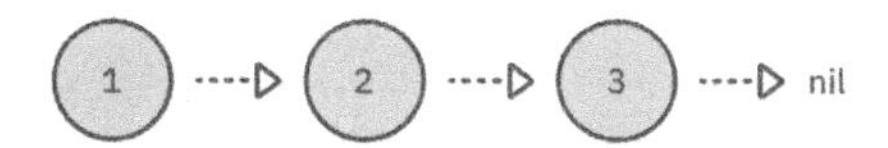

A linked list containing values 1, 2, and 3

In the console, you should see the following output:

```
---Example of creating and linking nodes---
1 -> 2 -> 3
```

As far as practicality goes, the current method of building lists leaves a lot to be desired. You can easily see that building long lists this way is impractical. A common way to alleviate this problem is to build a `LinkedList` that manages the `Node` objects. You'll do just that!

LinkedList

Create a new file in the **Sources** directory and name it **LinkedList.swift**. Add the following to the file:

```
public struct LinkedList<Value> {

  public var head: Node<Value>?
  public var tail: Node<Value>?

  public init() {}

  public var isEmpty: Bool {
    head == nil
  }
}

extension LinkedList: CustomStringConvertible {

  public var description: String {
    guard let head = head else {
      return "Empty list"
    }
    return String(describing: head)
  }
}
```

A linked list has the concept of a **head** and **tail**, which refers to the first and last nodes of the list, respectively:

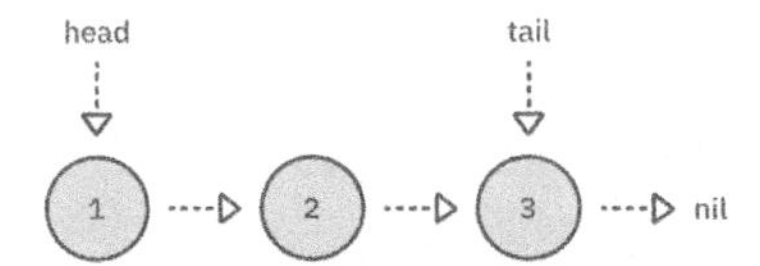

The head and tail of the list

Adding values to the list

As mentioned before, you're going to provide an interface to manage the `Node` objects. You'll first take care of adding values. There are three ways to add values to a linked list, each having unique performance characteristics:

1. **`push`**: Adds a value at the front of the list.
2. **`append`**: Adds a value at the end of the list.
3. **`insert(after:)`**: Adds a value after a particular list node.

You'll implement each of these in the next section and analyze their performance characteristics.

push operations

Adding a value at the front of the list is known as a `push` operation. This is also known as **head-first insertion**. The code for it is deliciously simple.

Add the following method to `LinkedList`:

```
public mutating func push(_ value: Value) {
  head = Node(value: value, next: head)
  if tail == nil {
    tail = head
  }
}
```

If you're pushing into an empty list, the new node is both the head and tail of the list.

In the playground page, add the following:

```
example(of: "push") {
  var list = LinkedList<Int>()
  list.push(3)
  list.push(2)
  list.push(1)

  print(list)
}
```

Your console output should show this:

```
---Example of push---
1 -> 2 -> 3
```

append operations

The next operation you'll look at is append. This adds a value at the end of the list, known as **tail-end insertion**.

In **LinkedList.swift**, add the following code just below push:

```
public mutating func append(_ value: Value) {

  // 1
  guard !isEmpty else {
    push(value)
    return
  }

  // 2
  tail!.next = Node(value: value)

  // 3
  tail = tail!.next
}
```

This code is relatively straightforward:

1. Like before, if the list is empty, you'll need to update both head and tail to the new node. Since append on an empty list is functionally identical to push, you invoke push to do the work for you.
2. You create a new node *after* the tail node in all other cases. Force unwrapping is guaranteed to succeed since you push in the isEmpty case with the above guard statement.
3. Since this is tail-end insertion, your new node is also the tail of the list.

Leap back into the playground and write the following at the bottom:

```
example(of: "append") {
  var list = LinkedList<Int>()
  list.append(1)
  list.append(2)
  list.append(3)

  print(list)
}
```

You should see the following output in the console:

```
---Example of append---
1 -> 2 -> 3
```

insert(after:) operations

The third and final operation for adding values is insert(after:). This operation inserts a value at a particular place in the list and requires two steps:

1. Finding a particular node in the list.
2. Inserting the new node.

First, you'll implement the code to find the node where you want to insert your value.

In **LinkedList.swift**, add the following code just below append:

```
public func node(at index: Int) -> Node<Value>? {
  // 1
  var currentNode = head
  var currentIndex = 0
```

```
  // 2
  while currentNode != nil && currentIndex < index {
    currentNode = currentNode!.next
    currentIndex += 1
  }

  return currentNode
}
```

node(at:) will try to retrieve a node in the list based on the given index. Since you can only access the nodes of the list from the head node, you'll have to make iterative traversals. Here's the play-by-play:

1. You create a new reference to head and track the current number of traversals.
2. Using a while loop, you move the reference down the list until you've reached the desired index. Empty lists or out-of-bounds indexes will result in a nil return value.

Now you need to insert the new node.

Add the following method just below node(at:):

```
// 1
@discardableResult
public mutating func insert(_ value: Value,
                            after node: Node<Value>)
                            -> Node<Value> {
  // 2
  guard tail !== node else {
    append(value)
    return tail!
  }
  // 3
  node.next = Node(value: value, next: node.next)
  return node.next!
}
```

Here's what you've done:

1. @discardableResult lets callers ignore the return value of this method without the compiler jumping up and down warning you about it.
2. In the case where this method is called with the tail node, you'll call the functionally equivalent append method. This will take care of updating tail.
3. Otherwise, you simply link up the new node with the rest of the list and return the new node.

Hop back to the playground page to test this out. Add the following to the bottom of the playground:

```
example(of: "inserting at a particular index") {
  var list = LinkedList<Int>()
  list.push(3)
  list.push(2)
  list.push(1)

  print("Before inserting: \(list)")
  var middleNode = list.node(at: 1)!
  for _ in 1...4 {
    middleNode = list.insert(-1, after: middleNode)
  }
  print("After inserting: \(list)")
}
```

You should see the following output:

```
---Example of inserting at a particular index---
Before inserting: 1 -> 2 -> 3
After inserting: 1 -> 2 -> -1 -> -1 -> -1 -> -1 -> 3
```

Performance analysis

Whew! You've made good progress so far. To recap, you've implemented the three operations that add values to a linked list and a method to find a node at a particular index.

	push	append	insert(after:)	node(at:)
Behaviour	insert at head	insert at tail	insert after a node	returns a node at given index
Time complexity	O(1)	O(1)	O(1)	O(i), where i is the given index

Next, you'll focus on the opposite action: removal operations.

Removing values from the list

There are three main operations for removing nodes:

1. **pop**: Removes the value at the front of the list.
2. **removeLast**: Removes the value at the end of the list.
3. **remove(at:)**: Removes a value anywhere in the list.

You'll implement all three and analyze their performance characteristics.

pop operations

Removing a value at the front of the list is often referred to as pop. This operation is almost as simple as push, so dive right in.

Add the following method to LinkedList:

```
@discardableResult
public mutating func pop() -> Value? {
  defer {
    head = head?.next
    if isEmpty {
      tail = nil
    }
  }
  return head?.value
}
```

pop returns the value that was removed from the list. This value is optional since the list may be empty.

By moving the head down a node, you've effectively removed the first node of the list. ARC will remove the old node from memory once the method finishes since no more references will be attached to it. If the list becomes empty, you set tail to nil.

Head back inside the playground page and test it out by adding the following code at the bottom:

```
example(of: "pop") {
  var list = LinkedList<Int>()
  list.push(3)
  list.push(2)
  list.push(1)

  print("Before popping list: \(list)")
```

```
    let poppedValue = list.pop()
    print("After popping list: \(list)")
    print("Popped value: " + String(describing: poppedValue))
}
```

You should see the following output:

```
---Example of pop---
Before popping list: 1 -> 2 -> 3
After popping list: 2 -> 3
Popped value: Optional(1)
```

removeLast operations

Removing the last node of the list is somewhat inconvenient. Although you have a reference to the `tail` node, you can't chop it off without having a reference to the node before it. Thus, you'll have to do an arduous traversal. Add the following code just below pop:

```
@discardableResult
public mutating func removeLast() -> Value? {
  // 1
  guard let head = head else {
    return nil
  }
  // 2
  guard head.next != nil else {
    return pop()
  }
  // 3
  var prev = head
  var current = head

  while let next = current.next {
    prev = current
    current = next
  }
  // 4
  prev.next = nil
  tail = prev
  return current.value
}
```

Here's what's happening in the code:

1. If `head` is `nil`, there's nothing to remove, so you return `nil`.
2. If the list only consists of one node, `removeLast` is functionally equivalent to `pop`. Since `pop` will handle updating the `head` and `tail` references, you'll just delegate this work to it.
3. You keep searching for a next node until `current.next` is `nil`. This signifies that `current` is the last node of the list.
4. Since `current` is the last node, you simply disconnect it using the `prev.next` reference. You also make sure to update the `tail` reference.

Head back to the playground page and add the following to the bottom:

```
example(of: "removing the last node") {
  var list = LinkedList<Int>()
  list.push(3)
  list.push(2)
  list.push(1)

  print("Before removing last node: \(list)")
  let removedValue = list.removeLast()

  print("After removing last node: \(list)")
  print("Removed value: " + String(describing: removedValue))
}
```

You should see the following at the bottom of the console:

```
---Example of removing the last node---
Before removing last node: 1 -> 2 -> 3
After removing last node: 1 -> 2
Removed value: Optional(3)
```

`removeLast` requires you to traverse all the way down the list. This makes for an $O(n)$ operation, which is relatively expensive.

remove(after:) operations

The final remove operation is removing a particular node at a particular point in the list. This is achieved much like `insert(after:)`; You'll first find the node immediately before the node you wish to remove and then unlink it.

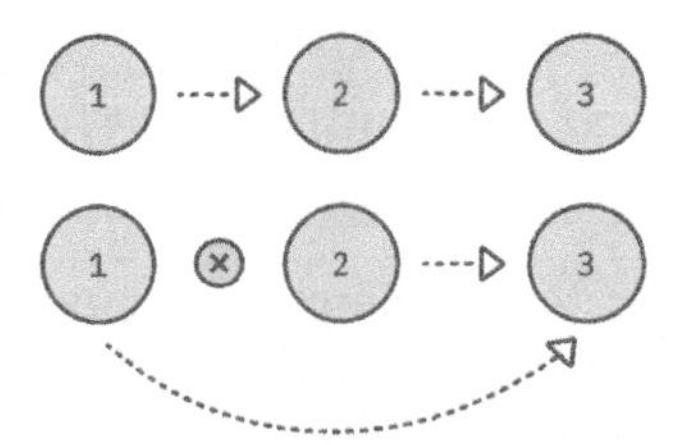

Removing the middle node

Navigate back to **LinkedList.swift** and add the following method below `removeLast`:

```
@discardableResult
public mutating func remove(after node: Node<Value>) -> Value? {
  defer {
    if node.next === tail {
      tail = node
    }
    node.next = node.next?.next
  }
  return node.next?.value
}
```

The unlinking of the nodes occurs in the `defer` block. Special care needs to be taken if the removed node is the tail node since the `tail` reference must be updated.

Head back to the playground to try it out. You know the drill:

```
example(of: "removing a node after a particular node") {
  var list = LinkedList<Int>()
  list.push(3)
  list.push(2)
  list.push(1)

  print("Before removing at particular index: \(list)")
  let index = 1
  let node = list.node(at: index - 1)!
  let removedValue = list.remove(after: node)

  print("After removing at index \(index): \(list)")
  print("Removed value: " + String(describing: removedValue))
}
```

You should see the following output in the console:

```
---Example of removing a node after a particular node---
Before removing at particular index: 1 -> 2 -> 3
After removing at index 1: 1 -> 3
Removed value: Optional(2)
```

Try adding more elements and play around with the value of index. Similar to `insert(at:)`, the time complexity of this operation is *O*(1), but it requires you to have a reference to a particular node beforehand.

Performance analysis

You've hit another checkpoint! To recap, you've implemented the three operations that remove values from a linked list:

	pop	removeLast	remove(after:)
Behaviour	remove at head	remove at tail	remove the immediate next node
Time complexity	O(1)	O(1)	O(1)

At this point, you've defined an interface for a linked list that most programmers around the world can relate to. However, there's work to be done to adorn the Swift semantics. In the next half of the chapter, you'll focus on making the interface as *Swifty* as possible.

Swift collection protocols

The Swift standard library has a set of protocols that help define what's expected of a particular type. Each of these protocols provides certain guarantees on characteristics and performance. From this set of protocols, you'll focus on four collection related protocols.

Here's a quick summary of what each protocol does:

- **Tier 1, Sequence**: A sequence type provides sequential access to its elements. It comes with an important caveat: Using the sequential access may destructively consume the elements so that you can't revisit them.

- **Tier 2, Collection**: A *collection type* is a sequence type that provides additional guarantees. A collection type is finite and allows for repeated nondestructive sequential access.
- **Tier 3, BidirectionalColllection**: A collection type can be a *bidirectional collection* type if it, as the name suggests, can allow for bidirectional travel up and down the sequence. This isn't possible for the linked list since you can only go from the head to the tail, but not the other way around.
- **Tier 4, RandomAccessCollection**: A bidirectional collection type can be a *random-access collection type* if it can guarantee that accessing an element at a particular index will take just as long as access an element at any other index. This is not possible for the linked list since accessing a node near the front of the list is substantially quicker than one further down the list.

There's more to be said for each of these. You'll learn more about each as you write conformances for them.

A linked list can earn two qualifications from the Swift collection protocols. First, since a linked list is a chain of nodes, adopting the `Sequence` protocol makes sense. Second, since the chain of nodes is a *finite* sequence, it makes sense to adopt the `Collection` protocol.

Becoming a Swift collection

In this section, you'll look into implementing the `Collection` protocol. A collection type is a finite sequence and provides nondestructive sequential access. A Swift `Collection` also allows for access via a **subscript**, a fancy term for saying an index can be mapped to a value in the collection.

Here's an example of using the subscript of a Swift `Array`:

```
array[5]
```

The index of an array is an `Int` value — value of 5 in this example. The subscript operation is defined with the square brackets. Using the subscript with an index will return you a value from the collection.

Custom collection indexes

A defining metric for performance of the `Collection` protocol methods is the speed of mapping an `Index` to a value. Unlike other storage options such as the Swift `Array`, the linked list cannot achieve O(1) subscript operations using integer indexes. Thus, your goal is to define a custom index that contains a reference to its respective node.

In **LinkedList.swift**, add the following extension:

```
extension LinkedList: Collection {

  public struct Index: Comparable {

    public var node: Node<Value>?

    static public func ==(lhs: Index, rhs: Index) -> Bool {
      switch (lhs.node, rhs.node) {
      case let (left?, right?):
        return left.next === right.next
      case (nil, nil):
        return true
      default:
        return false
      }
    }

    static public func <(lhs: Index, rhs: Index) -> Bool {
      guard lhs != rhs else {
        return false
      }
      let nodes = sequence(first: lhs.node) { $0?.next }
      return nodes.contains { $0 === rhs.node }
    }
  }
}
```

You'll use this custom index to fulfill `Collection` requirements. Write the following inside the extension to complete it:

```
// 1
public var startIndex: Index {
  Index(node: head)
}
// 2
public var endIndex: Index {
  Index(node: tail?.next)
}
// 3
```

```
public func index(after i: Index) -> Index {
  Index(node: i.node?.next)
}
// 4
public subscript(position: Index) -> Value {
  position.node!.value
}
```

1. The `startIndex` is reasonably defined by the `head` of the linked list.

2. `Collection` defines the `endIndex` as the index right after the last accessible value, so you give it `tail?.next`.

3. `index(after:)` dictates how the index can be incremented. You simply give it an index of the immediate next node.

4. The `subscript` is used to map an `Index` to the value in the collection. Since you've created the custom index, you can easily achieve this in constant time by referring to the node's value.

That wraps up the procedures for adopting `Collection`. Navigate back to the playground page and take it for a test drive:

```
example(of: "using collection") {
  var list = LinkedList<Int>()
  for i in 0...9 {
    list.append(i)
  }

  print("List: \(list)")
  print("First element: \(list[list.startIndex])")
  print("Array containing first 3 elements: \
(Array(list.prefix(3)))")
  print("Array containing last 3 elements: \
(Array(list.suffix(3)))")

  let sum = list.reduce(0, +)
  print("Sum of all values: \(sum)")
}
```

You should see the following output:

```
---Example of using collection---
List: 0 -> 1 -> 2 -> 3 -> 4 -> 5 -> 6 -> 7 -> 8 -> 9
First element: 0
Array containing first 3 elements: [0, 1, 2]
Array containing last 3 elements: [7, 8, 9]
Sum of all values: 45
```

Value semantics and copy-on-write

Another important quality of a Swift collection is that it has value semantics. This is implemented efficiently using copy-on-write, hereby referred to as *COW*. To illustrate the concept of value semantics, you'll explore the behavior using arrays.

Write the following at the bottom of the playground page:

```
example(of: "array cow") {
  let array1 = [1, 2]
  var array2 = array1

  print("array1: \(array1)")
  print("array2: \(array2)")

  print("---After adding 3 to array 2---")
  array2.append(3)
  print("array1: \(array1)")
  print("array2: \(array2)")
}
```

You should see the following output:

```
---Example of array cow---
array1: [1, 2]
array2: [1, 2]
---After adding 3 to array 2---
array1: [1, 2]
array2: [1, 2, 3]
```

The elements of `array1` are unchanged when `array2` is modified. Underneath the hood, `array2` makes a copy of the underlying storage when append is called:

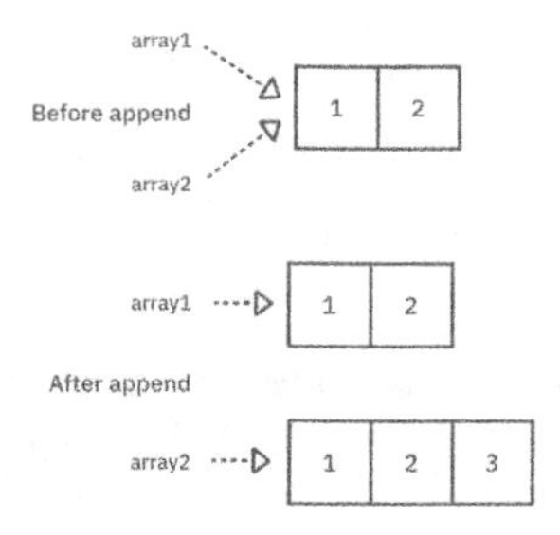

Now, check whether or not your linked list has value semantics. Write the following at the bottom of the playground page:

```
example(of: "linked list cow") {
  var list1 = LinkedList<Int>()
```

```
    list1.append(1)
    list1.append(2)
    var list2 = list1
    print("List1: \(list1)")
    print("List2: \(list2)")

    print("After appending 3 to list2")
    list2.append(3)
    print("List1: \(list1)")
    print("List2: \(list2)")
}
```

You should see the following output:

```
---Example of linked list cow---
List1: 1 -> 2
List2: 1 -> 2
After appending 3 to list2
List1: 1 -> 2 -> 3
List2: 1 -> 2 -> 3
```

Unfortunately, your linked list does not have value semantics! This is because your underlying storage uses a reference type (`Node`). This is a serious problem, as `LinkedList` is a struct and should use value semantics. Implementing COW will fix this problem.

The strategy to achieve value semantics with COW is reasonably straightforward. Before mutating the contents of the linked list, you want to perform a *copy* of the underlying storage and update all references (`head` and `tail`) to the new copy.

In **LinkedList.swift**, add the following method to `LinkedList`:

```
private mutating func copyNodes() {
  guard var oldNode = head else {
    return
  }

  head = Node(value: oldNode.value)
  var newNode = head

  while let nextOldNode = oldNode.next {
    newNode!.next = Node(value: nextOldNode.value)
    newNode = newNode!.next

    oldNode = nextOldNode
  }

  tail = newNode
}
```

This method will replace the existing nodes of your linked list with newly allocated ones with the same value.

Now find all other methods in `LinkedList` marked with the **`mutating`** keyword and call `copyNodes` at the top of every method.

There are six methods in total:

- `push`
- `append`
- `insert(after:)`
- `pop`
- `removeLast`
- `remove(after:)`

After you've completed the retrofits, the last `example` function call should yield the following output:

```
---Example of linked list cow---
List1: 1 -> 2
List2: 1 -> 2
After appending 3 to list2
List1: 1 -> 2
List2: 1 -> 2 -> 3
```

Which is what you want! Well, other than introducing a *O(n)* overhead on every mutating call...

Optimizing COW

The *O(n)* overhead on every mutating call is *unacceptable*. Two strategies help alleviate this problem. The first is to avoid copying when the nodes only have **one** owner.

isKnownUniquelyReferenced

In the Swift standard library lives a function named `isKnownUniquelyReferenced`. This function can be used to determine whether or not an object has exactly one reference to it. Test this out in the linked list COW example.

In the last `example` function call, find the line where you wrote `var list2 = list1` and update that to the following:

```
print("List1 uniquely referenced: \
(isKnownUniquelyReferenced(&list1.head))")
var list2 = list1
print("List1 uniquely referenced: \
(isKnownUniquelyReferenced(&list1.head))")
```

You should see two new lines in the console:

```
List1 uniquely referenced: true
List1 uniquely referenced: false
```

Using `isKnownUniquelyReferenced`, you can check whether or not the underlying node objects are shared! Since you've verified this behavior, remove the two `print` statements. Your path is clear. Add the following condition to the top of `copyNodes`:

```
guard !isKnownUniquelyReferenced(&head) else {
  return
}
```

You can be pleased that COW is still very much in effect:

```
---Example of linked list cow---
List1: 1 -> 2
List2: 1 -> 2
After appending 3 to list2
List1: 1 -> 2
List2: 1 -> 2 -> 3
```

With this change, your linked list performance will reclaim its previous performance with the benefits of COW.

A minor predicament

Add the following code inside your previous example code:

```
print("Removing middle node on list2")
if let node = list2.node(at: 0) {
  list2.remove(after: node)
}
print("List2: \(list2)")
```

You should see the following console output:

```
---Example of linked list cow---
List1: 1 -> 2
List2: 1 -> 2
After appending 3 to list2
List1: 1 -> 2
List2: 1 -> 2 -> 3
Removing middle node on list2
List2: 1 -> 2 -> 3
```

The remove operation is no longer working. The reason for this lies in the CoW optimization we made. Because every mutation can trigger a copy of the nodes, the `remove(after:)` implementation is making a removal on the wrong set of nodes. To rectify that, you'll write a specialized version of the `copyNodes` method. Head back into **LinkedList.swift** in your **Sources** directory and write the following just below the `copyNodes` method:

```
private mutating func copyNodes(returningCopyOf node:
Node<Value>?) -> Node<Value>? {
  guard !isKnownUniquelyReferenced(&head) else {
    return nil
  }
  guard var oldNode = head else {
    return nil
  }

  head = Node(value: oldNode.value)
  var newNode = head
  var nodeCopy: Node<Value>?

  while let nextOldNode = oldNode.next {
    if oldNode === node {
      nodeCopy = newNode
    }
    newNode!.next = Node(value: nextOldNode.value)
    newNode = newNode!.next
    oldNode = nextOldNode
  }

  return nodeCopy
}
```

This method shares many similarities with the previous implementation. The main difference is that it will return the newly copied node based on the passed in parameter. Update the `remove(after:)` method to the following:

```
@discardableResult
public mutating func remove(after node: Node<Value>) -> Value? {
```

```
  guard let node = copyNodes(returningCopyOf: node) else
{ return nil }
  defer {
    if node.next === tail {
      tail = node
    }
    node.next = node.next?.next
  }
  return node.next?.value
}
```

You're now using the method you just created and performing the removal on the newly copied node.

Sharing nodes

The second optimization is a *partial sharing* of nodes. As it turns out, there are certain scenarios where you can avoid a copy. A comprehensive evaluation of all the scenarios is beyond the scope of this book, but this will give you an idea about what's involved.

Take a look at the following example (no need to write this down):

```
var list1 = LinkedList<Int>()
(1...3).forEach { list1.append($0) }
var list2 = list1
```

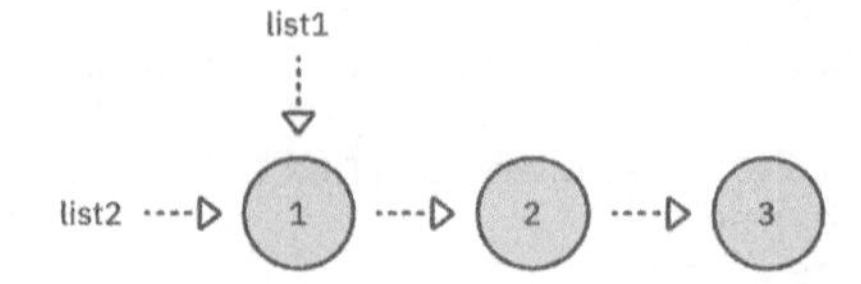

Now consider the consequence of doing a push operation on `list2` with cow *disabled*:

```
list2.push(0)
```

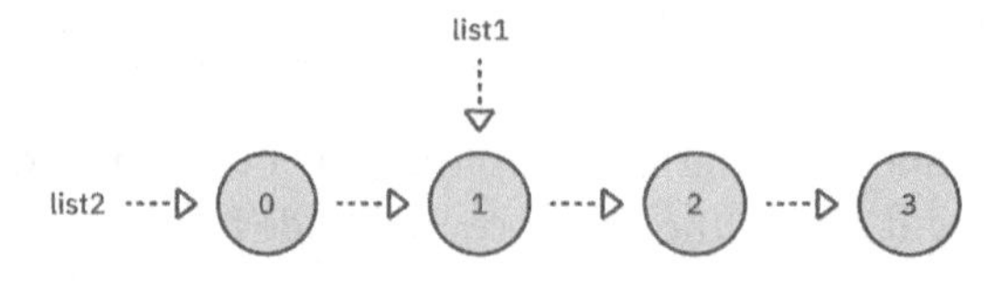

Is `list1` affected by `push` operation on `list2`? Not in this case! If you were to print the two lists, you'll get the following output:

```
List1: 1 -> 2 -> 3
List2: 0 -> 1 -> 2 -> 3
```

The result of pushing 100 to `list1` in this case is also safe:

```
list1.push(100)
```

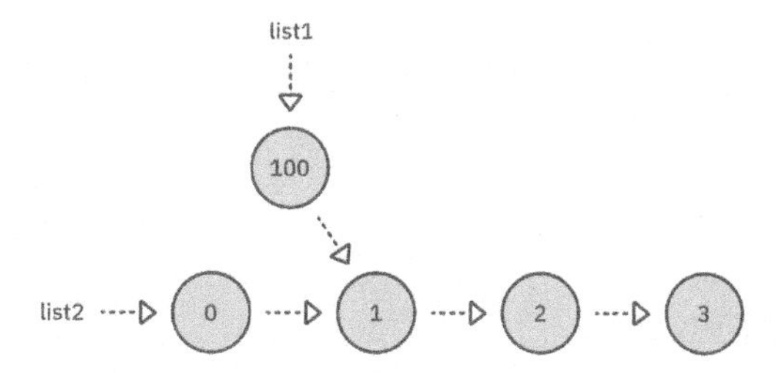

If you were to print the two lists now, you'd get the following output:

```
List1: 100 -> 1 -> 2 -> 3
List2: 0 -> 1 -> 2 -> 3
```

The unidirectional nature of the linked list means that head-first insertions can ignore the "COW tax"!

Key points

- Linked lists are linear and unidirectional. As soon as you move a reference from one node to another, you can't go back.
- Linked lists have a $O(1)$ time complexity for head first insertions. Arrays have $O(n)$ time complexity for head-first insertions.
- Conforming to Swift collection protocols such as `Sequence` and `Collection` automatically gives you access to many helpful methods.
- **Copy-on-write** behavior lets you achieve value semantics while maintaining good performance.

Chapter 7: Linked List Challenges

By Kelvin Lau

In this chapter, you'll work through five common scenarios for the linked list. These problems are relatively easy compared to most challenges, and they will serve to solidify your knowledge of data structures.

Open the starter project to begin. In it, you'll find the following challenges.

Challenge 1: Print in reverse

Create a function that prints the nodes of a linked list in reverse order. For example:

```
1 -> 2 -> 3 -> nil

// should print out the following:
3
2
1
```

Challenge 2: Find the middle node

Create a function that finds the middle node of a linked list. For example:

```
1 -> 2 -> 3 -> 4 -> nil
// middle is 3

1 -> 2 -> 3 -> nil
// middle is 2
```

Challenge 3: Reverse a linked list

Create a function that reverses a linked list. You do this by manipulating the nodes so that they're linked in the other direction. For example:

```
// before
1 -> 2 -> 3 -> nil

// after
3 -> 2 -> 1 -> nil
```

Challenge 4: Merge two lists

Create a function that takes two sorted linked lists and merges them into a single sorted linked list. Your goal is to return a new linked list that contains the nodes from two lists in sorted order. You may assume the sort order is ascending. For example:

```
// list1
1 -> 4 -> 10 -> 11

// list2
-1 -> 2 -> 3 -> 6

// merged list
-1 -> 1 -> 2 -> 3 -> 4 -> 6 -> 10 -> 11
```

Challenge 5: Remove all occurrences

Create a function that removes all occurrences of a specific element from a linked list. The implementation is similar to the `remove(at:)` method you implemented for the linked list. For example:

```
// original list
1 -> 3 -> 3 -> 3 -> 4

// list after removing all occurrences of 3
1 -> 4
```

Solutions

Solution to Challenge 1

A straightforward way to solve this problem is to use recursion. Since recursion allows you to build a call stack, you just need to call the `print` statements as the call stack unwinds.

Your first task is to recursively traverse to the end. Add the following helper function to your playground:

```
private func printInReverse<T>(_ node: Node<T>?) {

  // 1
  guard let node = node else { return }

  // 2
  printInReverse(node.next)
}
```

1. You first start off with the **base case**: the condition to terminating the recursion. If node is `nil`, then it means you've reached the end of the list.
2. This is your recursive call, calling the same function with the next node.

Printing

Where you add the `print` statement will determine whether you print the list in reverse order or not.

Update the function to the following:

```
private func printInReverse<T>(_ node: Node<T>?) {
  guard let node = node else { return }
  printInReverse(node.next)
  print(node.value)
}
```

Any code that comes after the recursive call is called only after the base case triggers (i.e., after the recursive function hits the end of the list). As the recursive statements unravel, the node data gets printed out.

Finally, you need to call the helper method from the original `printInReverse` function. Update that to look like this:

```
func printInReverse<T>(_ list: LinkedList<T>) {
  printInReverse(list.head)
}
```

Test it out!

Write the following at the bottom of the playground page:

```
example(of: "printing in reverse") {
  var list = LinkedList<Int>()
  list.push(3)
  list.push(2)
  list.push(1)

  print("Original list: \(list)")
  print("Printing in reverse:")
  printInReverse(list)
}
```

You should see the following output:

```
---Example of printing in reverse---
Original list: 1 -> 2 -> 3
Printing in reverse:
3
2
1
```

The time complexity of this algorithm is ***O(n)*** since you have to traverse each node of the list. The space complexity is likewise ***O(n)*** since you implicitly use the function call stack to process each element.

Solution to Challenge 2

One solution is to have two references traverse down the nodes of the list, where one is twice as fast as the other. Once the faster reference reaches the end, the slower reference will be in the middle. Update the function to the following:

```
func getMiddle<T>(_ list: LinkedList<T>) -> Node<T>? {
  var slow = list.head
  var fast = list.head

  while let nextFast = fast?.next {
    fast = nextFast.next
    slow = slow?.next
  }

  return slow
}
```

In the `while` declaration, you bind the next node to `nextFast`. If there is a next node, you update `fast` to the next node of `nextFast`, effectively traversing the list twice. The `slow` pointer is updated only once. This is known as the *runner's technique*.

Try it out!

Write the following at the bottom of the playground page:

```
example(of: "getting the middle node") {
  var list = LinkedList<Int>()
  list.push(3)
  list.push(2)
  list.push(1)

  print(list)

  if let middleNode = getMiddle(list) {
    print(middleNode)
  }
}
```

You should see the following output:

```
---Example of getting the middle node---
1 -> 2 -> 3
2 -> 3
```

The time complexity of this algorithm is ***O(n)*** since you traversed the list in a single pass. The runner's technique helps solve a variety of problems associated with the linked list.

Solution to Challenge 3

To reverse a linked list, you must visit each node and update the `next` reference to point in the other direction. This can be a tricky task since you'll need to manage multiple references to multiple nodes.

The easy way

You can trivially reverse a list by using the `push` method along with a new temporary list. Update the code in the playground:

```
extension LinkedList {

  mutating func reverse() {

    // 1
    let tmpList = LinkedList<Value>()
    for value in self {
      tmpList.push(value)
    }

    // 2
    head = tmpList.head
  }
}
```

1. You first start by pushing the current values in your list to a new `tmpList`. This will create a list in reverse order.
2. You point the `head` of the list to the reversed nodes.

O(n) time complexity, short and sweet!

But wait...

Although ***O(n)*** is the optimal time complexity for reversing a list, there's a significant resource cost in the previous solution. As it is now, `reverse` will have to allocate new nodes for each `push` method on the temporary list. You can avoid using the temporary list entirely and reverse the list by manipulating the `next` pointers of each node. The code ends up being more complicated, but you reap considerable benefits in terms of performance.

Update the reverse method to the following:

```
mutating func reverse() {
  tail = head
  var prev = head
  var current = head?.next
  prev?.next = nil

  // more to come...
}
```

You begin by assigning head to `tail`. Next, you create two references — `prev` and `current` — to keep track of traversal. The strategy is fairly straightforward: each node points to the next node down the list. You'll traverse the list and make each node point to the previous node instead:

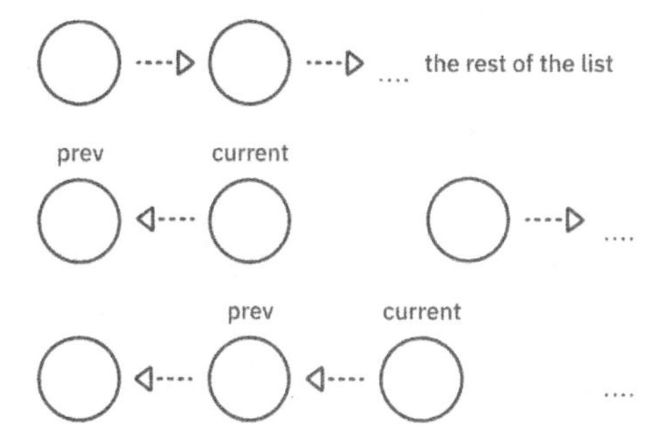

As you can see from the diagram, it gets a little tricky. By pointing `current` to `prev`, you've lost the link to the rest of the list. Therefore, you'll need to manage a third pointer. Add the following at the bottom of the `reverse` method:

```
while current != nil {
  let next = current?.next
  current?.next = prev
  prev = current
  current = next
}
```

Each time you perform the reversal, you create a new reference to the next node. After every reversal procedure, you move the two pointers to the next two nodes.

Once you've finished reversing all the pointers, you'll set the head to the last node of this list. Add the following at the end of the `reverse` method:

```
head = prev
```

Try it out!

Test the `reverse` method by writing the following at the bottom of the playground page:

```
example(of: "reversing a list") {
  var list = LinkedList<Int>()
  list.push(3)
  list.push(2)
  list.push(1)

  print("Original list: \(list)")
  list.reverse()
  print("Reversed list: \(list)")
}
```

You should see the following output:

```
---Example of reversing a list---
Original list: 1 -> 2 -> 3
Reversed list: 3 -> 2 -> 1
```

The time complexity of your new `reverse` method is still ***O(n)***, the same as the trivial implementation discussed earlier. However, you didn't need to use a temporary list or allocate new `Node` objects, which significantly improves the performance of this algorithm.

Solution to Challenge 4

The solution to this problem is to continuously pluck nodes from the two sorted lists and add them to a new list. Since the two lists are sorted, you can compare the `next` node of both lists to see which one should be the next one to add to the new list.

Setting up

You'll begin by checking the cases where one or both of the lists are empty. Add the following to `mergeSorted`:

```
guard !left.isEmpty else {
  return right
}

guard !right.isEmpty else {
  return left
}

var newHead: Node<T>?
```

If one is empty, you return the other. You also introduce a new reference to hold a sorted list of `Node` objects. The strategy is to merge the nodes in `left` and `right` onto `newHead` in sorted order.

Write the following below `newHead`:

```
// 1
var tail: Node<T>?
var currentLeft = left.head
var currentRight = right.head
// 2
if let leftNode = currentLeft, let rightNode = currentRight {
  if leftNode.value < rightNode.value {
    newHead = leftNode
    currentLeft = leftNode.next
  } else {
    newHead = rightNode
    currentRight = rightNode.next
  }
  tail = newHead
}
```

1. You create a pointer to the **tail** of the new list you're adding to. This allows for constant-time append operations.
2. You compare the first nodes of `left` and `right` to assign `newHead`.

Merging

Next, you'll need to iterate through both `left` and `right`, cherry picking the nodes to add to ensure that the new list is sorted. Add the following to the end of the function:

```
// 1
while let leftNode = currentLeft, let rightNode = currentRight {
  // 2
  if leftNode.value < rightNode.value {
    tail?.next = leftNode
    currentLeft = leftNode.next
  } else {
    tail?.next = rightNode
    currentRight = rightNode.next
  }
  tail = tail?.next
}
```

1. The `while` loop will continue until one of the list reaches the end.
2. Much like before, you compare the nodes to find out which node to connect to `tail`.

Since this loop depends on both `currentLeft` and `currentRight`, it will terminate even if nodes remain on either list.

Add the following to handle the remaining nodes:

```
if let leftNodes = currentLeft {
  tail?.next = leftNodes
}

if let rightNodes = currentRight {
  tail?.next = rightNodes
}
```

This appends the remainder of the nodes.

To wrap things up, you instantiate a new list. Instead of using using the `append` or `insert` methods to insert elements to the list, you'll simply set the reference of the `head` and `tail` of the list directly:

```
var list = LinkedList<T>()
list.head = newHead
list.tail = {
  while let next = tail?.next {
    tail = next
  }
  return tail
}()
return list
```

Try it out!

Write the following at the bottom of the playground:

```
example(of: "merging two lists") {
  var list = LinkedList<Int>()
  list.push(3)
  list.push(2)
  list.push(1)
  var anotherList = LinkedList<Int>()
  anotherList.push(-1)
  anotherList.push(-2)
  anotherList.push(-3)
  print("First list: \(list)")
  print("Second list: \(anotherList)")
  let mergedList = mergeSorted(list, anotherList)
  print("Merged list: \(mergedList)")
}
```

You should see the following output:

```
---Example of merging two lists---
First list: 1 -> 2 -> 3
Second list: -3 -> -2 -> -1
Merged list: -3 -> -2 -> -1 -> 1 -> 2 -> 3
```

This algorithm has a time complexity of ***O(m + n)***, where ***m*** is the # of nodes in the first list, and ***n*** is the # of nodes in the second list.

Solution to Challenge 5

This solution traverses down the list, removing all nodes that match the element you want to remove. Each time you perform a removal, you need to reconnect the predecessor node with the successor node. While this can get complicated, it's well worth it to practice this technique. Many data structures and algorithms will rely on clever uses of pointer arithmetic to build.

There are a few cases you need to consider. The first is to clear out the nodes from the front of the list.

Trimming the head

The first case to consider is when the head of the list contains the value that you want to remove. Suppose you want to remove **1** from the following list:

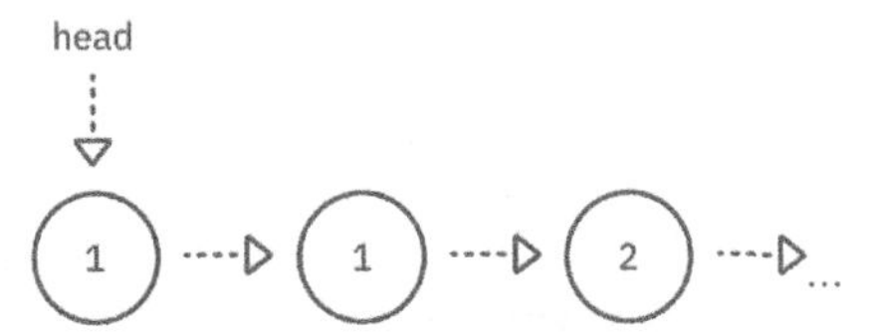

You'd want your new head to point to **2**.

Write the following inside the `remove` function:

```
while let head = head, head.value == value {
  head = head?.next
}
```

You first deal with the case where the head of the list contains the value you want to remove. Since it's possible to have a sequence of nodes with the same value, you use a `while` loop to ensure that you remove them all.

Unlinking the nodes

Like many of the algorithms associated with the linked list, you'll be leveraging your pointer arithmetic skills to unlink the nodes. Write the following at the bottom of `remove`:

```
var prev = head
var current = head?.next
while let currentNode = current {
  guard currentNode.value != value else {
    prev?.next = currentNode.next
    current = prev?.next
    continue
  }
  // more to come
}
```

You'll need to traverse the list using two pointers. The `else` block of the `guard` statement will trigger if it's necessary to remove the node.

You modify the list so that you bypass the node you don't want:

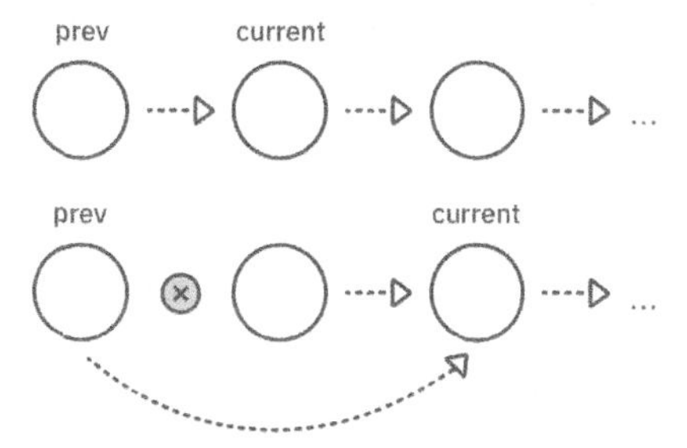

Keep traveling...

Can you tell what's missing? As it is right now, the `while` statement may never terminate. You need to move the `prev` and `current` pointers along. Write the following at the bottom of the `while` loop, after the `guard` statement:

```
prev = current
current = current?.next
```

Finally, you'll update the `tail` of the linked list. This is necessary when the original tail is a node containing the value you wanted to remove. Add the following to the end of `removeAll`:

```
tail = prev
```

And that's it for the implementation!

Try it out!

Write the following at the bottom of the playground page:

```
example(of: "deleting duplicate nodes") {
  var list = LinkedList<Int>()
  list.push(3)
  list.push(2)
  list.push(2)
  list.push(1)
  list.push(1)

  list.removeAll(3)
  print(list)
}
```

You should see the following output:

```
---Example of deleting duplicate nodes---
1 -> 1 -> 2 -> 2
```

This algorithm has a time complexity of ***O(n)*** since you'll need to go through all the elements.

Chapter 8: Queues

By Vincent Ngo

We are all familiar with waiting in line. Whether you are in line to buy tickets to your favorite movie or waiting for a printer to print a file, these real-life scenarios mimic the **queue** data structure.

Queues use **FIFO** or *first-in first-out* ordering, meaning the first element added will always be the first to be removed. Queues are handy when you need to maintain the order of your elements to process later.

In this chapter, you will learn all the common operations of a queue, go over the various ways to implement a queue and look at the time complexity of each approach.

Common operations

Let's establish a protocol for queues:

```
public protocol Queue {
  associatedtype Element
  mutating func enqueue(_ element: Element) -> Bool
  mutating func dequeue() -> Element?
  var isEmpty: Bool { get }
  var peek: Element? { get }
}
```

The protocol describes the core operations for a queue:

- **enqueue**: Insert an element at the back of the queue. Returns `true` if the operation was successful.
- **dequeue**: Remove the element at the front of the queue and return it.
- **isEmpty**: Check if the queue is empty.
- **peek**: Return the element at the front of the queue without removing it.

Notice that the queue only cares about removal from the front and insertion at the back. You don't need to know what the contents are in between. If you did, you would probably just use an array.

Example of a queue

The easiest way to understand how a queue works is to see a working example. Imagine a group of people waiting in line for a movie ticket.

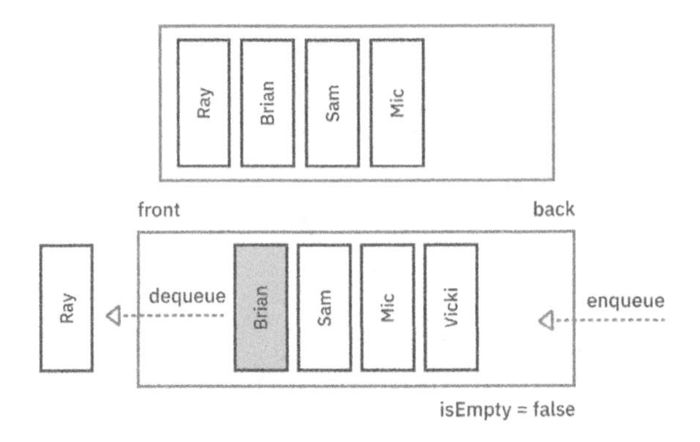

The queue currently holds Ray, Brian, Sam and Mic. Once Ray has received his ticket, he moves out of the line. By calling `dequeue()`, Ray is removed from the *front* of the queue.

Calling `peek` will return Brian since he is now at the front of the line.

Now comes Vicki, who just joined the line to buy a ticket. By calling `enqueue("Vicki")`, Vicki gets added to the *back* of the queue.

In the following sections, you will learn to create a queue in four different ways:

- Using an array
- Using a doubly linked list
- Using a ring buffer
- Using two stacks

Array-based implementation

The Swift standard library comes with a core set of highly optimized, primitive data structures that you can use to build higher-level abstractions. One of them is `Array`, a data structure that stores a contiguous, ordered list of elements. In this section, you will use an array to create a queue.

front back

Ray Brian Sam

A simple Swift array can be used to model the queue.

Open the starter playground. To the **QueueArray** page, add the following:

```
public struct QueueArray<T>: Queue {
  private var array: [T] = []
  public init() {}
}
```

Here, you've defined a generic `QueueArray` struct that adopts the `Queue` protocol. Note that the compiler infers the associated type `Element` from the type parameter `T`.

Next, you'll complete the implementation of QueueArray to conform to the Queue protocol.

Leveraging arrays

Add the following code to QueueArray:

```
public var isEmpty: Bool {
  array.isEmpty // 1
}

public var peek: T? {
  array.first // 2
}
```

Using the features of Array, you get the following for free:

1. Check if the queue is empty.
2. Return the element at the front of the queue.

These operations are all $O(1)$.

Enqueue

Adding an element to the back of the queue is easy. Just append an element to the array. Add the following:

```
public mutating func enqueue(_ element: T) -> Bool {
  array.append(element)
  return true
}
```

Enqueueing an element is, on average, an $O(1)$ operation. This is because the array has empty space at the back.

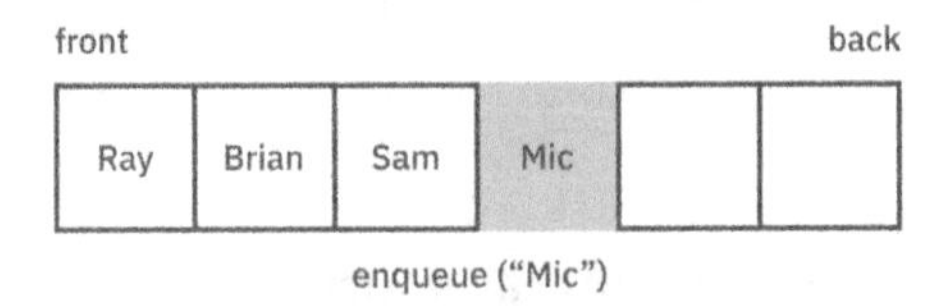

In the example above, notice that, once you add Mic, the array has two empty spaces.

After adding multiple elements, the array will eventually be full. When you want to use more than the allocated space, the array must resize to make additional room.

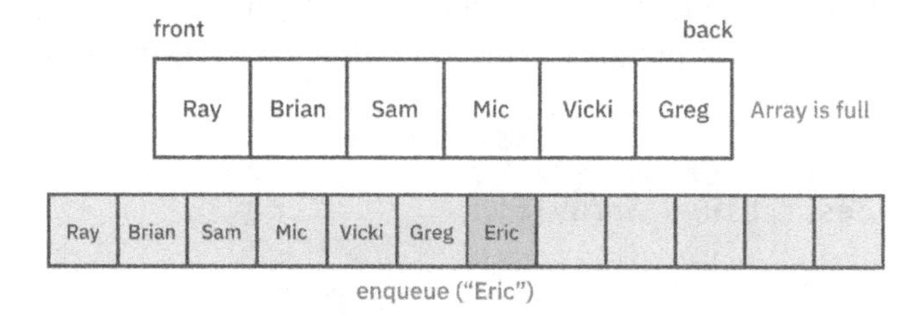

You might find it surprising that enqueueing is an $O(1)$ operation even though sizing is an $O(n)$ operation. Resizing, after all, requires the array to allocate new memory and copy all existing data over to the new array. The key is that this doesn't happen very often. This is because the capacity doubles each time it runs out of space. As a result, if you work out the **amortized cost** of the operation (the average cost), enqueueing is only $O(1)$. That said, the worst-case performance is $O(n)$ when the copy is performed.

Dequeue

Removing an item from the front requires a bit more work. Add the following:

```
public mutating func dequeue() -> T? {
  isEmpty ? nil : array.removeFirst()
}
```

If the queue is empty, `dequeue` simply returns `nil`. If not, it removes the element from the front of the array and returns it.

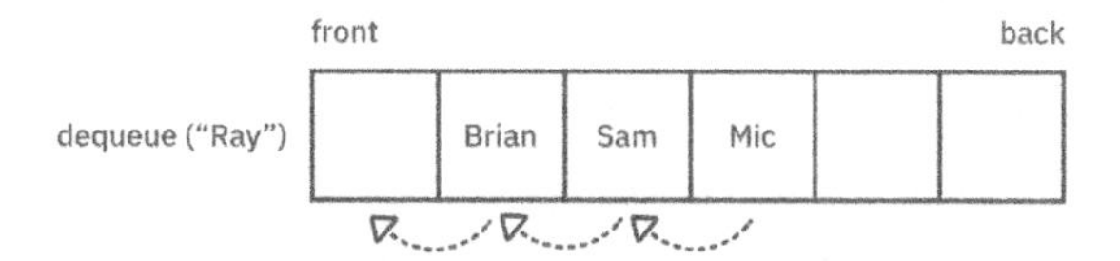

Removing an element from the front of the queue is an $O(n)$ operation. To dequeue, you remove the element from the beginning of the array. This is always a linear-time operation because it requires all the remaining elements in the array to be shifted in memory.

Debug and test

For debugging purposes, you'll have your queue adopt the `CustomStringConvertible` protocol. Add the following at the bottom of the page:

```
extension QueueArray: CustomStringConvertible {
  public var description: String {
    String(describing: array)
  }
}
```

Time to try out the queue that you just implemented! Add the following to the bottom of the page:

```
var queue = QueueArray<String>()
queue.enqueue("Ray")
queue.enqueue("Brian")
queue.enqueue("Eric")
queue
queue.dequeue()
queue
queue.peek
```

This code puts Ray, Brian and Eric in the queue, then removes Ray and peeks at Brian, but it doesn't remove him.

Strengths and weaknesses

Here is a summary of the algorithmic and storage complexity of the array-based queue implementation. Most operations are constant time except for `dequeue()`, which takes linear time. Storage space is also linear.

Array-Based Queue

Operations	Average case	Worst case
enqueue	O(1)	O(n)
dequeue	O(n)	O(n)
Space Complexity	O(n)	O(n)

You have seen how easy it is to implement an array-based queue by leveraging a Swift `Array`. Enqueue is, on average, very fast, thanks to an $O(1)$ append operation.

There are some shortcomings to the implementation. Removing an item from the front of the queue can be inefficient, as removal causes all elements to shift up by one. This makes a difference for very large queues. Once the array gets full, it has to resize and may have unused space. This could increase your memory footprint over time. Is it possible to address these shortcomings? Let's look at a linked list-based implementation and compare it to a `QueueArray`.

Doubly linked list implementation

Switch to the **QueueLinkedList** playground page. Within the page's **Sources** folder, you will notice a `DoublyLinkedList` class. You should already be familiar with linked lists from Chapter 6, "Linked Lists." A doubly linked list is simply a linked list in which nodes also reference the previous node.

Start by adding a generic `QueueLinkedList` to the very end of the page as shown below:

```
public class QueueLinkedList<T>: Queue {
  private var list = DoublyLinkedList<T>()
  public init() {}
}
```

This implementation is similar to `QueueArray`, but instead of an array, you create a `DoublyLinkedList`.

Next, let's start conforming to the `Queue` protocol.

Enqueue

To add an element to the back of the queue, simply add the following:

```
public func enqueue(_ element: T) -> Bool {
  list.append(element)
  return true
}
```

Behind the scenes, the doubly linked list will update its tail node's previous and next references to the new node. This is an $O(1)$ operation.

Dequeue

To remove an element from the queue, add the following:

```
public func dequeue() -> T? {
  guard !list.isEmpty, let element = list.first else {
    return nil
  }
  return list.remove(element)
}
```

This code checks to see if the list is not empty and the first element of the queue exists. If it doesn't, it returns `nil`. Otherwise, it removes and returns the element at the front of the queue.

Removing from the front of the list is also an $O(1)$ operation. Compared to the array implementation, you didn't have to shift elements one by one. Instead, in the diagram above, you simply update the `next` and `previous` pointers between the first two nodes of the linked list.

Checking the state of a queue

Similar to the array implementation, you can implement `peek` and `isEmpty` using the properties of the `DoublyLinkedList`. Add the following:

```
public var peek: T? {
  list.first?.value
}

public var isEmpty: Bool {
  list.isEmpty
}
```

Debug and test

For debugging purposes, you can add the following at the bottom of the page:

```
extension QueueLinkedList: CustomStringConvertible {
  public var description: String {
    String(describing: list)
  }
}
```

This conformance leverages `DoublyLinkedList`'s default implementation for the `CustomStringConvertible` protocol.

That's all there is to implementing a queue using a linked list! In the QueueLinkedList page of playground, you can try the example:

```
var queue = QueueLinkedList<String>()
queue.enqueue("Ray")
queue.enqueue("Brian")
queue.enqueue("Eric")
queue
queue.dequeue()
queue
queue.peek
```

This test code yields the same results as your `QueueArray` implementation.

Strengths and weaknesses

Let's summarize the algorithmic and storage complexity of the doubly linked list-based queue implementation.

Linked-List Based Queue

Operations	Average case	Worst case
enqueue	O(1)	O(1)
dequeue	O(1)	O(1)
Space Complexity	O(n)	O(n)

One of the main problems with `QueueArray` is that dequeuing an item takes linear time. With the linked list implementation, you reduced it to a constant operation, $O(1)$. All you needed to do was update the node's `previous` and `next` pointers.

The main weakness with `QueueLinkedList` is not apparent from the table. Despite $O(1)$ performance, it suffers from high overhead. Each element has to have extra storage for the forward and back reference. Moreover, every time you create a new element, it requires a relatively expensive dynamic allocation. By contrast, `QueueArray` does a faster bulk allocation.

Can you eliminate allocation overhead and main $O(1)$ dequeues? If you don't have to worry about your queue growing beyond a fixed size, you can use a different approach like the **ring buffer**. For example, you might have a game of *Monopoly* with five players. You can use a queue based on a ring buffer to keep track of whose turn is coming up next. You'll take a look at a ring buffer implementation next.

Ring buffer implementation

A ring buffer, also known as a **circular buffer**, is a fixed-size array. This data structure strategically wraps around to the beginning when there are no more items to remove at the end.

Going over a simple example of how a queue can be implemented using a ring buffer:

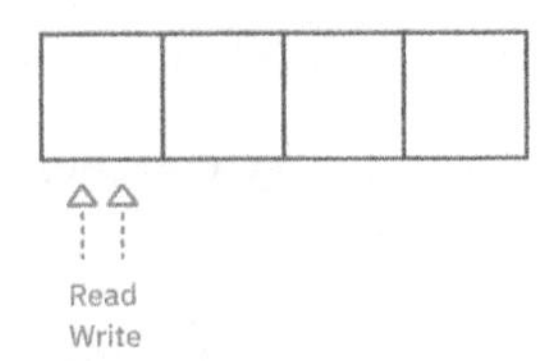

You first create a ring buffer that has a fixed size of **4**. The ring buffer has two pointers that keep track of two things:

1. The **read** pointer keeps track of the front of the queue.
2. The **write** pointer keeps track of the next available slot so that you can override existing elements that have already been read.

Let's enqueue an item:

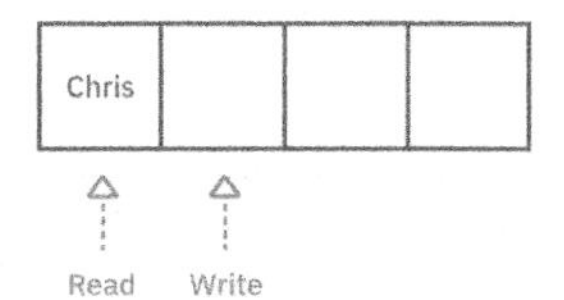

Each time you add an item to the queue, the **write** pointer increments by one. Let's add a few more elements:

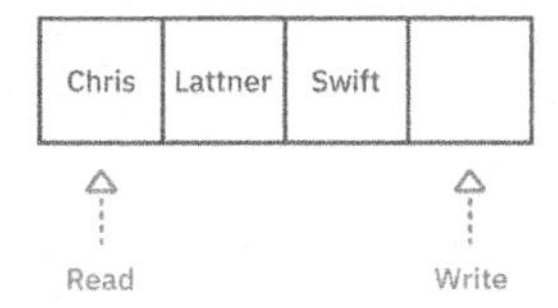

Notice that the **write** pointer moved two more spots and is ahead of the **read** pointer. This means that the queue is not empty.

Next, let's dequeue two items:

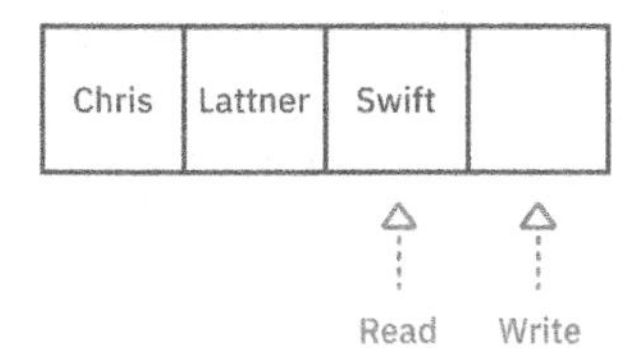

Dequeuing is the equivalent of reading a ring buffer. Notice how the **read** pointer moved twice.

Now, enqueue one more item to fill up the queue:

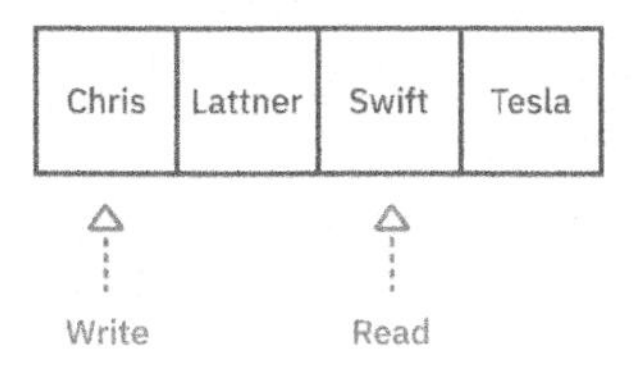

Since the **write** pointer reached the end, it simply wraps around to the starting index again. This is why the data structure is known as a circular buffer.

Finally, dequeue the two remaining items:

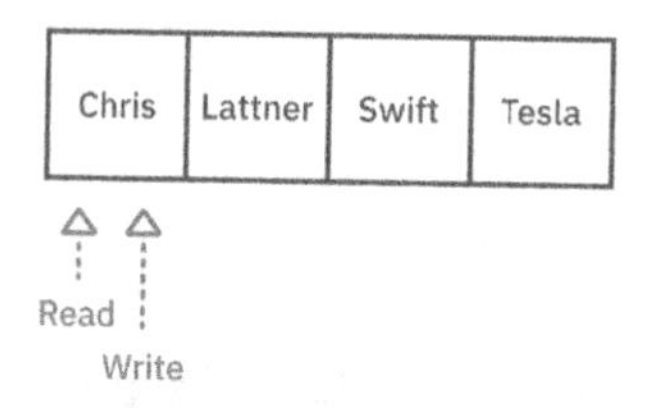

The **read** pointer wraps to the beginning, as well.

As a final observation, notice that whenever the read and write pointers are at the same index, the queue is **empty**.

Now that you have a better understanding of how ring buffers make a queue let's implement one!

Go to the **QueueRingBuffer** playground page. Within the page's **Sources** folder, you'll notice a `RingBuffer` class.

> **Note**: If you want to learn more about the implementation of this class, check out this full walk-through at https://github.com/raywenderlich/swift-algorithm-club/tree/master/Ring%20Buffer.

In the **QueueRingBuffer** page, add the following:

```
public struct QueueRingBuffer<T>: Queue {
  private var ringBuffer: RingBuffer<T>

  public init(count: Int) {
    ringBuffer = RingBuffer<T>(count: count)
  }

  public var isEmpty: Bool {
    ringBuffer.isEmpty
  }

  public var peek: T? {
    ringBuffer.first
  }
}
```

Here, you defined a generic `QueueRingBuffer`. Note that you must include a `count` parameter since the ring buffer has a fixed size.

To conform to the Queue protocol, you also created two properties isEmpty and peek. Instead of exposing ringBuffer, you provide helper variables to access the front of the queue and to check if the queue is empty. Both of these are *O*(1) operations.

Enqueue

Next, add the method below:

```
public mutating func enqueue(_ element: T) -> Bool {
  ringBuffer.write(element)
}
```

To append an element to the queue, you simply call write(_:) on the ringBuffer. This increments the write pointer by one.

Since the queue has a fixed size, you must now return true or false to indicate whether the element has been successfully added. enqueue(_:) is still an *O*(1) operation.

Dequeue

Next add the following:

```
public mutating func dequeue() -> T? {
  ringBuffer.read()
}
```

To remove an item from the front of the queue, you simply call read() on the ringBuffer. Behind the scenes, it checks if the ringBuffer is empty and, if so, returns nil. If not, it returns an item from the front of the buffer and increments the read pointer by one.

Debug and test

To see your results in the playground, add the following:

```
extension QueueRingBuffer: CustomStringConvertible {
  public var description: String {
   String(describing: ringBuffer)
  }
}
```

This code creates a string representation of the Queue by delegating to the underlying ring buffer.

That's all there is to it! Test your ring buffer-based queue by adding the following at the bottom of the page:

```
var queue = QueueRingBuffer<String>(count: 10)
queue.enqueue("Ray")
queue.enqueue("Brian")
queue.enqueue("Eric")
queue
queue.dequeue()
queue
queue.peek
```

This test code works just like the previous examples dequeuing Ray and peeking at Brian.

Strengths and weaknesses

How does the ring-buffer implementation compare? Let's look at a summary of the algorithmic and storage complexity.

Ring-Buffer Based Queue

Operations	Average case	Worst case
enqueue	O(1)	O(1)
dequeue	O(1)	O(1)
Space Complexity	O(n)	O(n)

The ring buffer-based queue has the same time complexity for enqueue and dequeue as the linked list implementation. The only difference is the space complexity. The ring buffer has a fixed size, which means that enqueue can fail.

So far, you have seen three implementations: a simple array, a doubly linked list and a ring buffer.

Although they appear to be eminently useful, you'll next look at a queue implemented using two stacks. You will see how its spatial locality is far superior to the linked list. It also doesn't need a fixed size like a ring buffer.

Double-stack implementation

Open the **QueueStack** playground page and start by adding a generic `QueueStack` as shown below:

```
public struct QueueStack<T> : Queue {
  private var leftStack: [T] = []
  private var rightStack: [T] = []
  public init() {}
}
```

The idea behind using two stacks is simple. Whenever you enqueue an element, it goes in the **right** stack.

When you need to dequeue an element, you reverse the right stack and place it in the **left** stack so that you can retrieve the elements using FIFO order.

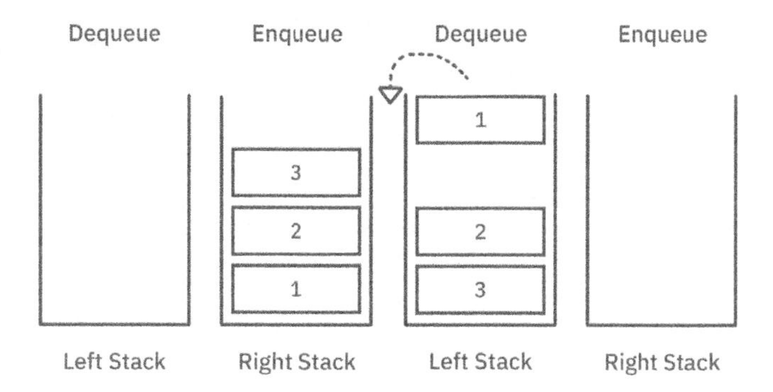

Leveraging arrays

Implement the common features of a queue, starting with the following:

```
public var isEmpty: Bool {
  leftStack.isEmpty && rightStack.isEmpty
}
```

To check if the queue is empty, check that both the left and right stacks are empty. This means that there are no elements left to dequeue, and no new elements have been enqueued.

Next, add the following:

```
public var peek: T? {
  !leftStack.isEmpty ? leftStack.last : rightStack.first
}
```

You know that peeking looks at the top element. If the left stack is not empty, the element on top of this stack is at the front of the queue.

If the left stack is empty, the right stack will be reversed and placed in the left stack.

In this case, the element at the *bottom* of the right stack is next in the queue. Note that the two properties `isEmpty` and `peek` are still $O(1)$ operations.

Enqueue

Next add the method below:

```
public mutating func enqueue(_ element: T) -> Bool {
  rightStack.append(element)
  return true
}
```

Recall that the **right** stack is used to enqueue elements.

You simply push to the stack by appending to the array. Previously, from implementing the `QueueArray`, you know that appending an element is an $O(1)$ operation.

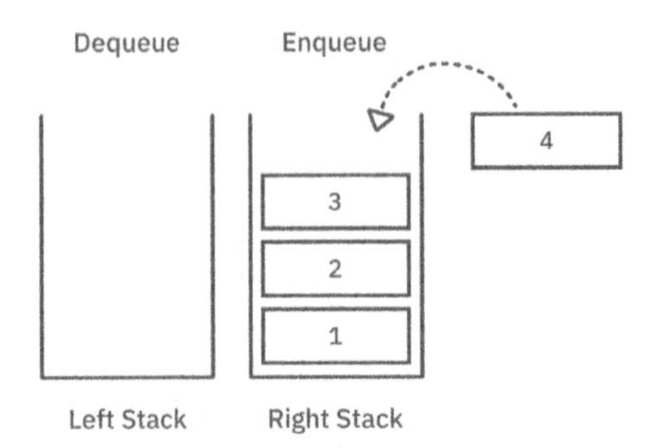

Dequeue

Removing an item from a two-stack-based implementation of a queue is tricky. Add the following method:

```
public mutating func dequeue() -> T? {
  if leftStack.isEmpty { // 1
    leftStack = rightStack.reversed() // 2
    rightStack.removeAll() // 3
  }
  return leftStack.popLast() // 4
}
```

1. Check to see if the left stack is empty.
2. If the left stack is empty, set it as the reverse of the right stack.

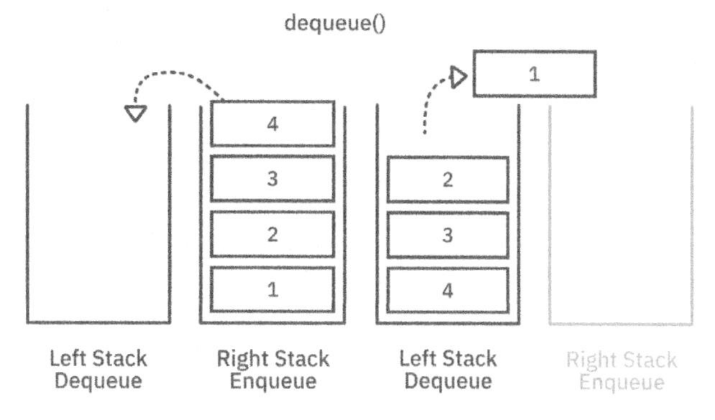

3. Invalidate your right stack. Since you have transferred everything to the left, just clear it.
4. Remove the last element from the left stack.

Remember, you only transfer the elements in the right stack when the left stack is empty!

> **Note**: Yes, reversing the contents of an array is an $O(n)$ operation. The overall dequeue cost is still amortized $O(1)$. Imagine having a large number of items in both the left and right stack. If you dequeue all of the elements, first it will remove all of the elements from the left stack, then reverse-copy the right stack only once, and then continue removing elements off the left stack.

Debug and test

To see your results in the playground, add the following:

```
extension QueueStack: CustomStringConvertible {
  public var description: String {
    String(describing: leftStack.reversed() + rightStack)
  }
}
```

Here, you simply combine the left stack with the reverse of the right stack, and you print all the elements.

Let's try out the double-stack implementation:

```
var queue = QueueStack<String>()
queue.enqueue("Ray")
queue.enqueue("Brian")
queue.enqueue("Eric")
queue
queue.dequeue()
queue
queue.peek
```

Like all of the examples before, this code enqueues Ray, Brian and Eric, dequeues Ray and then peeks at Brian.

Strengths and weaknesses

Let's look at a summary of the algorithmic and storage complexity of your two-stack-based implementation.

Double Stack Based Queue

Operations	Average case	Worst case
enqueue	O(1)	O(n)
dequeue	O(1)	O(n)
Space Complexity	O(n)	O(n)

Compared to the array-based implementation, by leveraging two stacks, you were able to transform `dequeue(_:)` into an amortized $O(1)$ operation.

Moreover, your two-stack implementation is fully dynamic and doesn't have the fixed size restriction that your ring-buffer-based queue implementation has. Worst-case performance is $O(n)$ when the right queue needs to be reversed or runs out of capacity. Running out of capacity doesn't happen very often thanks to doubling it every time it happens.

Finally, it beats the linked list in terms of spatial locality. This is because array elements are next to each other in memory blocks. So a large number of elements will be loaded in a cache on first access. Even though arrays require $O(n)$, for simple copy operations, it is a *very fast* $O(n)$ happening close to memory bandwidth.

Compare the two images below:

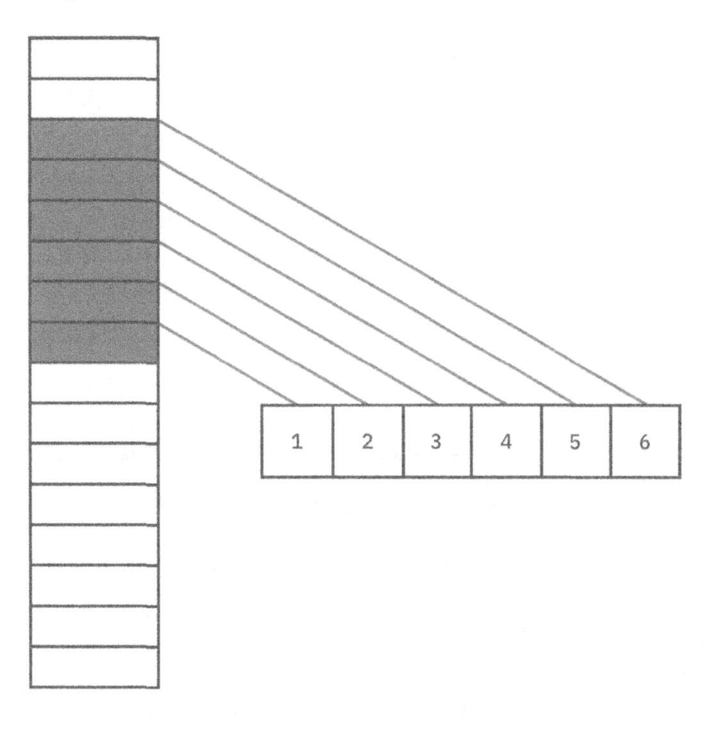

A linked list wherein the elements aren't in contiguous blocks of memory. This non-locality could lead to more cache misses, which will increase access time.

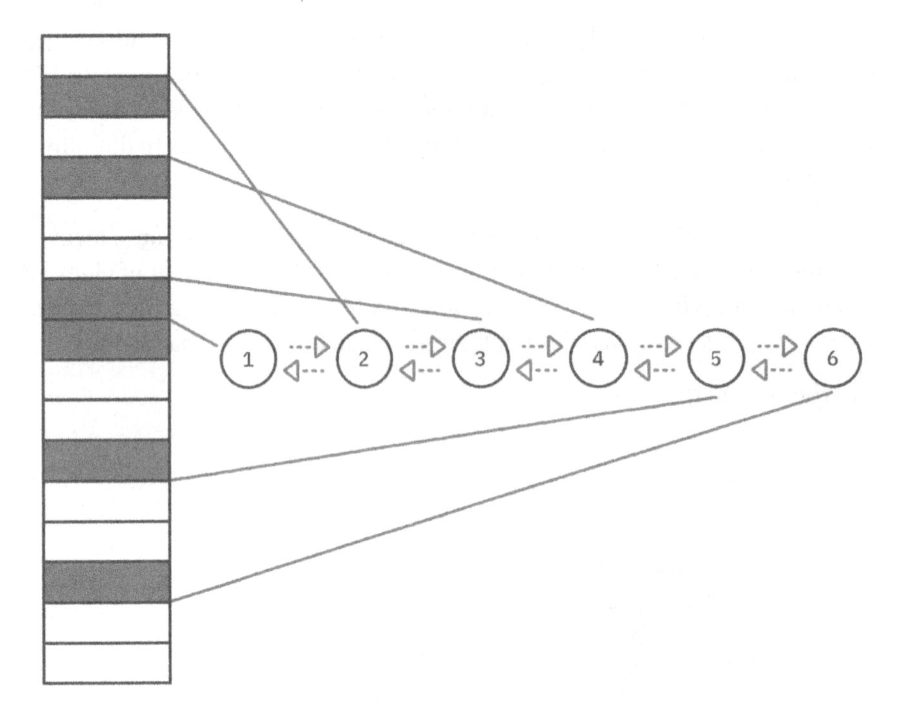

Key points

- Queue takes a **FIFO** strategy; an element added first must also be removed first.
- **Enqueue** inserts an element to the back of the queue.
- **Dequeue** removes the element at the front of the queue.
- Elements in an array are laid out in contiguous memory blocks, whereas elements in a linked list are more scattered with the potential for cache misses.
- Ring-buffer-queue-based implementation is suitable for queues with a fixed size.
- Compared to other data structures, leveraging two stacks improves the `dequeue(_:)` time complexity to amortized $O(1)$ operation.
- Double-stack implementation beats out linked list in terms of storage locality.

Chapter 9: Queue Challenges

By Vincent Ngo

Think you have a handle on queues? In this chapter, you will explore five different problems related to queues. This serves to solidify your fundamental knowledge of data structures in general.

Challenge 1: Stack vs. Queue

Explain the difference between a stack and a queue. Provide two real-life examples for each data structure.

Challenge 2: Step-by-step Diagrams

Given the following queue:

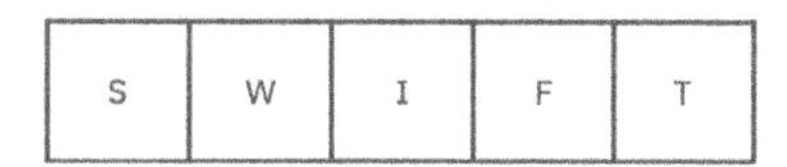

Provide step-by-step diagrams showing how the following series of commands affects the queue:

```
enqueue("R")
enqueue("O")
dequeue()
enqueue("C")
dequeue()
dequeue()
enqueue("K")
```

Do this for the following queue implementations:

1. Array-based
2. Linked list
3. Ring buffer
4. Stack-based

Assume that the array and ring buffer each have an initial size of 5.

Challenge 3: Whose turn is it?

Open the starter project, and navigate to **Challenge 3**'s playground page to begin.

Imagine that you are playing a game of Monopoly with your friends. The problem is that everyone always forgets whose turn it is! Create a Monopoly organizer that always tells you whose turn it is. Below is a protocol that you can conform to:

```
protocol BoardGameManager {

  associatedtype Player
  mutating func nextPlayer() -> Player?
}
```

Challenge 4: Reverse Queue

Navigate to **Challenge 4**'s playground page to begin.

Implement a method to reverse the contents of a queue.

> Hint: The `Stack` data structure has been included in the **Sources** folder.

```
extension QueueArray {

  func reversed() -> QueueArray {
    var queue = self
    // Solution here.
    return queue
  }
}
```

Challenge 5: Double-ended Queue

A double-ended queue — a.k.a. a **deque** — is, as its name suggests, a queue where elementscan be added or removed from the `front` or `back`.

- A queue **(FIFO order)** allows you to add elements to the back and remove them from the front.
- A stack **(LIFO order)** allows you to add elements to the back and remove them from the back.

Deque can be considered both a queue and a stack at the same time.

A simple `Deque` protocol has been provided to help you build your data structure. An enum `Direction` has been provided to help describe whether you are adding or removing an element from the front or back of the deque. You can use any data structure you prefer to construct a `Deque`.

Note:

In **DoubleLinkedList.swift** one additional property and function has been added:

- A property called `last` has been added to help get the tail element of a double-linked list.
- A function called `prepend(_:)` has been added to help you add an element to the front of a double-linked list.

```
enum Direction {
  case front
  case back
}

protocol Deque {
  associatedtype Element
  var isEmpty: Bool { get }
  func peek(from direction: Direction) -> Element?
  mutating func enqueue(_ element: Element,
                        to direction: Direction) -> Bool
  mutating func dequeue(from direction: Direction) -> Element?
}
```

Solutions

Solution to Challenge 1

Queues have a behavior of first-in-first-out. What comes in first must come out first. Items in the queue are inserted from the rear and removed from the front.

Queue Examples:

1. **Line in a movie theatre**: You would hate for people to cut the line at the movie theatre when buying tickets!
2. **Printer**: Multiple people could print documents from a printer in a similar first-come-first-serve manner.

Stacks have a behavior of last-in-first-out. Items on the stack are inserted at the top and removed from the top.

Stack Examples:

1. **Stack of plates**: Placing plates on top of each other and removing the top plate every time you use a plate. Isn't this easier than grabbing the one at the bottom?
2. **Undo functionality**: Imagine typing words on a keyboard. Clicking Ctrl-Z will undo the most recent text you typed.

Solution to Challenge 2

Array

Keep in mind whenever the array is full, and you try to add a new element, a new array will be created with **twice** the capacity with existing elements being copied over.

S	W	I	F	T

S	W	I	F	T	R				

enqueue ("R")

S	W	I	F	T	R	O			

enqueue ("O")

W	I	F	T	R	O				

dequeue ()

W	I	F	T	R	O	C			

enqueue ("C")

I	F	T	R	O	C				

dequeue ()

F	T	R	O	C					

dequeue ()

F	T	R	O	C	K				

enqueue ("K")

Linked list

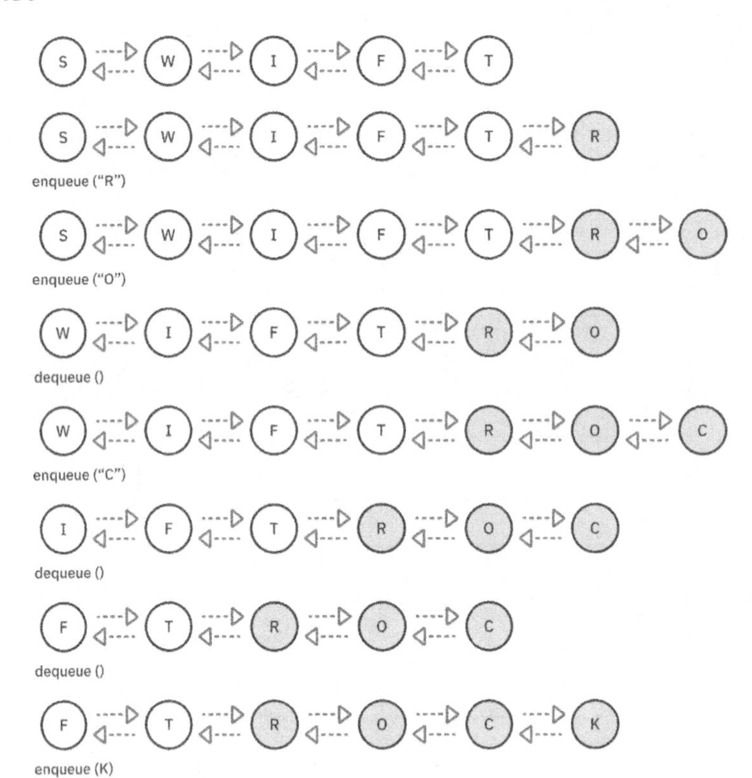
S W I F T
S W I F T R
enqueue ("R")
S W I F T R O
enqueue ("O")
W I F T R O
dequeue ()
W I F T R O C
enqueue ("C")
I F T R O C
dequeue ()
F T R O C
dequeue ()
F T R O C K
enqueue (K)

Ring buffer

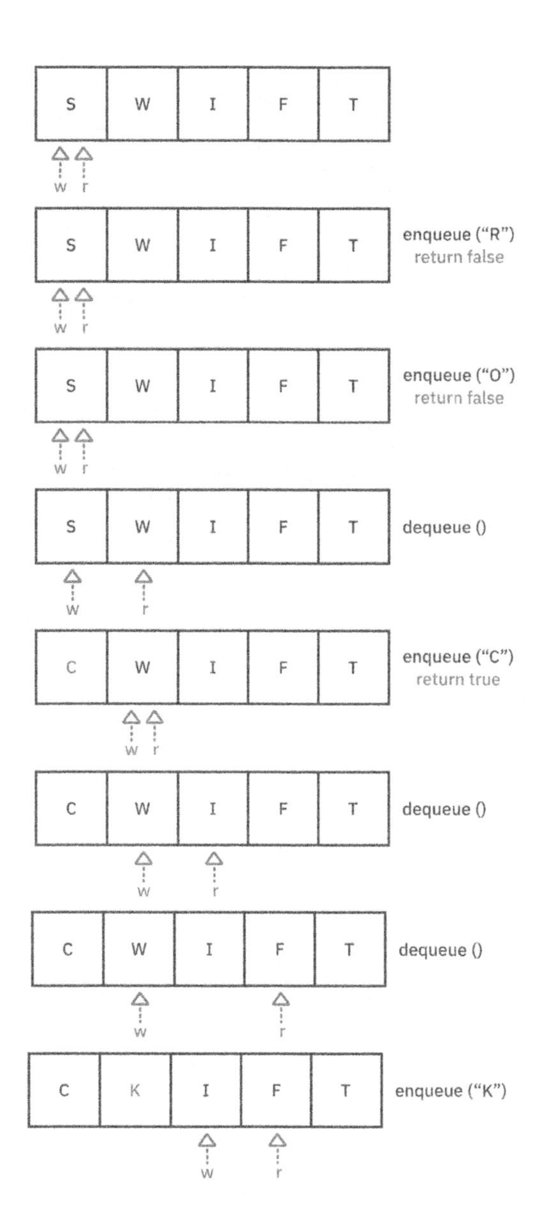
S W I F T
w r
S W I F T
enqueue ("R")
return false
w r
S W I F T
enqueue ("O")
return false
w r
S W I F T
dequeue ()
w r
C W I F T
enqueue ("C")
return true
w r
C W I F T
dequeue ()
w r
C W I F T
dequeue ()
w r
C K I F T
enqueue ("K")
w r

Double stack

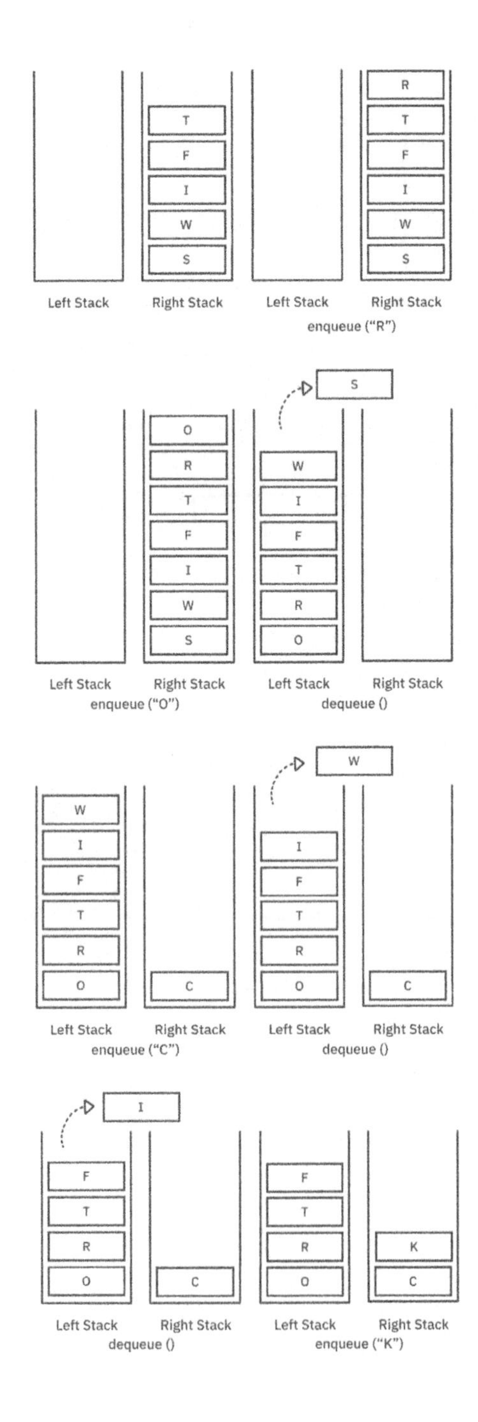

Solution to Challenge 3

Creating a board game manager is straightforward. All you care about is whose turn it is. A queue data structure is the perfect choice to adopt the `BoardGameManager` protocol!

```
extension QueueArray: BoardGameManager {

  public typealias Player = T

  public mutating func nextPlayer() -> T? {
    guard let person = dequeue() else { // 1
      return nil
    }
    enqueue(person) // 2
    return person // 3
  }
}
```

There are two requirements to adopt this protocol. You first set the `typealias` equal to the parameter type `T`. Next, you implement `nextPlayer`, which works as follows:

1. Get the next player by calling `dequeue`. If the queue is empty, return `nil`.
2. `enqueue` the same person, putting the player at the end of the queue.
3. Return the next player.

The time complexity depends on the queue implementation you pick. For the array-based queue, it is overall _O(*n*) time complexity. `dequeue` takes _O(*n*) time, because it has to shift the elements to the left every time you remove the first element. Test it out:

```
var queue = QueueArray<String>()
queue.enqueue("Vincent")
queue.enqueue("Remel")
queue.enqueue("Lukiih")
queue.enqueue("Allison")
print(queue)

print("===== boardgame =======")
queue.nextPlayer()
print(queue)
queue.nextPlayer()
print(queue)
queue.nextPlayer()
print(queue)
queue.nextPlayer()
print(queue)
```

Solution to Challenge 4

A queue uses first-in-first-out, whereas a stack uses last-in-first-out. You can use a stack to help reverse the contents of a queue. By inserting all the contents of the queue into a stack, you reverse the order once you pop every single element off the stack!

```
extension QueueArray {

  func reversed() -> QueueArray {
    var queue = self // 1
    var stack = Stack<T>() // 2
    while let element = queue.dequeue() { // 3
      stack.push(element)
    }
    while let element = stack.pop() { // 4
      queue.enqueue(element)
    }
    return queue // 5
  }
}
```

It doesn't matter what implementation of a queue you pick. As long as it conforms to the `Queue` protocol, you can generalize it to any queue!

For this solution, you can extend `QueueArray` by adding a `reversed` function. It works the following way:

1. Create a copy of the queue.
2. Create a stack.
3. `dequeue` all the elements in the queue onto the stack.
4. `pop` all the elements off the stack and insert them into the queue.
5. Return your reversed queue!

The time complexity is overall $O(n)$. You loop through the elements twice. Once for removing the elements off the queue, and once for removing the elements off the stack.

Testing it out:

```
var queue = QueueArray<String>()
queue.enqueue("1")
queue.enqueue("21")
queue.enqueue("18")
queue.enqueue("42")

print("before: \(queue)")
print("after: \(queue.reversed())")
```

Solution to Challenge 5

`Deque` is made up of common operations from the `Queue` and `Stack` data structures. There are many ways to implement a `Deque`. You could build one using a circular buffer, two stacks, an array, or a doubly linked list. The solution below makes use of a doubly linked list to construct a `Deque`.

First setup the doubly linked list deque as shown below:

```
class DequeDoubleLinkedList<Element>: Deque {

  private var list = DoublyLinkedList<Element>()
  public init() {}

}
```

Now you have to conform to the `Deque` protocol. First, implement `isEmpty` by checking if the linked list is empty. This is an $O(1)$ operation.

```
var isEmpty: Bool {
  list.isEmpty
}
```

Next, you need a way to look at the value from the front or back of the `Deque`.

```
func peek(from direction: Direction) -> Element? {
  switch direction {
  case .front:
    return list.first?.value
  case .back:
    return list.last?.value
  }
}
```

To `peek(_:)` at the element from the front or back, check the list's `first` and `last` values. This is an $O(1)$ operation since you need to look at the `head` and `tail` of the list.

Now you need a way to add elements to the front or back of the `Deque`.

```
func enqueue(_ element: Element, to direction: Direction) ->
Bool {
  switch direction {
  case .front:
    list.prepend(element)
  case .back:
    list.append(element)
  }
```

```
    return true
  }
```

Adding an element to the front or back of a Deque:

1. **Front**: prepend an element to the front of the list. Internally the linked list will update the new node as the head of the linked list.

2. **Back**: append an element to the back of the list. Similarly, the linked list will update the new node as the tail of the linked list.

These are both $O(1)$ operations, as all you have to do is update the head or tail previous and next pointers of a node.

Now that we have a way to add elements, how about a way to remove elements?

```
  func dequeue(from direction: Direction) -> Element? {
    let element: Element?
    switch direction {
    case .front:
      guard let first = list.first else { return nil }
      element = list.remove(first)
    case .back:
      guard let last = list.last else { return nil }
      element = list.remove(last)
    }
    return element
  }
```

Removing an element from the front or back of a Deque is simple. Since a doubly linked list references head and tail, you can grab their nodes and disconnect the node's previous and next pointers.

1. **Front**: Get the first **(head)** node in the list and remove it.

2. **Back**: Similarly, get the last **(tail)** node in the list and remove it.

Similar to enqueue(_:), this is an $O(1)$ operation.

Lastly, add the following CustomStringConvertible so you can test your Deque.

```
  extension DequeDoubleLinkedList: CustomStringConvertible {

    public var description: String {
      String(describing: list)
    }
  }
```

That's all there is to building a `Deque`! Add the following code below to test your implementation:

```
let deque = DequeDoubleLinkedList<Int>()
deque.enqueue(1, to: .back)
deque.enqueue(2, to: .back)
deque.enqueue(3, to: .back)
deque.enqueue(4, to: .back)

print(deque)

deque.enqueue(5, to: .front)

print(deque)

deque.dequeue(from: .back)
deque.dequeue(from: .back)
deque.dequeue(from: .back)
deque.dequeue(from: .front)
deque.dequeue(from: .front)
deque.dequeue(from: .front)

print(deque)
```

Section III: Trees

Trees are another way to organize information, introducing the concept of children and parents. You'll take a look at the most common tree types and see how they readily solve specific computational problems. Just like the last section, this section will introduce you to a concept with a chapter, followed by a Challenge chapter to help you hone the skills you are learning.

Trees are a handy way to organize information when performance is critical. Adding them as a tool to your toolbelt will undoubtedly prove to be useful throughout your career.

Chapter 10: Trees

By Kelvin Lau

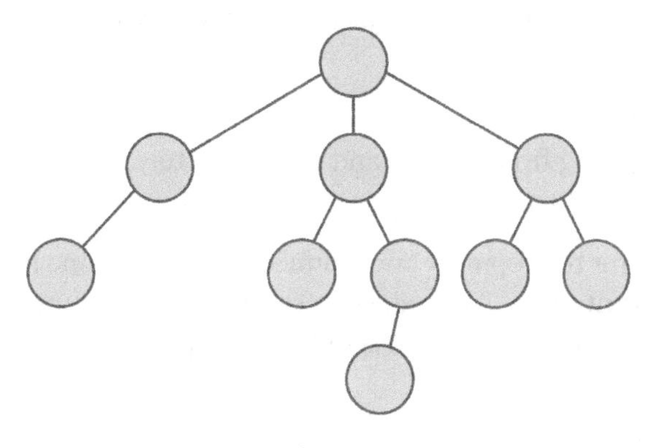

A tree

The **tree** is a data structure of profound importance. It is used in numerous facets of software development, such as:

- Representing hierarchical relationships.
- Managing sorted data.
- Facilitating fast lookup operations.

There are many types of trees, and they come in various shapes and sizes. In this chapter, you will learn the basics of using and implementing a tree.

Terminology

Many terms are associated with trees, and here are some you should know right off the bat.

Node

Like the linked list, trees are made up of **nodes**.

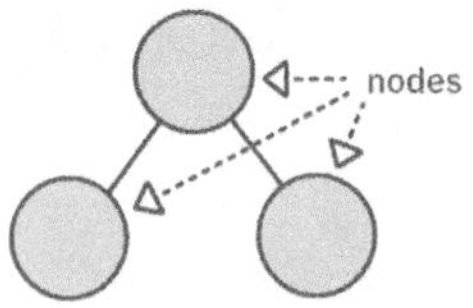

Each node can carry some data and keeps track of its *children*.

Parent and child

Trees are viewed starting from the top and branching towards the bottom, just like a real tree, only upside-down.

Every node (except for the topmost one) connects to exactly one node above it. That node is called a **parent** node. The nodes directly below and connected to it are called its **child** nodes. In a tree, every child has exactly one parent. That's what makes a tree, well, a tree.

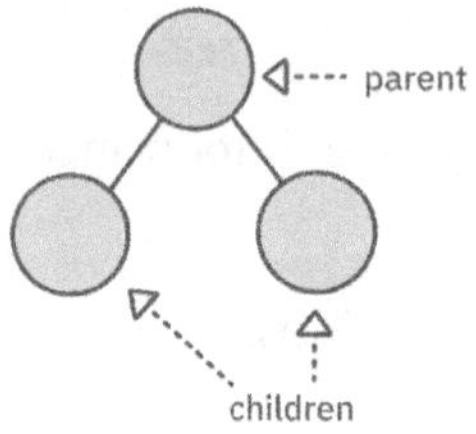

Root

The topmost node in the tree is called the **root** of the tree. It is the only node that has no parent:

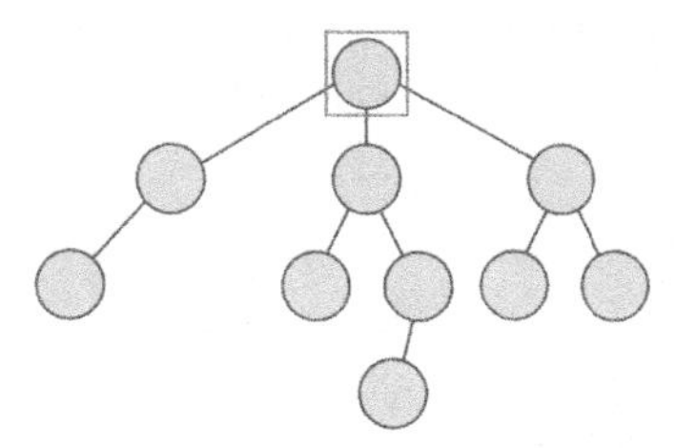

Leaf

A node is a **leaf** if it has no children:

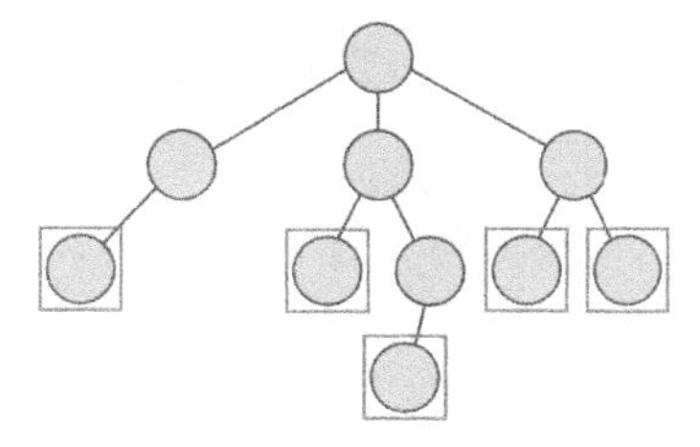

You will run into more terms later on, but this should be enough to get you started.

Implementation

Open up the starter playground for this chapter to get started. A tree consists of nodes, so your first task is to create a `TreeNode` class.

Create a new file named **TreeNode.swift** and write the following inside it:

```
public class TreeNode<T> {
  public var value: T
  public var children: [TreeNode] = []

  public init(_ value: T) {
    self.value = value
  }
}
```

Each node is responsible for a `value` and holds references to all its children using an array.

> **Note**: Using a class type to represent `TreeNode` will mean losing value semantics. On the other hand, it makes creating references to nodes trivial, which you'll use later on.

Next, add the following method inside the `TreeNode` class:

```
public func add(_ child: TreeNode) {
  children.append(child)
}
```

This method adds a child node to a node.

Time to give it a whirl. Head back to the playground page and write the following:

```
example(of: "creating a tree") {
  let beverages = TreeNode("Beverages")

  let hot = TreeNode("Hot")
  let cold = TreeNode("Cold")

  beverages.add(hot)
  beverages.add(cold)
}
```

Hierarchical structures are natural candidates for tree structures, so, here, you have defined three different nodes and organized them into a logical hierarchy. This arrangement corresponds to the following structure:

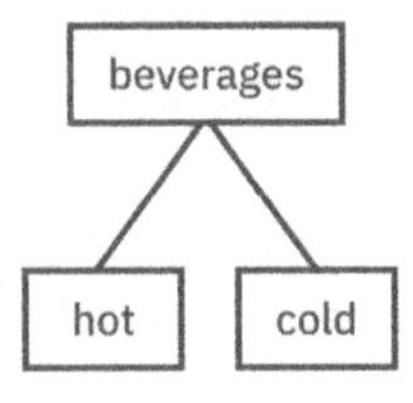

Traversal algorithms

Iterating through *linear* collections such as arrays or linked lists is straightforward. Linear collections have a clear start and end:

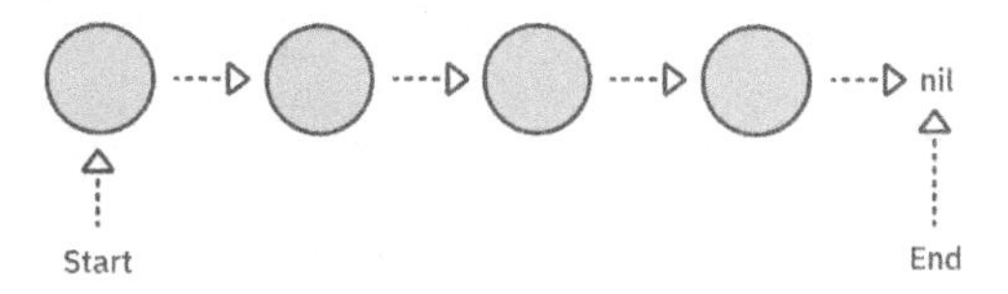

Iterating through trees is a bit more complicated:

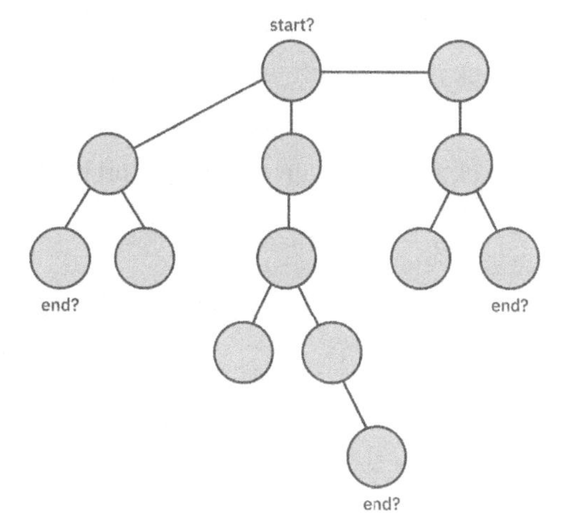

Should nodes on the left have precedence? How should the depth of a node relate to its precedence? Your traversal strategy depends on the problem that you're trying to solve. There are multiple strategies for different trees and different problems. In the next section, you will look at **depth-first traversal**, a technique that starts at the root and visits nodes as deep as it can before backtracking.

Depth-first traversal

Write the following at the bottom of **TreeNode.swift**:

```
extension TreeNode {
  public func forEachDepthFirst(visit: (TreeNode) -> Void) {
    visit(self)
    children.forEach {
      $0.forEachDepthFirst(visit: visit)
    }
  }
}
```

This simple code uses recursion to process the next node.

You could use your own stack if you didn't want your implementation to be recursive.

Time to test it out. Head back to the playground page and write the following:

```
func makeBeverageTree() -> TreeNode<String> {
  let tree = TreeNode("Beverages")

  let hot = TreeNode("hot")
  let cold = TreeNode("cold")

  let tea = TreeNode("tea")
  let coffee = TreeNode("coffee")
  let chocolate = TreeNode("cocoa")

  let blackTea = TreeNode("black")
  let greenTea = TreeNode("green")
  let chaiTea = TreeNode("chai")

  let soda = TreeNode("soda")
  let milk = TreeNode("milk")

  let gingerAle = TreeNode("ginger ale")
  let bitterLemon = TreeNode("bitter lemon")

  tree.add(hot)
  tree.add(cold)

  hot.add(tea)
  hot.add(coffee)
  hot.add(chocolate)

  cold.add(soda)
  cold.add(milk)

  tea.add(blackTea)
```

```
    tea.add(greenTea)
    tea.add(chaiTea)

    soda.add(gingerAle)
    soda.add(bitterLemon)

    return tree
}
```

This function creates the following tree:

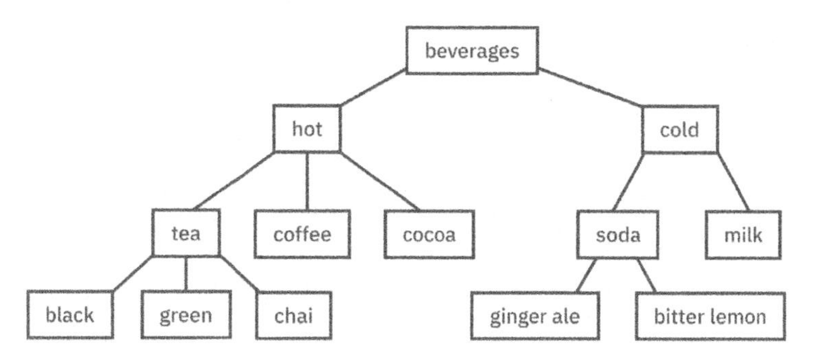

Next, add this:

```
example(of: "depth-first traversal") {
    let tree = makeBeverageTree()
    tree.forEachDepthFirst { print($0.value) }
}
```

This code produces the following depth-first output:

```
---Example of: depth-first traversal---
Beverages
hot
tea
black
green
chai
coffee
cocoa
cold
soda
ginger ale
bitter lemon
milk
```

In the next section, you will look at **level-order traversal**, a technique that visits each node of the tree based on the depth of the nodes.

Level-order traversal

Write the following at the bottom of **TreeNode.swift**:

```
extension TreeNode {
  public func forEachLevelOrder(visit: (TreeNode) -> Void) {
    visit(self)
    var queue = Queue<TreeNode>()
    children.forEach { queue.enqueue($0) }
    while let node = queue.dequeue() {
      visit(node)
      node.children.forEach { queue.enqueue($0) }
    }
  }
}
```

`forEachLevelOrder` visits each of the nodes in level-order:

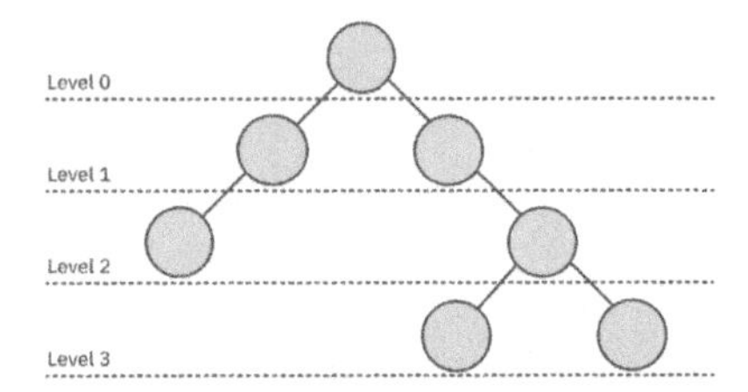

Note how you used a queue (not a stack) to ensure you visit nodes in the right level order. A simple recursion (which implicitly uses a stack) would not have worked!

Head back to the playground page and write the following:

```
example(of: "level-order traversal") {
  let tree = makeBeverageTree()
  tree.forEachLevelOrder { print($0.value) }
}
```

In the console, you will see the following output:

```
---Example of: level-order traversal---
Beverages
hot
cold
tea
coffee
cocoa
soda
milk
black
green
```

```
chai
ginger ale
bitter lemon
```

Search

You already have a method that iterates through all the nodes, so building a search algorithm shouldn't take long. Write the following at the bottom of **TreeNode.swift**:

```
extension TreeNode where T: Equatable {
  public func search(_ value: T) -> TreeNode? {
    var result: TreeNode?
    forEachLevelOrder { node in
      if node.value == value {
        result = node
      }
    }
    return result
  }
}
```

Head back to the playground page to test your code. To save some time, copy the previous example and modify it to test the `search` method:

```
example(of: "searching for a node") {
  // tree from the last example

  if let searchResult1 = tree.search("ginger ale") {
    print("Found node: \(searchResult1.value)")
  }
  if let searchResult2 = tree.search("WKD Blue") {
    print(searchResult2.value)
  } else {
    print("Couldn't find WKD Blue")
  }
}
```

You will see the following console output:

```
---Example of: searching for a node---
Found node: ginger ale
Couldn't find WKD Blue
```

Here, you used your level-order traversal algorithm. Since this code visits all nodes, the last match will win if there are multiple matches. This instability means that you will get different objects back depending on what traversal you use.

Key points

- Trees share similarities to linked lists, but a tree node can link to many child nodes where linked-list nodes may only link to one successor node.
- Every tree node, except for the root node, has exactly one parent node.
- A root node has no parent nodes.
- Leaf nodes have no child nodes.
- Be comfortable with the tree terminology such as **parent**, **child**, **leaf** and **root**. Many of these terms are common tongue for fellow programmers and will help explain other tree structures.
- Traversals, such as **depth-first** and **level-order** traversals, aren't specific to the general tree. They work on other kinds of trees, although their implementation will be slightly different based on how the tree is structured.

Chapter 11: Tree Challenges

By Kelvin Lau

Challenge 1: Print a tree in level order

Print all the values in a tree in an order based on their level. Nodes in the same level should be printed on the same line. For example, consider the following tree:

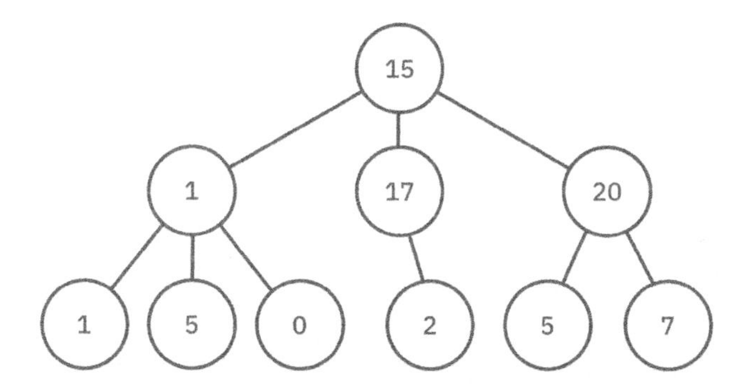

Your algorithm should print the following:

```
15
1 17 20
1 5 0 2 5 7
```

> **Hint**: Consider using a `Queue` included for you in the **Sources** folder of the starter playground.

Challenge 2: Parents and ownership

Consider the original definition of a tree node:

```
public class TreeNode<T> {
  public var value: T
  public var children: [TreeNode] = []

  public init(_ value: T) {
    self.value = value
  }
}
```

How can you modify this definition to include a parent? What considerations should you make about ownership?

Solutions

Solution to Challenge 1

A straightforward way to print the nodes in level-order is to leverage the level-order traversal using a `Queue` data structure. The tricky bit is determining when a newline should occur. Here's the solution:

```
func printEachLevel<T>(for tree: TreeNode<T>) {
  // 1
  var queue = Queue<TreeNode<T>>()
  var nodesLeftInCurrentLevel = 0
  queue.enqueue(tree)

  // 2
  while !queue.isEmpty {

    // 3
    nodesLeftInCurrentLevel = queue.count

    // 4
    while nodesLeftInCurrentLevel > 0 {
      guard let node = queue.dequeue() else { break }
      print("\(node.value) ", terminator: "")
      node.children.forEach { queue.enqueue($0) }
      nodesLeftInCurrentLevel -= 1
    }

    // 5
    print()
  }
}
```

1. You begin by initializing a `Queue` data structure to facilitate the level-order traversal. You also create `nodesLeftInCurrentLevel` to keep track of the number of nodes you'll need to work on before you print a new line.
2. Your level-order traversal continues until your queue is empty.
3. Inside the first `while` loop, you begin by setting `nodesLeftInCurrentLevel` to the current elements in the queue.

4. Using another `while` loop, you dequeue the first `nodesLeftInCurrentLevel` number of elements from the queue. Every element you dequeue is printed out **without** establishing a new line. You also enqueue all the children of the node.

5. At this point, you generate the new line using `print()`. In the next iteration, `nodesLeftInCurrentLevel` will be updated with the count of the queue, representing the number of children from the previous iteration.

This algorithm has a time complexity of ***O(n)***. Since you initialize the `Queue` data structure as an intermediary container, this algorithm also uses ***O(n)*** space.

Solution to Challenge 2

You can add a property `parent` to the `TreeNode` like so:

```
public class TreeNode<T> {

  public weak var parent: TreeNode?

  // etc...
}
```

Use an optional type since the root node does not have a parent. Give it weak ownership to avoid reference cycles. By convention, a node has a strong ownership relationship with its children but a weak non-ownership relationship with its parent. Continuing the linked list analogy, having nodes with a parent is analogous to a doubly-linked list. There is more bookkeeping overhead to worry about, but it allows quick upward traversal of the tree.

Chapter 12: Binary Trees

By Kelvin Lau

In the previous chapter, you looked at a basic tree where each node can have many children. A **binary tree** is a tree where each node has at most **two** children, often referred to as the **left** and **right** children:

parent

left child right child

Binary trees serve as the basis for many tree structures and algorithms. In this chapter, you'll build a binary tree and learn about the three most important tree traversal algorithms.

Implementation

Open the starter project for this chapter. Create a new file and name it **BinaryNode.swift**. Add the following inside this file:

```
public class BinaryNode<Element> {

  public var value: Element
  public var leftChild: BinaryNode?
  public var rightChild: BinaryNode?

  public init(value: Element) {
    self.value = value
  }
}
```

In the main playground page, add the following:

```
var tree: BinaryNode<Int> = {
  let zero = BinaryNode(value: 0)
  let one = BinaryNode(value: 1)
  let five = BinaryNode(value: 5)
  let seven = BinaryNode(value: 7)
  let eight = BinaryNode(value: 8)
  let nine = BinaryNode(value: 9)

  seven.leftChild = one
  one.leftChild = zero
  one.rightChild = five
  seven.rightChild = nine
  nine.leftChild = eight

  return seven
}()
```

This code defines the following tree by executing the closure:

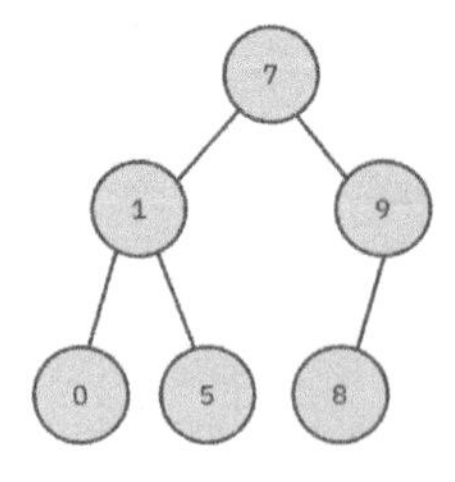

Building a diagram

Building a mental model of a data structure can be quite helpful in learning how it works. To that end, you'll implement a reusable algorithm that helps visualize a binary tree in the console.

> **Note**: This algorithm is based on an implementation by Károly Lőrentey in his book *Optimizing Collections*, available from https://www.objc.io/books/optimizing-collections/.

Add the following to the bottom of **BinaryNode.swift**:

```
extension BinaryNode: CustomStringConvertible {

  public var description: String {
    diagram(for: self)
  }

  private func diagram(for node: BinaryNode?,
                       _ top: String = "",
                       _ root: String = "",
                       _ bottom: String = "") -> String {
    guard let node = node else {
      return root + "nil\n"
    }
    if node.leftChild == nil && node.rightChild == nil {
      return root + "\(node.value)\n"
    }
    return diagram(for: node.rightChild,
                   top + " ", top + "┌──", top + "│ ")
         + root + "\(node.value)\n"
         + diagram(for: node.leftChild,
                   bottom + "│ ", bottom + "└──", bottom + " ")
  }
}
```

`diagram` will recursively create a string representing the binary tree. To try it out, head back to the playground and write the following:

```
example(of: "tree diagram") {
  print(tree)
}
```

You should see the following console output:

```
---Example of tree diagram---
 ┌──nil
┌──9
│ └──8
7
│ ┌──5
└──1
 └──0
```

You'll use this diagram for other binary trees in this book.

Traversal algorithms

Previously, you looked at a *level-order* traversal of a tree. With a few tweaks, you can make this algorithm work for binary trees as well. However, instead of re-implementing level-order traversal, you'll look at three traversal algorithms for binary trees: *in-order*, *pre-order* and *post-order* traversals.

In-order traversal

In-order traversal visits the nodes of a binary tree in the following order, starting from the root node:

- If the current node has a left child, recursively visit this child first.
- Then, visit the node itself.
- If the current node has a right child, recursively visit this child.

Here's what an in-order traversal looks like for your example tree:

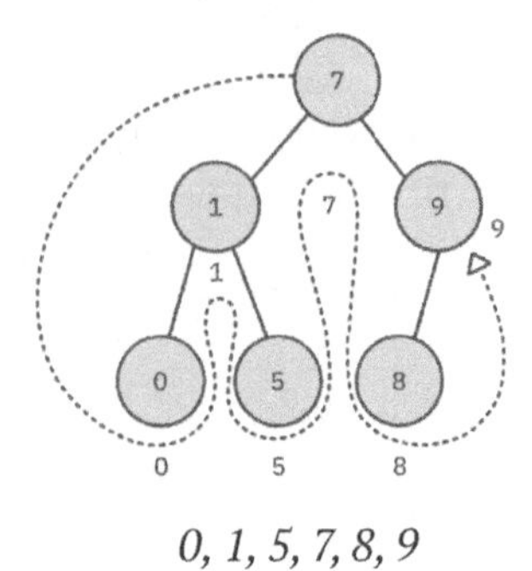

0, 1, 5, 7, 8, 9

You may have noticed that this prints the example tree in ascending order. If the tree nodes are structured in a certain way, in-order traversal visits them in ascending order! You'll learn more about *binary search trees* in the next chapter.

Open up **BinaryNode.swift** and add the following code to the bottom of the file:

```
extension BinaryNode {

  public func traverseInOrder(visit: (Element) -> Void) {
    leftChild?.traverseInOrder(visit: visit)
    visit(value)
    rightChild?.traverseInOrder(visit: visit)
  }
}
```

Following the rules laid out above, you first traverse to the left-most node before visiting the value. You then traverse to the right-most node. Head back to the playground page to test this out. Add the following at the bottom of the page:

```
example(of: "in-order traversal") {
  tree.traverseInOrder { print($0) }
}
```

You should see the following in the console:

```
---Example of in-order traversal---
0
1
5
7
8
9
```

Pre-order traversal

Pre-order traversal always visits the current node first, then recursively visits the left and right child:

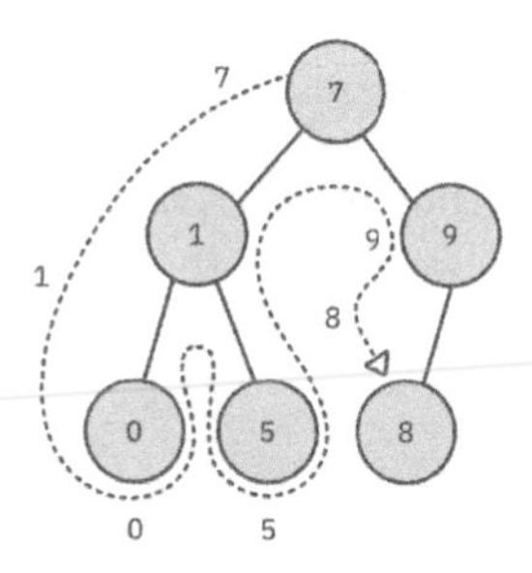

Write the following just below your in-order traversal method:

```
public func traversePreOrder(visit: (Element) -> Void) {
  visit(value)
  leftChild?.traversePreOrder(visit: visit)
  rightChild?.traversePreOrder(visit: visit)
}
```

Test it out with the following code:

```
example(of: "pre-order traversal") {
  tree.traversePreOrder { print($0) }
}
```

You should see the following output in the console:

```
---Example of pre-order traversal---
7
1
0
5
9
8
```

Post-order traversal

Post-order traversal only visits the current node after the left and right child have been visited recursively.

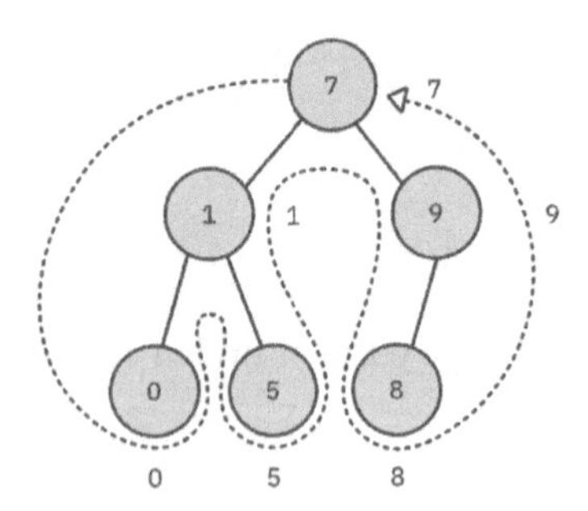

In other words, given any node, you'll visit its children before visiting itself. An interesting consequence of this is that the root node is always visited last.

Back inside **BinaryNode.swift**, write the following below `traversePreOrder`:

```
public func traversePostOrder(visit: (Element) -> Void) {
  leftChild?.traversePostOrder(visit: visit)
  rightChild?.traversePostOrder(visit: visit)
  visit(value)
}
```

Navigate back to the playground page to try it out:

```
example(of: "post-order traversal") {
  tree.traversePostOrder { print($0) }
}
```

You should see the following in the console:

```
---Example of post-order traversal---
0
5
1
8
9
7
```

Each of these traversal algorithms has a time and space complexity of $O(n)$. You saw that in-order traversal visits the nodes in ascending order. Binary trees can guarantee this by adhering to some rules during insertion. In the next chapter, you'll look at a binary tree with these stricter semantics: the binary search tree.

Key points

- The binary tree is the foundation of some of the most important tree structures. The binary **search** tree and AVL tree are binary trees that impose restrictions on the insertion/deletion behaviors.
- **In-order**, **pre-order** and **post-order** traversals aren't just important only for the binary tree; if you're processing data in any tree, you'll use these traversals regularly.

Chapter 13: Binary Tree Challenges

By Kelvin Lau

Binary trees are a surprisingly popular topic in algorithm interviews. Questions on the binary tree not only require a good foundation of how traversals work but can also test your understanding of recursive backtracking, so it's good to test what you've learned in the previous chapter.

Open the starter project to begin these challenges.

Challenge 1: Height of a Tree

Given a binary tree, find the height of the tree. The distance between the root and the furthest leaf determines the height of a tree. The height of a binary tree with a single node is zero since the single node is both the root and the furthest leaf.

Challenge 2: Serialization

A common task in software development is serializing an object into another data type. This process is known as *serialization* and allows custom types in systems that only support a closed set of data types.

An example of serialization is JSON. Your task is to devise a way to serialize a binary tree into an array and deserialize the array back into the same binary tree.

To clarify this problem, consider the following binary tree:

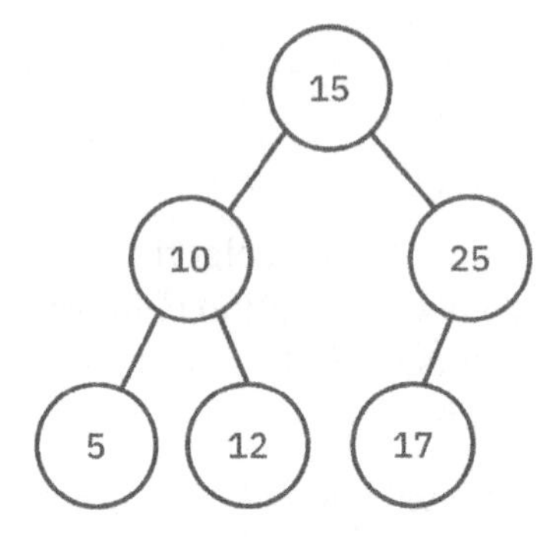

A particular algorithm may output the serialization as `[15, 10, 5, nil, nil, 12, nil, nil, 25, 17, nil, nil, nil]`. The deserialization process should transform the array back into the same binary tree. Note that there are many ways to perform serialization. You may choose any way you wish.

Solutions

Solution to Challenge 1

A recursive approach for finding the height of a binary tree is quite simple:

```
func height<T>(of node: BinaryNode<T>?) -> Int {

  // 1
  guard let node = node else {
    return -1
  }

  // 2
  return 1 + max(height(of: tree.leftChild), height(of:
tree.rightChild))
}
```

1. This is the base case for the recursive solution. If the node is `nil`, you'll return -1.
2. Here, you recursively call the height function. For every node you visit, you add one to the height of the highest child.

This algorithm has a time complexity of **O(*n*)** since you need to traverse through all the nodes. This algorithm incurs a space cost of **O(*n*)** since you need to make the same *n* recursive calls to the call stack.

Solution to Challenge 2

There are many ways to serialize or deserialize a binary tree. Your first task when encountering this question is to decide on the traversal strategy.

For this solution, you'll explore how to solve this challenge by choosing the **pre-order** traversal strategy.

Traversal

Write the following code in your playground page:

```
extension BinaryNode {

  public func traversePreOrder(visit: (Element?) -> Void) {
    visit(value)
    if let leftChild = leftChild {
      leftChild.traversePreOrder(visit: visit)
    } else {
      visit(nil)
    }
    if let rightChild = rightChild {
      rightChild.traversePreOrder(visit: visit)
    } else {
      visit(nil)
    }
  }
}
```

This function implements **pre-order** traversal. As the code suggests, pre-order traversal will traverse each node and visit the node before traversing the children.

It's important to point out that you need to visit the `nil` nodes since it's essential to record those for serialization and deserialization.

As with all traversal functions, this algorithm goes through every tree element once, so it has a time complexity of ***O(n)***.

Serialization

For serialization, you simply traverse the tree and store the values into an array. The elements of the array have type `T?` since you need to keep track of the `nil` nodes. Write the following in your playground page:

```
func serialize<T>(_ node: BinaryNode<T>) -> [T?] {
  var array: [T?] = []
  node.traversePreOrder { array.append($0) }
```

```
  return array
}
```

`serialize` will return a new array containing the values of the tree in pre-order.

The time complexity of the serialization step is ***O(n)***. Since you're creating a new array, this also incurs a ***O(n)*** space cost.

Deserialization

In the serialization process, you performed a pre-order traversal and assembled the values into an array. The deserialization process is to take each value of the array and reassemble it back to the tree.

Your goal is to iterate through the array and reassemble the tree in pre-order format. Write the following at the bottom of your playground page:

```
// 1
func deserialize<T>(_ array: inout [T?])
  -> BinaryNode<T>? {

  // 2
  guard let value = array.removeFirst() else {
    return nil
  }

  // 3
  let node = BinaryNode(value: value)
  node.leftChild = deserialize(&array)
  node.rightChild = deserialize(&array)
  return node
}
```

Here's how the code works:

1. The deserialize function takes an `inout` array of values. This is important because you'll be able to make mutations to the array in each recursive step and allow future recursive calls to see the changes.
2. This is the base case. If `removeFirst` returns `nil`, there are no more elements in the array; thus, you'll end recursion here.
3. You reassemble the tree by creating a node from the current value and recursively calling `deserialize` to assign nodes to the left and right children. Notice this is very similar to the pre-order traversal, except you build nodes rather than extract their values.

Your algorithm is now ready for testing! Write the following at the bottom of your playground:

```
var array = serialize(tree)
let node = deserialize(&array)
print(node!)
```

You should see the following in your console:

```
  ┌──nil
┌──9
│ └──8
7
│ ┌──5
└──1
  └──0

  ┌──nil
┌──9
│ └──8
7
│ ┌──5
└──1
  └──0
```

Your deserialized tree mirrors the sample tree in the provided playground. This is the behavior you want.

However, as alluded to earlier, the time complexity of this function isn't desirable. Since you're calling `removeFirst` as many times as elements in the array, this algorithm has a $O(n^2)$ time complexity. Fortunately, there's an easy way to remedy that.

Write the following function just after the `deserialize` function you created earlier:

```
func deserialize<T>(_ array: [T?]) -> BinaryNode<T>? {
  var reversed = Array(array.reversed())
  return deserialize(&reversed)
}
```

This is a helper function that first reverses the array before calling the main `deserialize` function. In the other `deserialize` function, find the `removeFirst` function call and change it to the following:

```
guard !array.isEmpty, let value = array.removeLast() else {
  return nil
}
```

This tiny change has a big effect on performance. `removeFirst` is an ***O(n)*** operation because, after every removal, every element after the removed element must shift left to take up the missing space. In contrast, `removeLast` is an ***O(1)*** operation.

Finally, find and update the call site of `deserialize` to use the new helper function that reverses the array:

```
let node = deserialize(&array) // old

let node = deserialize(array) // new
```

You should see the same tree before and after the deserialization process. The time complexity for this solution is now ***O(n)***. Because you've created a new reversed array and chose a recursive solution, this algorithm has a space complexity of ***O(n)***.

Chapter 14: Binary Search Trees

By Kelvin Lau

A **binary search tree**, or **BST**, is a data structure that facilitates fast lookup, insert and removal operations. Consider the following decision tree where picking a side forfeits all the possibilities of the other side, cutting the problem in half.

Once you make a decision and choose a branch, there is no looking back. You keep going until you make a final decision at a leaf node. Binary trees let you do the same thing. Specifically, a binary search tree imposes two rules on the binary tree you saw in the previous chapter:

- The value of a **left child** must be less than the value of its **parent**.
- Consequently, the value of a **right child** must be greater than or equal to the value of its **parent**.

Binary search trees use this property to save you from performing unnecessary checking. As a result, lookup, insert and removal have an average time complexity of $O(\log n)$, which is considerably faster than linear data structures such as arrays and linked lists.

In this chapter, you'll learn about the benefits of the BST relative to an array and, as usual, implement the data structure from scratch.

Case study: array vs. BST

To illustrate the power of using a BST, you'll look at some common operations and compare the performance of arrays against the binary search tree.

Consider the following two collections:

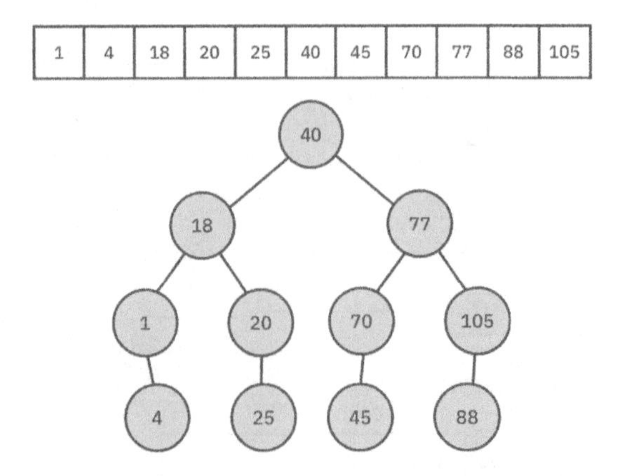

Lookup

There's only one way to do element lookups for an unsorted array. You need to check every element in the array from the start:

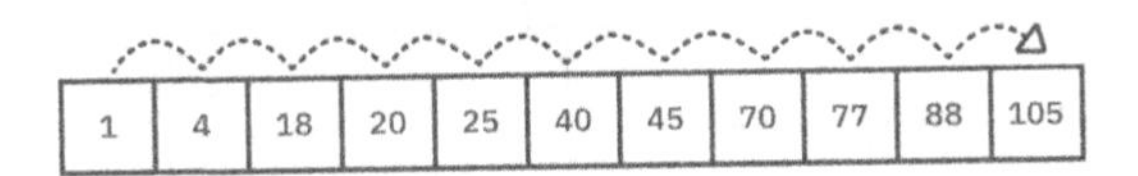

Searching for 105

That's why `array.contains(_:)` is an $O(n)$ operation.

This is not the case for binary search trees:

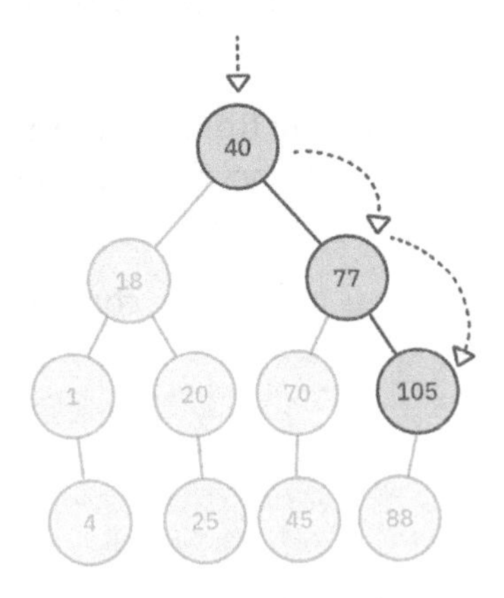

Searching for 105

Every time the search algorithm visits a node in the BST, it can safely make these two assumptions:

- If the search value is **less than** the current value, it must be in the **left** subtree.
- If the search value is **greater than** the current value, it must be in the **right** subtree.

By leveraging the rules of the BST, you can avoid unnecessary checks and cut the search space in half every time you make a decision. That's why element lookup in a BST is an $O(\log n)$ operation.

Insertion

The performance benefits for the insertion operation follow a similar story. Assume you want to insert **0** into a collection:

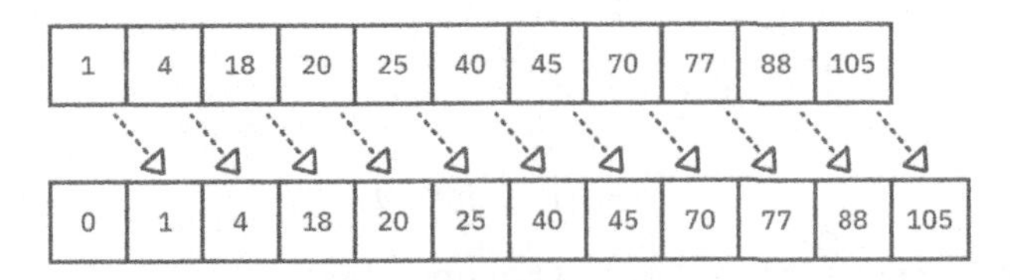

Inserting 0 in sorted order

Inserting values into an array is like butting into an existing line: Everyone in the line behind your chosen spot needs to make space for you by shuffling back.

In the above example, zero is inserted in front of the array, causing all other elements to shift backward by one position. Inserting into an array has a time complexity of $O(n)$.

Insertion into a binary search tree is much more comforting:

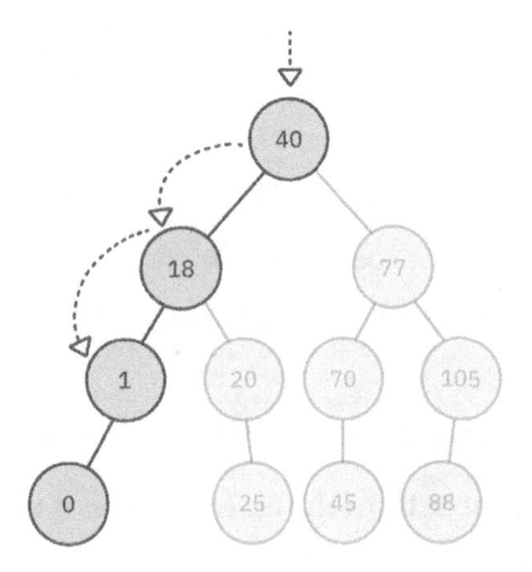

By leveraging the rules for the BST, you only needed to make three traversals to find the location for the insertion, and you didn't have to shuffle all the elements around! Inserting elements in a BST is again an $O(\log n)$ operation.

Removal

Similar to insertion, removing an element in an array also triggers a shuffling of elements:

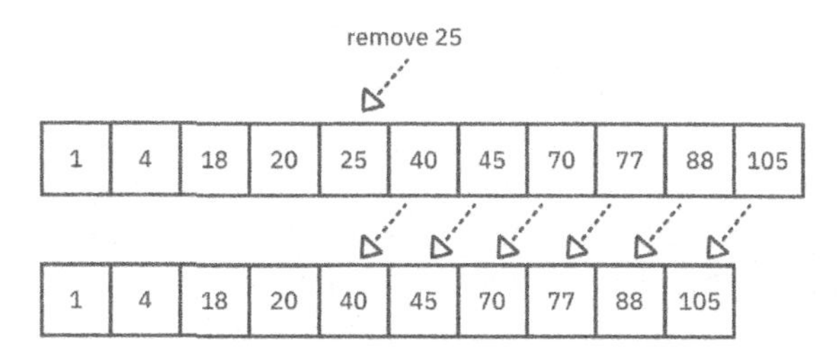

Removing 25 from the array

This behavior also plays nicely with the lineup analogy. If you leave the middle of the line, everyone behind you needs to shuffle forward to take up the empty space.

Here's what removing a value from a BST looks like:

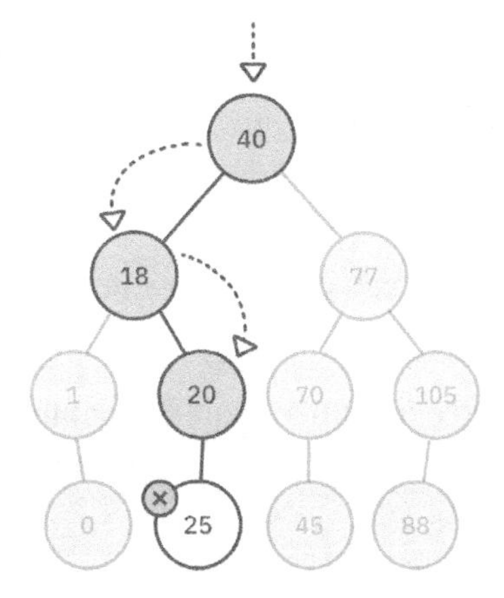

Nice and easy! There are complications to manage when the node you're removing has children, but you'll look into that later. Even with those complications, removing an element from a BST is still an $O(\log n)$ operation.

Binary search trees drastically reduce the number of steps for add, remove and lookup operations. Now that you understand the benefits of using a binary search tree, you can move on to the actual implementation.

Implementation

Open up the starter project for this chapter. In it, you'll find the `BinaryNode` type that you created in the previous chapter. Create a new file named **BinarySearchTree.swift** and add the following inside the file:

```
public struct BinarySearchTree<Element: Comparable> {

  public private(set) var root: BinaryNode<Element>?

  public init() {}
}

extension BinarySearchTree: CustomStringConvertible {

  public var description: String {
    guard let root = root else { return "empty tree" }
    return String(describing: root)
  }
}
```

By definition, binary search trees can only hold values that are `Comparable`.

> **Note**: You could relax the `Comparable` requirement by using closures for comparison. Use `Comparable` here to keep things simple and focus on the core concepts of binary trees.

Next, you'll look at the `insert` method.

Inserting elements

Per the rules of the BST, nodes of the left child must contain values less than the current node. Nodes of the right child must contain values greater than or equal to the current node. You'll implement the `insert` method while respecting these rules.

Add the following to **BinarySearchTree.swift**:

```
extension BinarySearchTree {

  public mutating func insert(_ value: Element) {
    root = insert(from: root, value: value)
  }

  private func insert(from node: BinaryNode<Element>?, value:
Element)
      -> BinaryNode<Element> {
    // 1
    guard let node = node else {
      return BinaryNode(value: value)
    }
    // 2
    if value < node.value {
      node.leftChild = insert(from: node.leftChild, value:
value)
    } else {
      node.rightChild = insert(from: node.rightChild, value:
value)
    }
    // 3
    return node
  }
}
```

The first `insert` method is exposed to users, while the second one will be used as a private helper method:

1. This is a recursive method, so it requires a base case for terminating the recursion. If the current node is `nil`, you've found the insertion point and can return a new `BinaryNode`.

2. Because `Element` types are comparable, you can perform a comparison. This `if` statement controls which way the next `insert` call should traverse. If the new value is less than the current value, you call `insert` on the **left** child. If the new value is greater than or equal to the current value, you'll call `insert` on the **right** child.

3. Return the current node. This makes assignments of the form `node = insert(from: node, value: value)` possible as `insert` will either create `node` (if it was `nil`) or return `node` (it it was not `nil`).

Head back to the playground page and add the following at the bottom:

```
example(of: "building a BST") {
  var bst = BinarySearchTree<Int>()
  for i in 0..<5 {
    bst.insert(i)
  }
  print(bst)
}
```

You should see the following output:

```
---Example of: building a BST---
    ┌──4
  ┌──3
  │ └──nil
 ┌──2
 │ └──nil
┌──1
│ └──nil
0
└──nil
```

That tree looks a bit *unbalanced*, but it does follow the rules. However, this tree layout has undesirable consequences. When working with trees, you always want to achieve a balanced format:

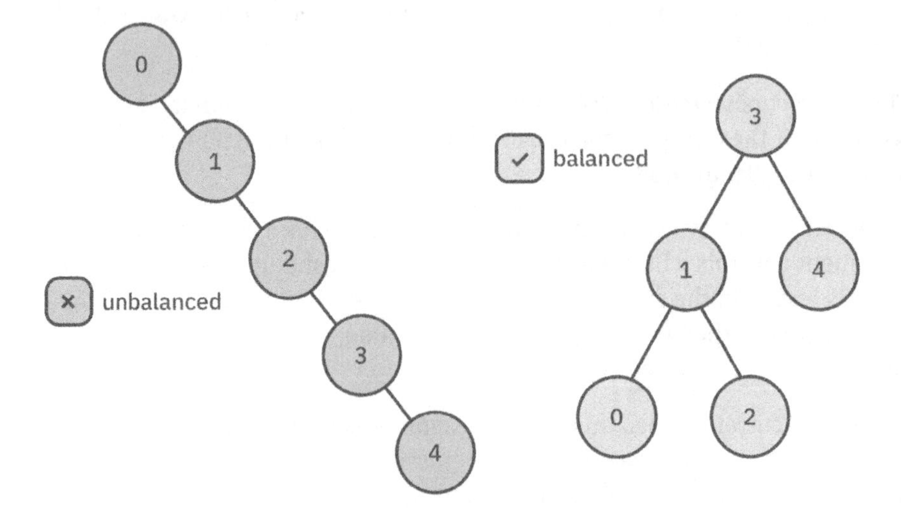

An unbalanced tree affects performance. If you insert **5** into the unbalanced tree you've created, it becomes an *O*(*n*) operation:

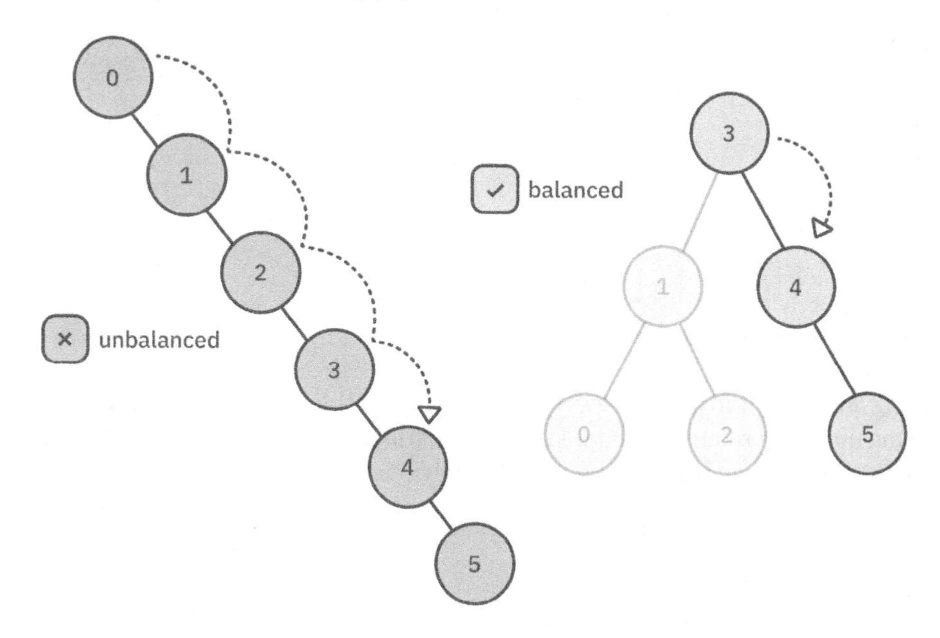

You can create structures known as *self-balancing* trees that use clever techniques to maintain a balanced structure, but we'll save those details for Chapter 16, "AVL Trees". For now, you'll build a sample tree with a bit of care to keep it from becoming unbalanced.

Add the following computed variable at the **top** of the playground page:

```
var exampleTree: BinarySearchTree<Int> {
  var bst = BinarySearchTree<Int>()
  bst.insert(3)
  bst.insert(1)
  bst.insert(4)
  bst.insert(0)
  bst.insert(2)
  bst.insert(5)
  return bst
}
```

Replace your `example` function with the following:

```
example(of: "building a BST") {
  print(exampleTree)
}
```

You should see the following in the console:

```
---Example of: building a BST---
  ┌──5
 ┌──4
 │ └──nil
3
 │ ┌──2
 └──1
  └──0
```

Much nicer!

Finding elements

Finding an element in a BST requires you to traverse through its nodes. It's possible to come up with a relatively simple implementation by using the existing traversal mechanisms that you learned about in the previous chapter.

Add the following to the bottom of **BinarySearchTree.swift**:

```
extension BinarySearchTree {

  public func contains(_ value: Element) -> Bool {
    guard let root = root else {
      return false
    }
    var found = false
    root.traverseInOrder {
      if $0 == value {
        found = true
      }
    }
    return found
  }
}
```

Next, head back to the playground page to test this out:

```
example(of: "finding a node") {
  if exampleTree.contains(5) {
    print("Found 5!")
  } else {
    print("Couldn't find 5")
  }
}
```

You should see the following in the console:

```
---Example of: finding a node---
Found 5!
```

In-order traversal has a time complexity of $O(n)$; thus, this implementation of `contains` has the same time complexity as an exhaustive search through an unsorted array. However, you can do better.

Optimizing contains

You can rely on the rules of the BST to avoid needless comparisons. Back in **BinarySearchTree.swift**, update the `contains` method to the following:

```
public func contains(_ value: Element) -> Bool {
  // 1
  var current = root
  // 2
  while let node = current {
    // 3
    if node.value == value {
      return true
    }
    // 4
    if value < node.value {
      current = node.leftChild
    } else {
      current = node.rightChild
    }
  }
  return false
}
```

1. Start by setting `current` to the `root` node.
2. While `current` is not `nil`, check the current node's value.
3. If the `value` is equal to what you're trying to find, return `true`.
4. Otherwise, decide whether you're going to check the left or the right child.

This implementation of `contains` is an $O(\log n)$ operation in a balanced binary search tree.

Removing elements

Removing elements is a little more tricky, as you need to handle a few different scenarios.

Case 1: Leaf node

Removing a leaf node is straightforward; simply detach the leaf node.

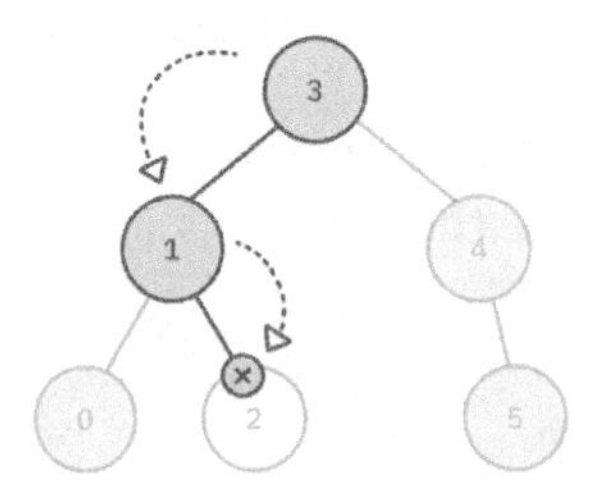

Removing 2

For non-leaf nodes, however, there are extra steps you must take.

Case 2: Nodes with one child

When removing nodes with **one** child, you'll need to reconnect that one child with the rest of the tree:

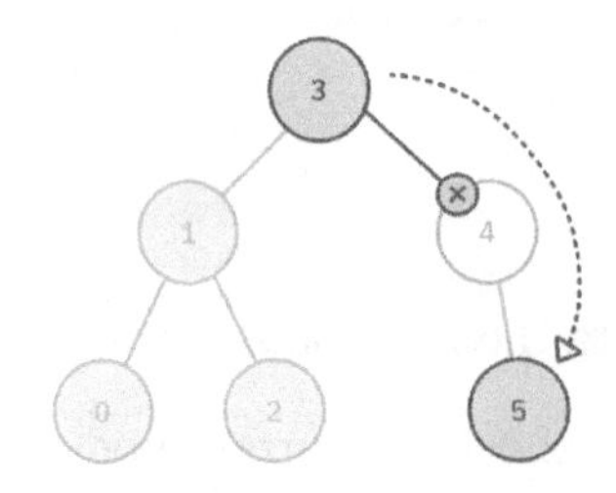

Removing 4, which has 1 child

Case 3: Nodes with two children

Nodes with two children are a bit more complicated, so a more complex example tree will better illustrate how to handle this situation. Assume that you have the following tree and that you want to remove the value **25**:

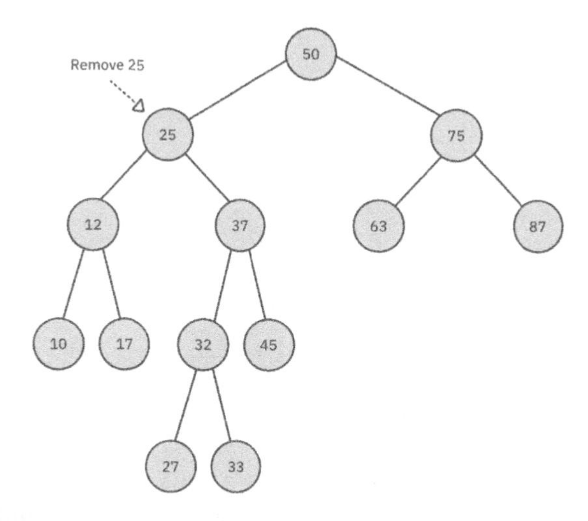

Simply deleting the node presents a dilemma:

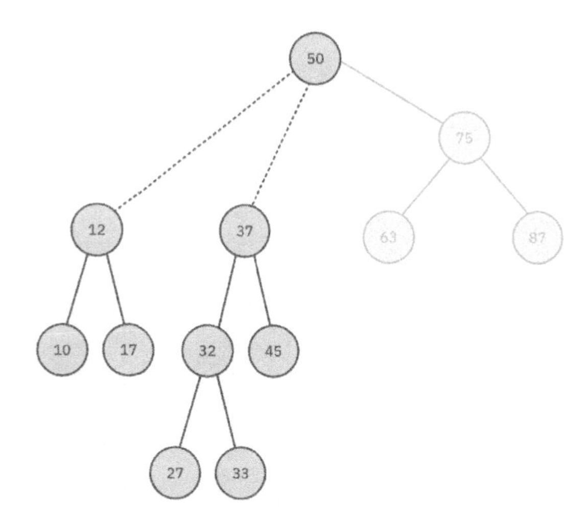

You have two child nodes (**12** and **37**) to reconnect, but the parent node only has space for one child. To solve this problem, you'll implement a clever workaround by performing a swap.

When removing a node with two children, replace the node you removed with the smallest node in its *right* subtree. Based on the rules of the BST, this is the **leftmost** node of the right subtree:

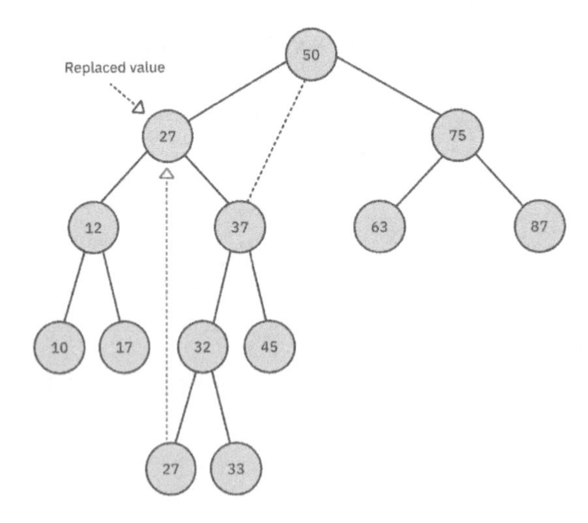

It's important to note that this produces a **valid** binary search tree. Because the new node was the smallest in the right subtree, all nodes in the right subtree will still be greater than or equal to the new node. And because the new node came from the right subtree, all nodes in the left subtree will be less than the new node.

After performing the swap, you can simply remove the value you copied, just a leaf node.

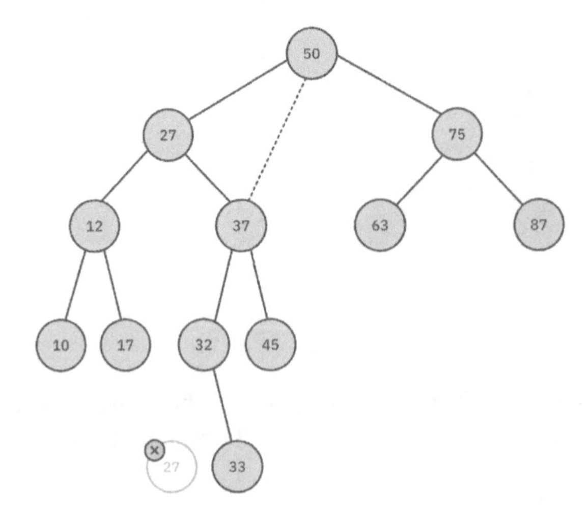

This will take care of removing nodes with two children.

Implementation

Open up **BinarySearchTree.swift** to implement `remove`. Add the following code at the bottom of the file:

```
private extension BinaryNode {

  var min: BinaryNode {
    leftChild?.min ?? self
  }
}

extension BinarySearchTree {

  public mutating func remove(_ value: Element) {
    root = remove(node: root, value: value)
  }

  private func remove(node: BinaryNode<Element>?, value:
Element)
    -> BinaryNode<Element>? {
    guard let node = node else {
      return nil
    }
    if value == node.value {
      // more to come
    } else if value < node.value {
      node.leftChild = remove(node: node.leftChild, value:
value)
    } else {
      node.rightChild = remove(node: node.rightChild, value:
value)
    }
    return node
  }
}
```

This should look familiar to you. You're using the same recursive setup with a private helper method as you did for `insert`. You've also added a recursive `min` property to `BinaryNode` to find the minimum node in a subtree. The different removal cases are handled in the `if value == node.value` clause:

```
// 1
if node.leftChild == nil && node.rightChild == nil {
  return nil
}
// 2
if node.leftChild == nil {
  return node.rightChild
}
// 3
if node.rightChild == nil {
  return node.leftChild
}
// 4
node.value = node.rightChild!.min.value
node.rightChild = remove(node: node.rightChild, value:
node.value)
```

1. If the node is a leaf node, you simply return `nil`, thereby removing the current node.
2. If the node has no left child, you return `node.rightChild` to reconnect the right subtree.
3. If the node has no right child, you return `node.leftChild` to reconnect the left subtree.
4. This is the case in which the node to be removed has both a left and right child. You replace the node's value with the smallest value from the right subtree. You then call `remove` on the right child to remove this swapped value.

Head back to the playground page and test `remove` by writing the following:

```
example(of: "removing a node") {
  var tree = exampleTree
  print("Tree before removal:")
  print(tree)
  tree.remove(3)
  print("Tree after removing root:")
  print(tree)
}
```

You should see the following output in the console:

```
---Example of: removing a node---
Tree before removal:
 ┌──5
┌──4
│ └──nil
3
└──┌──2
 └──1
  └──0

Tree after removing root:
┌──5
4
└──┌──2
 └──1
  └──0
```

Key points

- The binary search tree is a powerful data structure for holding **sorted** data.
- Elements of the binary search tree must be comparable. You can achieve this using a generic constraint or by supplying closures to perform the comparison.
- The time complexity for `insert`, `remove` and `contains` methods in a BST is $O(log\ n)$.
- Performance will degrade to $O(n)$ as the tree becomes unbalanced. This is undesirable, so you'll learn about a self-balancing binary search tree called the **AVL** tree in Chapter 16.

Chapter 15: Binary Search Tree Challenges

By Kelvin Lau

Think you've gotten the hang of binary search trees? Try out these three challenges to lock the concepts down.

Challenge 1: Binary tree or binary search tree?

Create a function that checks if a binary tree is a binary search tree.

Challenge 2: Equatable

The binary search tree currently lacks `Equatable` conformance. Your challenge is to adopt the `Equatable` protocol.

Challenge 3: Is it a subtree?

Create a method that checks if the current tree contains all the elements of another tree. You may require that elements are `Hashable`.

Solutions

Solution to Challenge 1

A binary search tree is a tree where every left child is less than or equal to its parent, and every right child is greater than its parent.

An algorithm that verifies whether a tree is a binary search tree involves going through all the nodes and checking for this property.

Write the following in your playground page:

```
extension BinaryNode where Element: Comparable {

  var isBinarySearchTree: Bool {
    isBST(self, min: nil, max: nil)
  }

  // 1
  private func isBST(_ tree: BinaryNode<Element>?,
                     min: Element?,
                     max: Element?) -> Bool {
    // 2
    guard let tree = tree else {
      return true
    }

    // 3
    if let min = min, tree.value <= min {
      return false
    } else if let max = max, tree.value > max {
      return false
    }

    // 4
    return isBST(tree.leftChild, min: min, max: tree.value) &&
           isBST(tree.rightChild, min: tree.value, max: max)
  }
}
```

`isBinarySearchTree` is the interface that will be exposed for external use. Meanwhile, the magic happens in the `isBST` function:

1. `isBST` is responsible for recursively traversing through the tree and checking for the BST property. It needs to keep track of progress via a reference to a `BinaryNode`, and also keep track of the `min` and `max` values to verify the BST property.

2. This is the base case. If `tree` is `nil`, then there are no nodes to inspect. A `nil` node is a binary search tree, so you'll return `true` in that case.

3. This is essentially a bounds check. If the current value exceeds the bounds of the `min` and `max`, the current node violates binary search tree rules.

4. This line contains the recursive calls. When traversing through the left children, the current value is passed in as the `max` value. This is because any nodes on the left side cannot be greater than the parent. Vice versa, when traversing to the right, the `min` value is updated to the current value. Any nodes on the right side must be greater than the parent. If any of the recursive calls evaluate `false`, the `false` value will propagate back to the top.

The time complexity of this solution is ***O(n)*** since you need to traverse through the entire tree once. There is also a ***O(n)*** space cost since you're making *n* recursive calls.

Solution to Challenge 2

Conforming to `Equatable` is relatively straightforward. For two binary trees to be equal, both trees must have the same elements in the same order. Here's what the solution looks like:

```
extension BinarySearchTree: Equatable {

  // 1
  public static func ==(lhs: BinarySearchTree,
                        rhs: BinarySearchTree) -> Bool {
    isEqual(lhs.root, rhs.root)
  }

  // 2
  private static func isEqual<Element: Equatable>(
    _ node1: BinaryNode<Element>?,
    _ node2: BinaryNode<Element>?) -> Bool {

  // 3
  guard let leftNode = node1,
        let rightNode = node2 else {
    return node1 == nil && node2 == nil
  }

  // 4
  return leftNode.value == rightNode.value &&
    isEqual(leftNode.leftChild, rightNode.leftChild) &&
    isEqual(leftNode.rightChild, rightNode.rightChild)
  }
}
```

Here's an explanation of the code:

1. This is the function that the `Equatable` protocol requires. Inside the function, you'll return the result from the `isEqual` helper function.
2. `isEqual` will recursively check two nodes and their descendants for equality.
3. This is the base case. If one or more of the nodes are `nil`, then there's no need to continue checking. If both nodes are `nil`, they are equal. Otherwise, one is `nil` and one isn't `nil`, so they must not be equal.
4. Here, you check the value of the left and right nodes for equality. You also recursively check the left children and right children for equality.

The time complexity of this function is ***O(n)***. The space complexity of this function is ***O(n)***.

Solution to Challenge 3

Your goal is to create a method that checks if the current tree contains all the elements of another tree. In other words, the values in the current tree must be a superset of the values of the other tree. Here's what the solution looks like:

```
// 1
extension BinarySearchTree where Element: Hashable {

  public func contains(_ subtree: BinarySearchTree) -> Bool {

    // 2
    var set: Set<Element> = []
    root?.traverseInOrder {
      set.insert($0)
    }

    // 3
    var isEqual = true

    // 4
    subtree.root?.traverseInOrder {
      isEqual = isEqual && set.contains($0)
    }
    return isEqual
  }
}
```

1. You'll make use of a `Set` for this solution. To insert elements into a `Set`, the elements must be `Hashable`, so you first constrain the extension where `Element` is `Hashable`.

2. Inside the `contains` function, you begin by inserting all the elements of the current tree into the set.

3. `isEqual` is to store the end result. You need this because `traverseInOrder` takes a closure, and you cannot directly return from inside the closure.

4. For every element in the subtree, you check if the set contains the value. If at any point `set.contains($0)` evaluates as `false`, you'll make sure `isEqual` stays `false` even if subsequent elements evaluate as `true` by assigning `isEqual && set.contains($0)` to itself.

The time complexity for this algorithm is ***O(n)***. The space complexity for this algorithm is ***O(n)***.

Chapter 16: AVL Trees

By Kelvin Lau

In the previous chapter, you learned about the $O(\log n)$ performance characteristics of the binary search tree. However, you also learned that *unbalanced* trees can deteriorate the performance of the tree, all the way down to $O(n)$. In 1962, Georgy Adelson-Velsky and Evgenii Landis came up with the first *self-balancing* binary search tree: The **AVL Tree**. In this chapter, you'll dig deeper into how the balance of a binary search tree can impact performance and implement the AVL tree from scratch!

Understanding balance

A balanced tree is the key to optimizing the performance of the binary search tree. In this section, you'll learn about the three main states of balance.

Perfect balance

The ideal form of a binary search tree is the **perfectly balanced** state. In technical terms, this means every level of the tree is filled with nodes, from top to bottom.

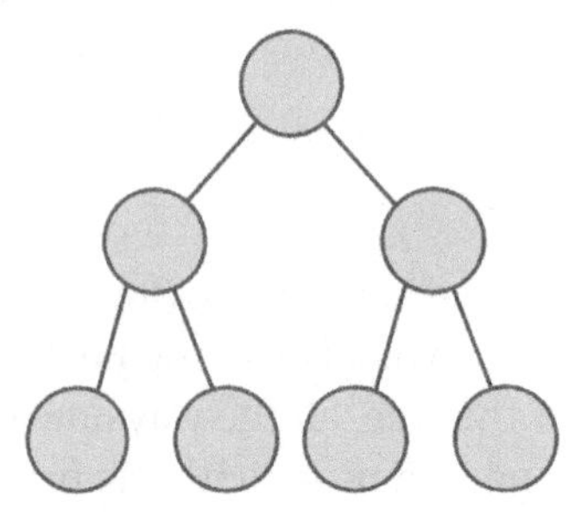

Perfectly balanced tree

Not only is the tree perfectly symmetrical, the nodes at the bottom level are completely filled. This is the requirement for being perfectly balanced.

"Good-enough" balance

Although achieving perfect balance is ideal, it is rarely possible. A perfectly balanced tree must contain the exact number of nodes to fill every level to the bottom, so it can only be perfect with a particular number of elements.

For example, a tree with 1, 3 or 7 nodes can be perfectly balanced, but a tree with 2, 4, 5 or 6 cannot be perfectly balanced since the last level of the tree will not be filled.

Balanced tree

The definition of a balanced tree is that every level of the tree must be filled, except for the bottom level. In most cases of binary trees, this is the best you can do.

Unbalanced

Finally, there's the **unbalanced** state. Binary search trees in this state suffer from various levels of performance loss, depending on the degree of imbalance.

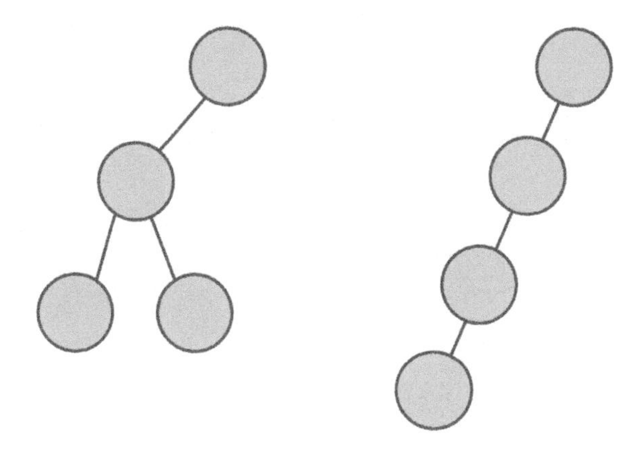

Unbalanced trees

Keeping the tree balanced gives the **find**, **insert** and **remove** operations an $O(\log n)$ time complexity. AVL trees maintain balance by adjusting the structure of the tree when the tree becomes unbalanced. You'll learn how this works as you progress through the chapter.

Implementation

Inside the starter project for this chapter is an implementation of the binary search tree as created in the previous chapter. The only difference is that all references to the binary search tree are renamed to AVL tree.

Binary search trees and AVL trees share much of the same implementation; in fact, all that you'll add is the balancing component. Open the starter project to begin.

Measuring balance

To keep a binary tree balanced, you'll need a way to measure the balance of the tree. The AVL tree achieves this with a `height` property in each node. In tree-speak, the **height** of a node is the **longest** distance from the current node to a leaf node:

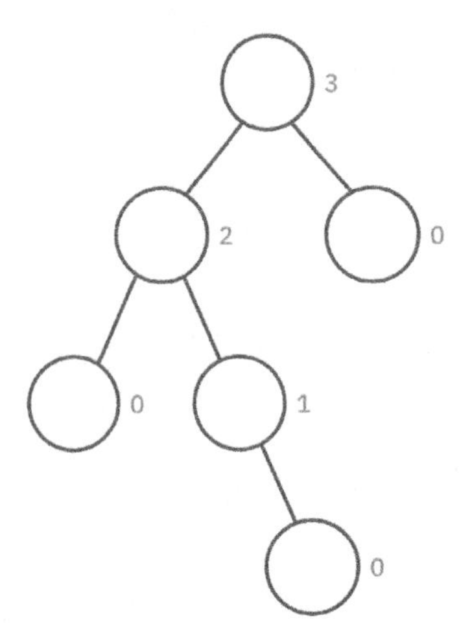

Nodes marked with heights

Open the starter playground for this chapter and add the following property to `AVLNode` in the compiled sources folder:

```
public var height = 0
```

You'll use the *relative* heights of a node's children to determine whether a particular node is balanced. The height of the left and right children of each node must differ at most by 1. This number is known as the **balance factor**.

Write the following just below the `height` property of `AVLNode`:

```
public var balanceFactor: Int {
  leftHeight - rightHeight
}

public var leftHeight: Int {
  leftChild?.height ?? -1
}

public var rightHeight: Int {
  rightChild?.height ?? -1
}
```

The `balanceFactor` computes the height difference of the left and right child. If a particular child is `nil`, its height is considered to be `-1`.

Here's an example of an AVL tree:

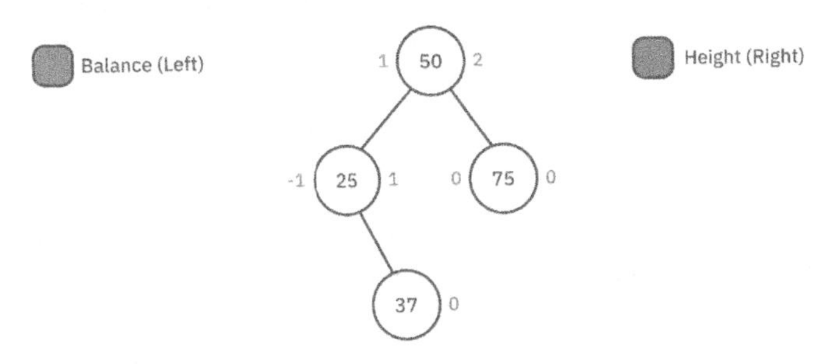

AVL tree with balance factors and heights

The diagram shows a balanced tree — all levels except the bottom one are filled. The numbers to the right of the node represent the `height` of each node, while the numbers to the left represent the `balanceFactor`.

Here's an updated diagram with **40** inserted:

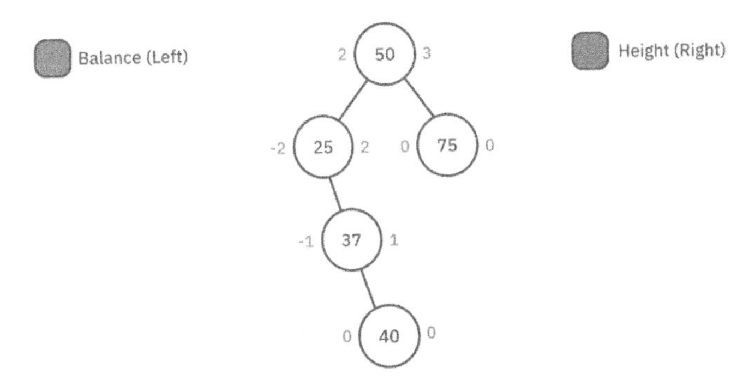

Unbalanced tree

Inserting **40** into the tree turns it into an unbalanced tree. Notice how the `balanceFactor` changes. A `balanceFactor` of **2** or **-2** or something more extreme indicates of an unbalanced tree. By checking after each insertion or deletion, though, you can guarantee that it is never more extreme than a magnitude of two.

Although more than one node may have a bad balancing factor, you only need to perform the balancing procedure on the bottom-most node containing the invalid balance factor: the node containing **25**.

That's where rotations come in.

Rotations

The procedures used to balance a binary search tree are known as **rotations**. There are four rotations in total for the four different ways that a tree can become unbalanced. These are known as **left** rotation, **left-right** rotation, **right** rotation and **right-left** rotation.

Left rotation

The imbalance caused by inserting **40** into the tree can be solved by a **left rotation**. A generic left rotation of node **x** looks like this:

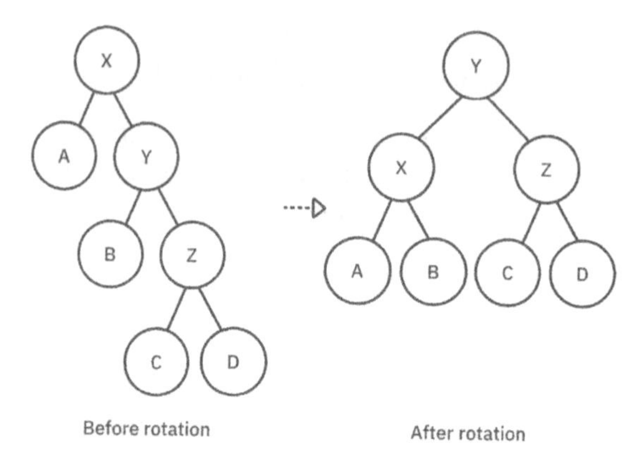

Left rotation applied on node x

Before going into specifics, there are two takeaways from this before-and-after comparison:

- In-order traversal for these nodes remains the same.
- The *depth* of the tree is reduced by one level after the rotation.

Add the following method to `AVLTree`, just below `insert(from:value:)`:

```
private func leftRotate(_ node: AVLNode<Element>)
  -> AVLNode<Element> {

  // 1
  let pivot = node.rightChild!
  // 2
  node.rightChild = pivot.leftChild
  // 3
  pivot.leftChild = node
  // 4
  node.height = max(node.leftHeight, node.rightHeight) + 1
```

```
    pivot.height = max(pivot.leftHeight, pivot.rightHeight) + 1
    // 5
    return pivot
}
```

Here are the steps needed to perform a left rotation:

1. The right child is chosen as the **pivot**. This node will replace the rotated node as the root of the subtree (it will move up a level).
2. The node to be rotated will become the left child of the pivot (it moves down a level). This means that the current left child of the pivot must be moved elsewhere.

   In the generic example shown in the earlier image, this is node **b**. Because **b** is smaller than **y** but greater than **x**, it can replace **y** as the right child of **x**. So you update the rotated node's `rightChild` to the pivot's `leftChild`.
3. The pivot's `leftChild` can now be set to the rotated node.
4. You update the heights of the rotated node and the pivot.
5. Finally, you return the pivot so that it can replace the rotated node in the tree.

Here are the before-and-after effects of the left rotation of **25** from the previous example:

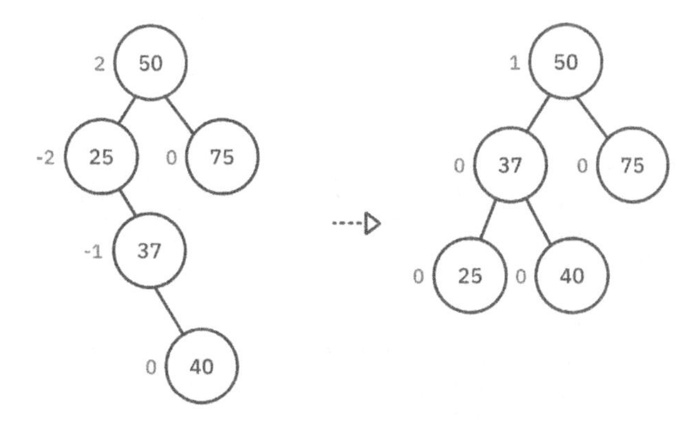

Before left rotate on 25

After left rotate on 25

Right rotation

Right rotation is the symmetrical opposite of left rotation. When a series of left children is causing an imbalance, it's time for a right rotation.

A generic right rotation of node **x** looks like this:

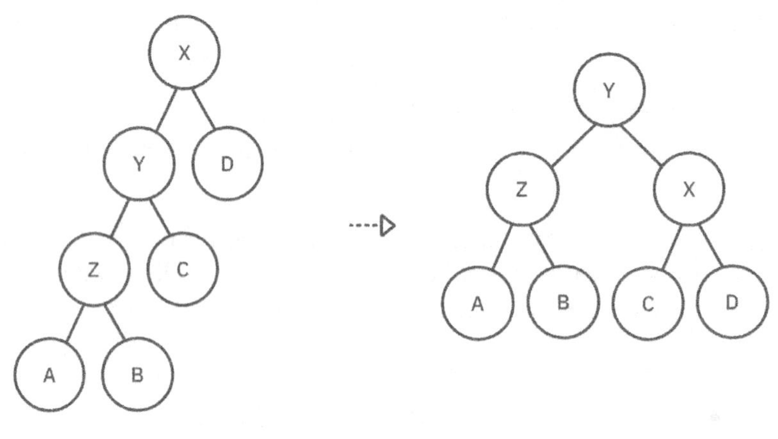

Right rotation applied on node x

To implement this, add the following code just after `leftRotate`:

```
private func rightRotate(_ node: AVLNode<Element>)
  -> AVLNode<Element> {

  let pivot = node.leftChild!
  node.leftChild = pivot.rightChild
  pivot.rightChild = node
  node.height = max(node.leftHeight, node.rightHeight) + 1
  pivot.height = max(pivot.leftHeight, pivot.rightHeight) + 1
  return pivot
}
```

This algorithm is nearly identical to the implementation of `leftRotate`, except the references to the left and right children are swapped.

Right-left rotation

You may have noticed that the left and right rotations balance nodes that are all left children or all right children. Consider the case in which **36** is inserted into the original example tree.

The right-left rotation:

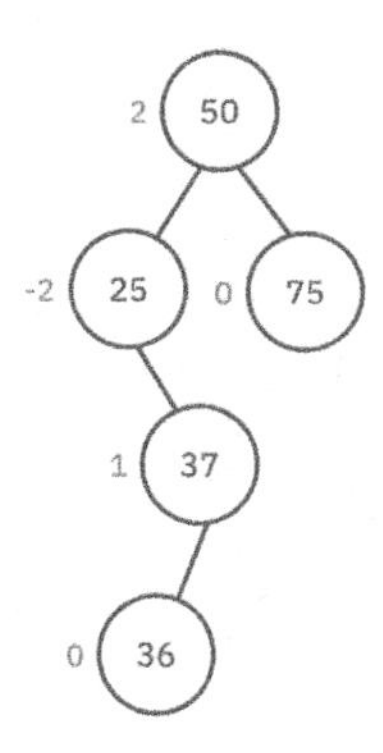

Inserted 36 as left child of 37

Doing a left rotation, in this case, won't result in a balanced tree. The way to handle cases like this is to perform a right rotation on the right child *before* doing the left rotation. Here's what the procedure looks like:

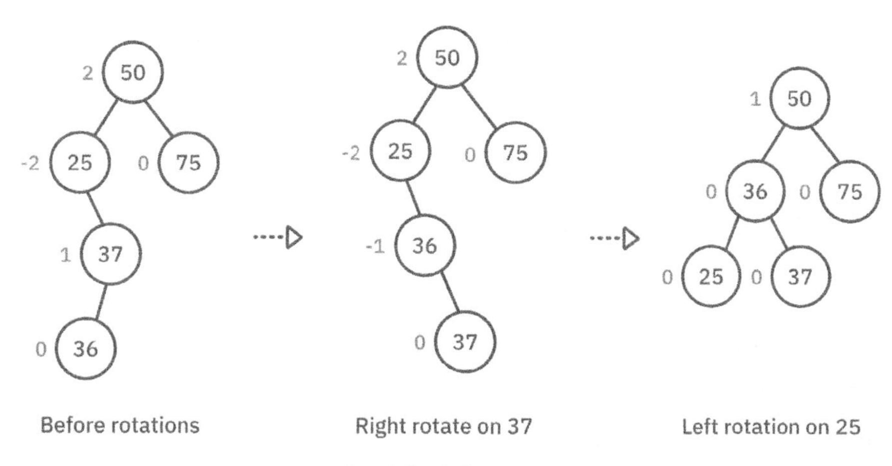

The right-left rotation

1. You apply a right rotation to **37**.
2. Now that nodes **25**, **36** and **37** are all right children; you can apply a left rotation to balance the tree.

Add the following code just after `rightRotate`:

```
private func rightLeftRotate(_ node: AVLNode<Element>)
  -> AVLNode<Element> {

  guard let rightChild = node.rightChild else {
```

```
      return node
    }
    node.rightChild = rightRotate(rightChild)
    return leftRotate(node)
  }
```

Don't worry just yet about when to call this. You'll get to that in a second. You first need to handle the last case, left-right rotation.

Left-right rotation

Left-right rotation is the symmetrical opposite of the right-left rotation. Here's an example:

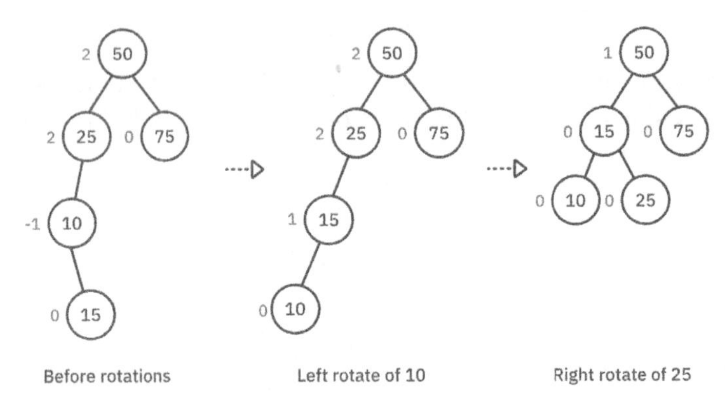

The left-right rotation

1. You apply a left rotation to node **10**.
2. Now that nodes **25**, **15** and **10** are all left children; you can apply a right rotation to balance the tree.

Add the following code just after `rightLeftRotate`:

```
private func leftRightRotate(_ node: AVLNode<Element>)
  -> AVLNode<Element> {

  guard let leftChild = node.leftChild else {
    return node
  }
  node.leftChild = leftRotate(leftChild)
  return rightRotate(node)
}
```

That's it for rotations. Next, you'll figure out when to apply these rotations at the correct location.

Balance

The next task is to design a method that uses balanceFactor to decide whether a node requires balancing or not. Write the following method below leftRightRotate:

```
private func balanced(_ node: AVLNode<Element>)
  -> AVLNode<Element> {

  switch node.balanceFactor {
  case 2:
    // ...
  case -2:
    // ...
  default:
    return node
  }
}
```

There are three cases to consider.

1. A balanceFactor of **2** suggests that the left child is "heavier" (contains more nodes) than the right child. This means that you want to use either right or left-right rotations.
2. A balanceFactor of **-2** suggests that the right child is heavier than the left child. This means that you want to use either left or right-left rotations.
3. The default case suggests that the particular node is balanced. There's nothing to do here except to return the node.

The sign of the balanceFactor can be used to determine if a single or double rotation is required:

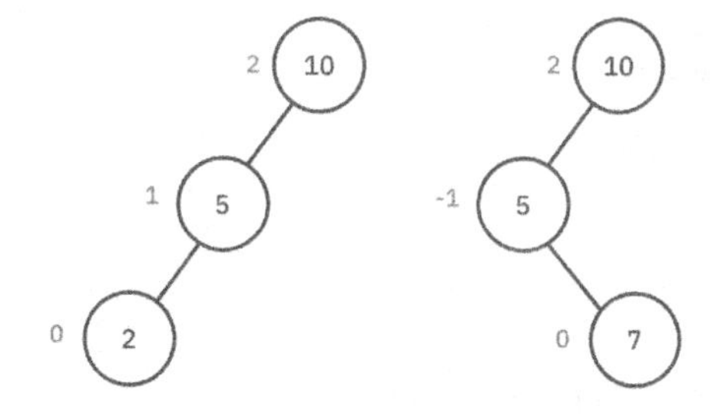

Right rotate or left-right rotate?

Update the balanced function to the following:

```
private func balanced(_ node: AVLNode<Element>)
  -> AVLNode<Element> {

  switch node.balanceFactor {
  case 2:
    if let leftChild = node.leftChild,
           leftChild.balanceFactor == -1 {
      return leftRightRotate(node)
    } else {
      return rightRotate(node)
    }
  case -2:
    if let rightChild = node.rightChild,
           rightChild.balanceFactor == 1 {
      return rightLeftRotate(node)
    } else {
      return leftRotate(node)
    }
  default:
    return node
  }
}
```

balanced inspects the balanceFactor to determine the proper course of action. All that's left is to call balance at the proper spot.

Revisiting insertion

You've already done the majority of the work. The remainder is fairly straightforward. Update insert(from:value:) to the following:

```
private func insert(from node: AVLNode<Element>?,
                    value: Element) -> AVLNode<Element> {
  guard let node = node else {
    return AVLNode(value: value)
  }
  if value < node.value {
    node.leftChild = insert(from: node.leftChild, value: value)
  } else {
    node.rightChild = insert(from: node.rightChild, value:
value)
  }
  let balancedNode = balanced(node)
  balancedNode.height = max(balancedNode.leftHeight,
balancedNode.rightHeight) + 1
  return balancedNode
}
```

Instead of returning the node directly after inserting, you pass it into balanced. Passing it ensures every node in the call stack is checked for balancing issues. You also update the node's height.

That's all there is to it! Head into the playground page and test it out. Add the following to the playground:

```
example(of: "repeated insertions in sequence") {
  var tree = AVLTree<Int>()
  for i in 0..<15 {
    tree.insert(i)
  }
  print(tree)
}
```

You should see the following output in the console:

```
---Example of: repeated insertions in sequence---
  ┌──14
 ┌──13
 │ └──12
┌──11
│ │ ┌──10
│ └──9
│   └──8
7
│  ┌──6
│ ┌──5
│ │ └──4
└──3
  │ ┌──2
  └──1
    └──0
```

Take a moment to appreciate the uniform spread of the nodes. If the rotations weren't applied, this would have become a long, unbalanced link of right children.

Revisiting remove

Retrofitting the `remove` operation for self-balancing is just as easy as fixing insert. In `AVLTree`, find `remove` and replace the final `return` statement with the following:

```
let balancedNode = balanced(node)
balancedNode.height = max(balancedNode.leftHeight,
balancedNode.rightHeight) + 1
return balancedNode
```

Head back to the playground page and add the following code at the bottom of the file:

```
example(of: "removing a value") {
  var tree = AVLTree<Int>()
  tree.insert(15)
  tree.insert(10)
  tree.insert(16)
  tree.insert(18)
  print(tree)
  tree.remove(10)
  print(tree)
}
```

You should see the following console output:

```
---Example of: removing a value---
 ┌──18
┌──16
│ └──nil
15
└──10

┌──18
16
└──15
```

Removing **10** caused a left rotation on **15**. Feel free to try out a few more test cases of your own.

Whew! The AVL tree is the culmination of your search for the ultimate binary search tree. The self-balancing property guarantees that the `insert` and `remove` operations function at optimal performance with an *O*(log *n*) time complexity.

Key points

- A self-balancing tree avoids performance degradation by performing a balancing procedure whenever you add or remove elements in the tree.
- AVL trees preserve balance by readjusting parts of the tree when the tree is no longer balanced.
- Balance is achieved by four types of tree rotations on node insertion and removal.

Where to go from here?

While AVL trees were the first self-balancing implementations of a BST, others, such as the red-black tree and splay tree, have since joined the party. If you're interested, you check those out in the raywenderlich.com Swift Algorithm Club. Find them at at: https://github.com/raywenderlich/swift-algorithm-club/tree/master/Red-Black%20Tree and https://github.com/raywenderlich/swift-algorithm-club/tree/master/Splay%20Tree respectively.

Chapter 17: AVL Tree Challenges

By Kelvin Lau

Here are three challenges that revolve around AVL trees. Solve these to make sure you have the concepts down.

Challenge 1: Number of leaves

How many **leaf** nodes are there in a perfectly balanced tree of height 3? What about a perfectly balanced tree of height `h`?

Challenge 2: Number of nodes

How many **nodes** are there in a perfectly balanced tree of height 3? What about a perfectly balanced tree of height `h`?

Challenge 3: A tree traversal protocol

Since there are many variants of binary trees, it makes sense to group shared functionality in a protocol. The traversal methods are a good candidate for this.

Create a `TraversableBinaryNode` protocol that provides a default implementation of the traversal methods so that conforming types get these methods for free. Have `AVLNode` conform to this.

> **Note**: You'll need to make `AVLNode` a final class because the protocol will have `Self` requirements.

Solutions

Solution to Challenge 1

A perfectly balanced tree is a tree where all the leaves are in the same level, and that level is completely filled:

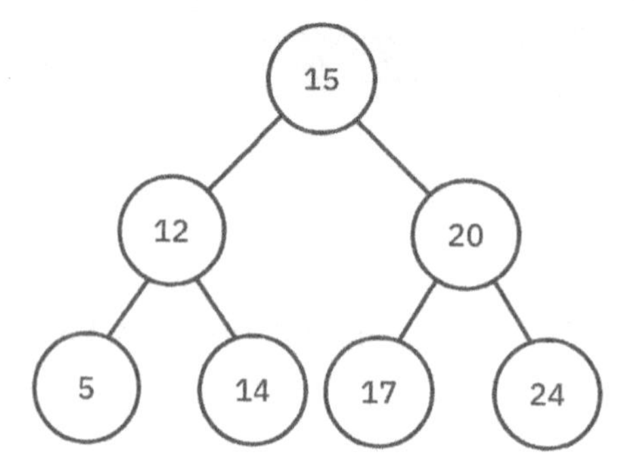

Recall that a tree with just a root node has a height of zero. Thus, the tree in the example above has a height of two. You can extrapolate that a tree with a height of three would have **eight** leaf nodes.

Since each node has two children, the number of leaf nodes doubles as the height increases. You can calculate the number of leaf nodes with a simple equation:

```
func leafNodes(inTreeOfHeight height: Int) -> Int {
  Int(pow(2.0, Double(height)))
}
```

Solution to Challenge 2

Since the tree is perfectly balanced, the number of nodes in a perfectly balanced tree of height 3 can be expressed by the following:

```
func nodes(inTreeOfHeight height: Int) -> Int {
  var totalHeight = 0
  for currentHeight in 0...height {
    totalHeight += Int(pow(2.0, Double(currentHeight)))
  }
  return totalHeight
}
```

Although this certainly gives you the correct answer, there is a faster way. If you examine the results of a sequence of height inputs, you'll realize that the total number of nodes is one less than the number of leaf nodes of the next level.

Thus, a faster version of this is the following:

```
func nodes(inTreeOfHeight height: Int) -> Int {
  Int(pow(2.0, Double(height + 1))) - 1
}
```

Solution to Challenge 3

First, create the following protocol:

```
protocol TraversableBinaryNode {

  associatedtype Element
  var value: Element { get }
  var leftChild: Self? { get }
  var rightChild: Self? { get }
  func traverseInOrder(visit: (Element) -> Void)
  func traversePreOrder(visit: (Element) -> Void)
  func traversePostOrder(visit: (Element) -> Void)
}
```

Then add a protocol extension to provide implementations for the traversal methods:

```
extension TraversableBinaryNode {

  func traverseInOrder(visit: (Element) -> Void) {
    leftChild?.traverseInOrder(visit: visit)
    visit(value)
    rightChild?.traverseInOrder(visit: visit)
  }

  func traversePreOrder(visit: (Element) -> Void) {
    visit(value)
    leftChild?.traversePreOrder(visit: visit)
    rightChild?.traversePreOrder(visit: visit)
  }

  func traversePostOrder(visit: (Element) -> Void) {
    leftChild?.traversePostOrder(visit: visit)
    rightChild?.traversePostOrder(visit: visit)
    visit(value)
  }
}
```

Next, head into **AVLNode.swift** update the type declaration to include the `final` keyword:

```
public final class AVLNode<Element>
```

Finally, add the following at the bottom of the playground:

```
extension AVLNode: TraversableBinaryNode {}

example(of: "using TraversableBinaryNode") {
  var tree = AVLTree<Int>()
  for i in 0..<15 {
    tree.insert(i)
  }
  tree.root?.traverseInOrder { print($0) }
}
```

Verify that you're getting the following results in the console:

```
---Example of: using TraversableBinaryNode---
0
1
2
3
4
5
6
7
8
9
10
11
12
13
14
```

Chapter 18: Tries

By Kelvin Lau

The **trie** (pronounced as *try*) is a tree that specializes in storing data that can be represented as a collection, such as English words:

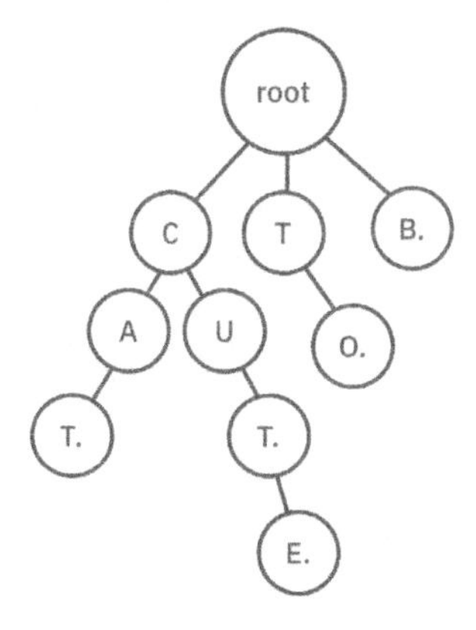

A trie containing the words CAT, CUT, CUTE, TO, and B

Each string character maps to a node where the last node (marked in the above diagram with a dot) is terminating. The benefits of a trie are best illustrated by looking at it in the context of prefix matching.

In this chapter, you'll first compare the performance of the trie to the array. Then you'll implement the trie from scratch!

Example

You are given a collection of strings. How would you build a component that handles prefix matching? Here's one way:

```
class EnglishDictionary {

  private var words: [String]

  func words(matching prefix: String) -> [String] {
    words.filter { $0.hasPrefix(prefix) }
  }
}
```

`words(matching:)` will go through the collection of strings and return the strings that match the prefix.

This algorithm is reasonable if the number of elements in the `words` array is small. But if you're dealing with more than a few thousand words, the time it takes to go through the `words` array will be unacceptable. The time complexity of `words(matching:)` is $O(k*n)$, where k is the longest string in the collection, and n is the number of words you need to check.

Imagine the number of words Google needs to parse

The trie data structure has excellent performance characteristics for this problem; as a tree with nodes that support multiple children, each node can represent a single character.

You form a word by tracing the collection of characters from the root to a node with a special indicator — a terminator — represented by a black dot. An interesting characteristic of the trie is that multiple words can share the same characters.

To illustrate the performance benefits of the trie, consider the following example in which you need to find the words with the prefix `CU`.

First, you travel to the node containing `C`. That quickly excludes other branches of the trie from the search operation:

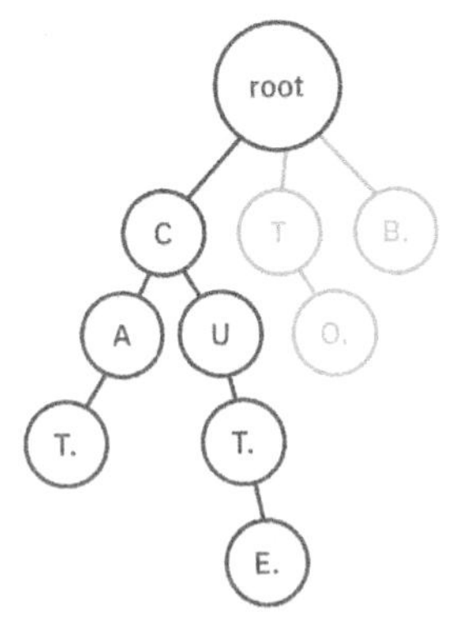

Next, you need to find the words that have the next letter `U`. You traverse to the `U` node:

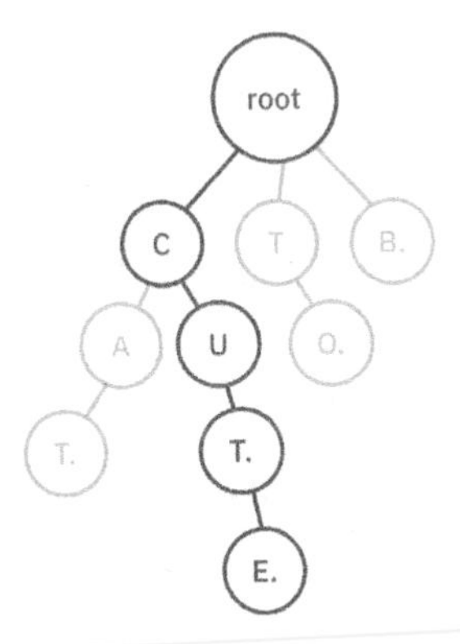

Since that's the end of your prefix, the trie would return all collections formed by the chain of nodes from the `U` node. In this case, the words `CUT` and `CUTE` would be returned. Imagine if this trie contained hundreds of thousands of words.

The number of comparisons you can avoid by employing a trie is substantial.

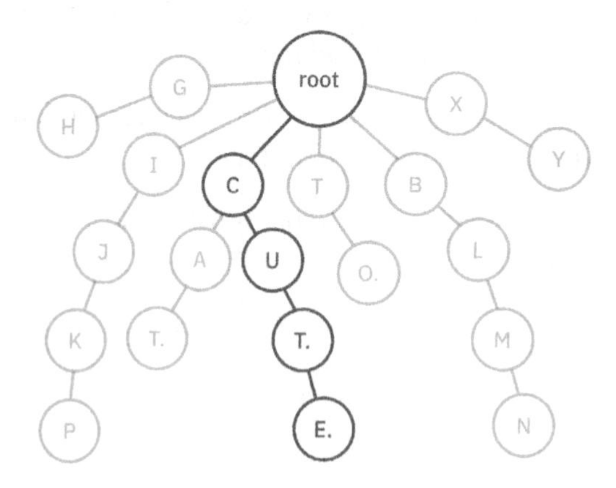

Implementation

As always, open up the starter playground for this chapter.

TrieNode

You'll begin by creating the node for the trie. In the **Sources** directory, create a new file named **TrieNode.swift**. Add the following to the file:

```
public class TrieNode<Key: Hashable> {

  // 1
  public var key: Key?

  // 2
  public weak var parent: TrieNode?

  // 3
  public var children: [Key: TrieNode] = [:]

  // 4
  public var isTerminating = false

  public init(key: Key?, parent: TrieNode?) {
    self.key = key
```

```
    self.parent = parent
  }
}
```

This interface is slightly different compared to the other nodes you've encountered:

1. `key` holds the data for the node. This is optional because the root node of the trie has no key.
2. A `TrieNode` holds a weak reference to its parent. This reference simplifies the `remove` method later on.
3. In binary search trees, nodes have a left and right child. In a trie, a node needs to hold multiple different elements. You've declared a `children` dictionary to help with that.
4. As discussed earlier, `isTerminating` acts as an indicator for the end of a collection.

Trie

Next, you'll create the trie itself, which will manage the nodes. In the **Sources** folder, create a new file named **Trie.swift**. Add the following to the file:

```
public class Trie<CollectionType: Collection>
    where CollectionType.Element: Hashable {

  public typealias Node = TrieNode<CollectionType.Element>

  private let root = Node(key: nil, parent: nil)

  public init() {}
}
```

You can use the `Trie` class for all types that adopt the `Collection` protocol, including `String`. In addition to this requirement, each element inside the collection must be `Hashable`. This additional restriction is required because you'll use the collection's elements as keys for the `children` dictionary in `TrieNode`.

Next, you'll implement four operations for the trie: `insert`, `contains`, `remove` and a prefix match.

Insert

Tries work with any type that conforms to `Collection`. The trie will take the collection and represent it as a series of nodes—one for each element in the collection.

Add the following method to `Trie`:

```
public func insert(_ collection: CollectionType) {
  // 1
  var current = root

  // 2
  for element in collection {
    if current.children[element] == nil {
      current.children[element] = Node(key: element, parent:
current)
    }
    current = current.children[element]!
  }

  // 3
  current.isTerminating = true
}
```

Here's what's going on:

1. `current` keeps track of your traversal progress, which starts with the root node.
2. A trie stores each collection element in a separate node. For each element of the collection, you first check if the node currently exists in the `children` dictionary. If it doesn't, you create a new node. During each loop, you move `current` to the next node.
3. After iterating through the `for` loop, `current` should be referencing the node representing the end of the collection. You mark that node as the terminating node.

The time complexity for this algorithm is $O(k)$, where k is the number of elements in the collection you're trying to insert. This cost is because you need to traverse through or create each node representing each new collection element.

Contains

`contains` is very similar to `insert`. Add the following method to `Trie`:

```
public func contains(_ collection: CollectionType) -> Bool {
  var current = root
  for element in collection {
    guard let child = current.children[element] else {
      return false
    }
    current = child
  }
  return current.isTerminating
}
```

Here, you traverse the trie in a way similar to `insert`. You check every element of the collection to see if it's in the tree. When you reach the last element of the collection, it must be a terminating element. If not, the collection wasn't added, and what you've found is a subset of a larger collection.

The time complexity of `contains` is $O(k)$, where k is the number of elements in the collection that you're using for the search. This time complexity comes from traversing through k nodes to determine whether the collection is in the trie.

To test out `insert` and `contains`, navigate to the playground page and add the following code:

```
example(of: "insert and contains") {
  let trie = Trie<String>()
  trie.insert("cute")
  if trie.contains("cute") {
    print("cute is in the trie")
  }
}
```

You should see the following console output:

```
---Example of: insert and contains---
cute is in the trie
```

Remove

Removing a node in the trie is a bit more tricky. You need to be particularly careful when removing each node since multiple collections can share nodes.

Write the following method just below `contains`:

```
public func remove(_ collection: CollectionType) {
  // 1
  var current = root
  for element in collection {
    guard let child = current.children[element] else {
      return
    }
    current = child
  }
  guard current.isTerminating else {
    return
  }
  // 2
  current.isTerminating = false
  // 3
  while let parent = current.parent,
        current.children.isEmpty && !current.isTerminating {
      parent.children[current.key!] = nil
      current = parent
  }
}
```

Taking it comment-by-comment:

1. This part should look familiar, as it's the implementation of `contains`. You use it here to check if the collection is part of the trie and point `current` to the last node of the collection.

2. You set `isTerminating` to `false` so the current node can be removed by the loop in the next step.

3. This is the tricky part. Since nodes can be shared, you don't want to remove elements that belong to another collection. If there are no other children in the current node, it means that other collections do not depend on the current node.

   You also check to see if the current node is terminating. If it is, then it belongs to another collection. As long as `current` satisfies these conditions, you continually backtrack through the `parent` property and remove the nodes.

The time complexity of this algorithm is $O(k)$, where k represents the number of elements of the collection that you're trying to remove.

Head back to the playground page and add the following to the bottom:

```
example(of: "remove") {
  let trie = Trie<String>()
  trie.insert("cut")
  trie.insert("cute")

  print("\n*** Before removing ***")
  assert(trie.contains("cut"))
  print("\"cut\" is in the trie")
  assert(trie.contains("cute"))
  print("\"cute\" is in the trie")

  print("\n*** After removing cut ***")
  trie.remove("cut")
  assert(!trie.contains("cut"))
  assert(trie.contains("cute"))
  print("\"cute\" is still in the trie")
}
```

You should see the following output added to the console:

```
---Example of: remove---

*** Before removing ***
"cut" is in the trie
"cute" is in the trie

*** After removing cut ***
"cute" is still in the trie
```

Prefix matching

The most iconic algorithm for the trie is the prefix-matching algorithm. Write the following at the bottom of **Trie.swift**:

```
public extension Trie where CollectionType:
RangeReplaceableCollection {

}
```

Your prefix-matching algorithm will sit inside this extension, where `CollectionType` is constrained to `RangeReplaceableCollection`. This conformance is required because the algorithm will need access to the `append` method of `RangeReplaceableCollection` types.

Next, add the following method inside the extension:

```
func collections(startingWith prefix: CollectionType) ->
[CollectionType] {
  // 1
  var current = root
  for element in prefix {
    guard let child = current.children[element] else {
      return []
    }
    current = child
  }

  // 2
  return collections(startingWith: prefix, after: current)
}
```

1. You start by verifying that the trie contains the prefix. If not, you return an empty array.

2. After you've found the node that marks the end of the prefix, you call a recursive helper method `collections(startingWith:after:)` to find all the sequences after the `current` node.

Next, add the code for the helper method:

```
private func collections(startingWith prefix: CollectionType,
                         after node: Node) -> [CollectionType] {
  // 1
  var results: [CollectionType] = []

  if node.isTerminating {
    results.append(prefix)
  }

  // 2
  for child in node.children.values {
    var prefix = prefix
    prefix.append(child.key!)
    results.append(contentsOf: collections(startingWith: prefix,
                                           after: child))
  }

  return results
}
```

1. You create an array to hold the results. If the current node a terminating, you add it to the results.

2. Next, you need to check the current node's children. For every child node, you recursively call `collections(startingWith:after:)` to seek out other terminating nodes.

`collection(startingWith:)` has a time complexity of $O(k*m)$, where k represents the longest collection matching the prefix and m represents the number of collections that match the prefix.

Recall that arrays have a time complexity of $O(k*n)$, where n is the number of elements in the collection.

For large sets of data in which each collection is uniformly distributed, tries have far better performance than using arrays for prefix matching.

Time to take the method for a spin. Navigate back to the playground page and add the following:

```
example(of: "prefix matching") {
  let trie = Trie<String>()
  trie.insert("car")
  trie.insert("card")
  trie.insert("care")
  trie.insert("cared")
  trie.insert("cars")
  trie.insert("carbs")
  trie.insert("carapace")
  trie.insert("cargo")

  print("\nCollections starting with \"car\"")
  let prefixedWithCar = trie.collections(startingWith: "car")
  print(prefixedWithCar)

  print("\nCollections starting with \"care\"")
  let prefixedWithCare = trie.collections(startingWith: "care")
  print(prefixedWithCare)
}
```

You should see the following output in the console:

```
---Example of: prefix matching---

Collections starting with "car"
["car", "carbs", "care", "cared", "cars", "carapace", "cargo",
"card"]

Collections starting with "care"
["care", "cared"]
```

Key points

- Tries provide great performance metrics in regards to prefix matching.
- Tries are relatively memory efficient since individual nodes can be shared between many different values. For example, "car," "carbs," and "care" can share the first three letters of the word.

Chapter 19: Trie Challenges

By Kelvin Lau

Challenge 1: How much faster?

Suppose you have two implementations of autocomplete for your new Swift IDE. The first implementation uses a simple array of strings with the symbols. The second implementation uses a trie of strings. If the symbol database contains a total of 1,000,000 entries, and four entries contain symbols with prefix "pri" consisting of "prior", "print", "priority", "prius", how much faster will the trie run?

> **Note**: Make the simplifying assumption that all `O(1)` operations take the same time and that `n * O(1) == O(n)`,

Challenge 2: Additional properties

The current implementation of the trie is missing some notable operations. Your task for this challenge is to augment the current implementation of the trie by adding the following:

1. A `collections` property that returns all the collections in the trie.
2. A `count` property that tells you how many collections are currently in the trie.
3. A `isEmpty` property that returns `true` if the trie is empty, `false` otherwise.

Solutions

Solution to Challenge 1

The answer is that the trie of strings runs "way faster".

With those assumptions:

```
1,000,000 * 3 * O(1) / 4 * 8 * O(1) = 93,750 times faster
```

1,000,000 is the database size; 3 is the prefix length; 4 is the number of matches; 8 is the length of the entry "priority".

Solution to Challenge 2

You'll implement the `collections` property as a stored property. Inside **Trie.swift**, add the following new property:

```
public private(set) var collections: Set<CollectionType> = []
```

This property is a `Set` that will store all the keys in the trie.

The `private(set)` scope modifier prevents the property from being tampered with outside the class definition. For this `Set` to be useful, you'll need to constrain further the trie such that the collection it holds is also `Hashable`.

Update the class declaration to the following:

```
public class Trie<CollectionType: Collection & Hashable>
  where CollectionType.Element: Hashable
```

Next, in the `insert` method, find the line `current.isTerminating = true` and replace it with:

```
if current.isTerminating {
  return
} else {
  current.isTerminating = true
  collections.insert(collection)
}
```

In the `remove` function, find the line `current.isTerminating = false` and add the following just below that line:

```
collections.remove(collection)
```

Adding the `count` and `isEmpty` properties is straightforward now that you're keeping track of all the collections:

```
public var count: Int {
  collections.count
}

public var isEmpty: Bool {
  collections.isEmpty
}
```

Chapter 20: Binary Search

By Kelvin Lau

Binary search is one of the most efficient searching algorithms with time complexity of *O(log n)*. This is comparable with searching for an element inside a **balanced** binary search tree.

Two conditions that need to be met before binary search may be used:

- The collection must be able to perform index manipulation in constant time. This means that the collection must be a `RandomAccessCollection`.
- The collection must be **sorted**.

Example

The benefits of binary search are best illustrated by comparing it with linear search. Swift's `Array` type uses linear search to implement its `firstIndex(of:)` method. It traverses through the whole collection or until it finds the first element:

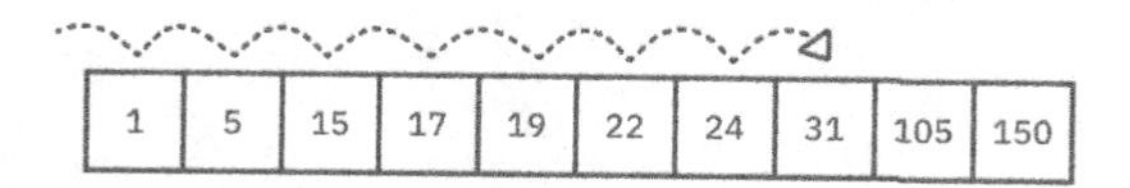

Linear search for the value 31.

Binary search handles things differently by taking advantage of the fact that the collection is already sorted.

Here's an example of applying binary search to find the value **31**:

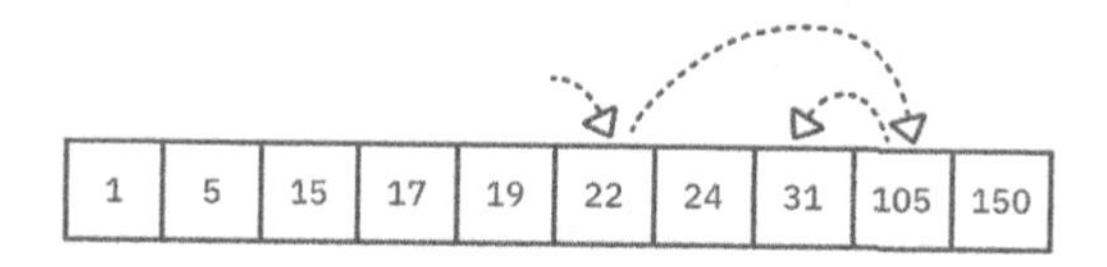

Binary search for the value 31.

Instead of eight steps to find 31, it only takes three. Here's how it works:

Step 1: Find middle index

The first step is to find the middle index of the collection. Finding it is fairly straightforward:

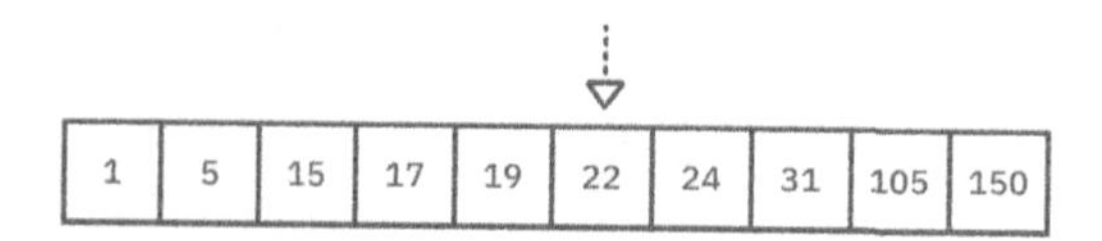

Step 2: Check the element at the middle index

The next step is to check the element stored at the middle index. If it matches the value you're looking for, return the index. Otherwise, continue to Step 3.

Step 3: Recursively call binary search

The final step is to call the binary search recursively. However, this time, you'll only consider the elements exclusively to the **left** or to the **right** of the middle index, depending on the value you're searching for. If the value you're searching for is less than the middle value, you search the left subsequence. If it is greater than the middle value, you search the right subsequence.

Each step effectively removes half of the comparisons you would otherwise need to perform.

In the example where you're looking for the value **31** (which is greater than the middle element **22**), you apply binary search on the right subsequence:

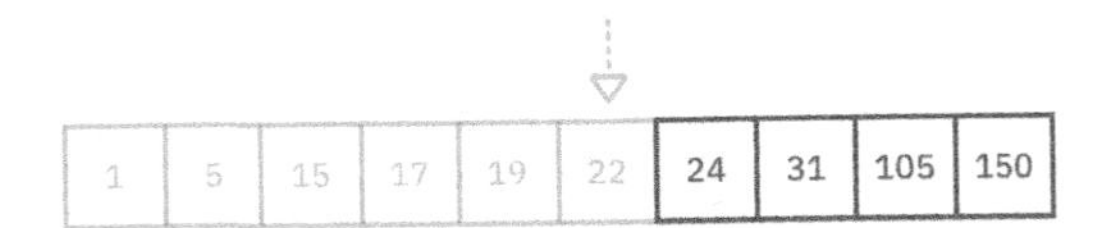

You continue these three steps until you can no longer split up the collection into left and right halves or until you find the value inside the collection.

Binary search achieves an *O(log n)* time complexity this way.

Implementation

Open the starter playground for this chapter. Create a new file in the **Sources** folder named **BinarySearch.swift**. Add the following to the file:

```
// 1
public extension RandomAccessCollection where Element:
Comparable {
  // 2
  func binarySearch(for value: Element, in range: Range<Index>?
= nil)
      -> Index? {
    // more to come
  }
}
```

Things are relatively simple so far:

1. Since binary search only works for types that conform to `RandomAccessCollection`, you add the method in an extension on `RandomAccessCollection`. This extension is constrained as you need to be able to compare elements.

2. Binary search is recursive, so you need to pass in a range to search. The parameter `range` is optional, so you can start the search without specifying a range. In this case, where `range` is `nil`, the entire collection will be searched.

Next, implement `binarySearch` as follows:

```
// 1
let range = range ?? startIndex..<endIndex
// 2
guard range.lowerBound < range.upperBound else {
  return nil
}
// 3
let size = distance(from: range.lowerBound, to:
range.upperBound)
let middle = index(range.lowerBound, offsetBy: size / 2)
// 4
if self[middle] == value {
  return middle
// 5
} else if self[middle] > value {
  return binarySearch(for: value, in: range.lowerBound..<middle)
} else {
  return binarySearch(for: value, in: index(after:
middle)..<range.upperBound)
}
```

Here are the steps:

1. First, you check if `range` was `nil`. If so, you create a range that covers the entire collection.

2. Then, you check if the range contains at least one element. If it doesn't, the search has failed, and you return `nil`.

3. Now that you're sure you have elements in the range, you find the middle index in the range.

4. You then compare the value at this index with the value that you're searching for. If the values match, you return the middle index.

5. If not, you recursively search either the left or right half of the collection.

That wraps up the implementation of binary search! Head back to the playground page to test it out. Write the following at the top of the playground page:

```
let array = [1, 5, 15, 17, 19, 22, 24, 31, 105, 150]

let search31 = array.firstIndex(of: 31)
let binarySearch31 = array.binarySearch(for: 31)

print("firstIndex(of:): \(String(describing: search31))")
print("binarySearch(for:): \(String(describing:
binarySearch31))")
```

You should see the following output in the console:

```
index(of:): Optional(7)
binarySearch(for:): Optional(7)
```

This is the index of the value you're looking for.

Binary search is a powerful algorithm to learn and comes up often in programming interviews. Whenever you read something along the lines of "Given a sorted array...", consider using the binary search algorithm. Also, if you are given a problem that looks like it is going to be $O(n^2)$ to search, consider doing some up-front sorting so you can use binary searching to reduce it down to the cost of the sort at $O(n \log n)$.

Key points

- Binary search is only a valid algorithm on **sorted** collections.
- Sometimes, it may be beneficial to sort a collection to leverage the binary search capability for looking up elements.
- The `firstIndex(of:)` method on sequences uses linear search, with $O(n)$ time complexity. Binary search has $O(\log n)$ time complexity, which scales much better for large data sets if you are doing repeated lookups.

Chapter 21: Binary Search Challenges

By Kelvin Lau

Challenge 1: Binary search as a free function

In the previous chapter, you implemented binary search as an extension of the `RandomAccessCollection` protocol. Since binary search only works on sorted collections, exposing the function as part of `RandomAccessCollection` will have a chance of misuse.

Your challenge is to implement binary search as a free function.

Challenge 2: Searching for a range

Write a function that searches a **sorted** array and finds the range of indices for a particular element. For example:

```
let array = [1, 2, 3, 3, 3, 4, 5, 5]
findIndices(of: 3, in: array)
```

`findIndices` should return the range `2..<5` since those are the start and end indices for the value `3`.

Solutions

Solution to Challenge 1

In this challenge, you'll implement binary search as a free function. Here's what the function looks like:

```
func binarySearch<Elements: RandomAccessCollection>(
  for element: Elements.Element,
  in collection: Elements,
  in range: Range<Elements.Index>? = nil) -> Elements.Index?
  where Elements.Element: Comparable {

  let range = range ??
collection.startIndex..<collection.endIndex
  guard range.lowerBound < range.upperBound else {
    return nil
  }
  let size = collection.distance(from: range.lowerBound,
                                 to: range.upperBound)
  let middle = collection.index(range.lowerBound, offsetBy: size
/ 2)
  if collection[middle] == element {
    return middle
  } else if collection[middle] > element {
    return binarySearch(for: element, in: collection, in:
range.lowerBound..<middle)
  } else {
    return binarySearch(for: element,
                        in: collection,
                        in: collection.index(after:
middle)..<range.upperBound)
  }
}
```

Solution to Challenge 2

An unoptimized but elegant solution is quite simple:

```
func findIndices(of value: Int, in array: [Int]) -> Range<Int>?
{
  guard let leftIndex = array.firstIndex(of: value) else {
    return nil
  }
  guard let rightIndex = array.lastIndex(of: value) else {
    return nil
  }
  return leftIndex..<rightIndex
}
```

The time complexity of this solution is *O*(*n*), which may not seem to be a cause for concern. However, the solution can be optimized to an *O*(_log *n*) time complexity solution.

Binary search is an algorithm that identifies values in a **sorted** collection, so keep that in mind whenever the problem promises a sorted collection. The binary search you implemented in the theory chapter is not powerful enough to reason whether the index is a start or end index. You'll modify the binary search that you learned to accommodate for this new rule.

Write the following in your playground:

```
func findIndices(of value: Int,
                 in array: [Int]) -> CountableRange<Int>? {
  guard let startIndex = startIndex(of: value,
                                    in: array,
                                    range: 0..<array.count) else
{
    return nil
  }
  guard let endIndex = endIndex(of: value,
                                in: array,
                                range: 0..<array.count) else {
    return nil
  }
  return startIndex..<endIndex
}

func startIndex(of value: Int,
                in array: [Int],
                range: CountableRange<Int>) -> Int {
  // more to come
}
```

```
func endIndex(of value: Int,
              in array: [Int],
              range: CountableRange<Int>) -> Int {
  // more to come
}
```

This time, `findIndices` will use specialized binary searches. `startIndex` and `endIndex` will be the ones that do the heavy lifting with a customized binary search. You will modify the binary search to inspect whether the adjacent value (depending on whether you're looking for the start or end index) differs from the current value. Update the `startIndex` method to the following:

```
func startIndex(of value: Int,
                in array: [Int],
                range: CountableRange<Int>) -> Int? {
  // 1
  let middleIndex = range.lowerBound +
                    (range.upperBound - range.lowerBound) / 2

  // 2
  if middleIndex == 0 || middleIndex == array.count - 1 {
    if array[middleIndex] == value {
      return middleIndex
    } else {
      return nil
    }
  }

  // 3
  if array[middleIndex] == value {
    if array[middleIndex - 1] != value {
      return middleIndex
    } else {
      return startIndex(of: value,
                        in: array,
                        range: range.lowerBound..<middleIndex)
    }
  } else if value < array[middleIndex]  {
    return startIndex(of: value,
                      in: array,
                      range: range.lowerBound..<middleIndex)
  } else {
    return startIndex(of: value,
                      in: array,
                      range: middleIndex..<range.upperBound)
  }
}
```

Here's what you do with this code:

1. You start by calculating the middle value of the indices contained in `range`.
2. This is the base case of this recursive function. If the middle index is the first or last accessible index of the array, you don't need to call binary search any further. You'll determine whether or not the current index is a valid bound for the given value.
3. Here, you check the value at the index and make your recursive calls. If the value at `middleIndex` is equal to the value you're given, you check to see if the predecessor is also the same value. If it isn't, you know that you've found the starting bound. Otherwise, you'll continue by recursively calling `startIndex`.

The `endIndex` method is similar. Update the `endIndex` implementation to the following:

```
func endIndex(of value: Int,
              in array: [Int],
              range: CountableRange<Int>) -> Int? {
  let middleIndex = range.lowerBound +
                    (range.upperBound - range.lowerBound) / 2

  if middleIndex == 0 || middleIndex == array.count - 1 {
    if array[middleIndex] == value {
      return middleIndex + 1
    } else {
      return nil
    }
  }

  if array[middleIndex] == value {
    if array[middleIndex + 1] != value {
      return middleIndex + 1
    } else {
      return endIndex(of: value,
                      in: array,
                      range: middleIndex..<range.upperBound)
    }
  } else if value < array[middleIndex]  {
    return endIndex(of: value,
                    in: array,
                    range: range.lowerBound..<middleIndex)
  } else {
    return endIndex(of: value,
                    in: array,
                    range: middleIndex..<range.upperBound)
  }
}
```

Test out your solution by writing the following at the bottom of the playground:

```
let array = [1, 2, 3, 3, 3, 4, 5, 5]
if let indices = findIndices(of: 3, in: array) {
  print(indices)
}
```

You should see the following output in the console:

```
2..<5
```

This function improves the time complexity from $O(n)$ to $O(\log n)$.

Chapter 22: Heaps

By Vincent Ngo

Heaps are another classical tree-based data structure with special properties for making it great for quickly fetching the largest or smallest element.

In this chapter, you will focus on creating and manipulating heaps. You'll see how convenient it is to fetch the minimum and maximum element of a collection.

What is a heap?

A heap is a **complete** binary tree, also known as a binary heap, that can be constructed using an array.

> **Note**: Don't confuse these heaps with memory heaps. The term heap is sometimes confusingly used in computer science to refer to a pool of memory. Memory heaps are a different concept and not what you are studying here.

Heaps come in two flavors:

1. **Max** heap, in which elements with a **higher** value have a higher priority.
2. **Min** heap, in which elements with a **lower** value have a higher priority.

The heap property

A heap has an essential characteristic that must always be satisfied. This characteristic is known as the **heap invariant** or **heap property**.

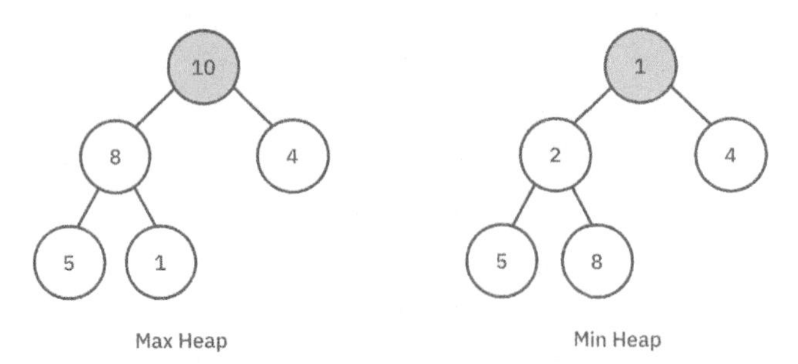

In a **max heap**, parent nodes must always contain a value that is *greater than or equal to* the value in its children. The root node will always contain the highest value.

In a **min heap**, parent nodes must always contain a value that is *less than or equal to* the value in its children. The root node will always contain the lowest value.

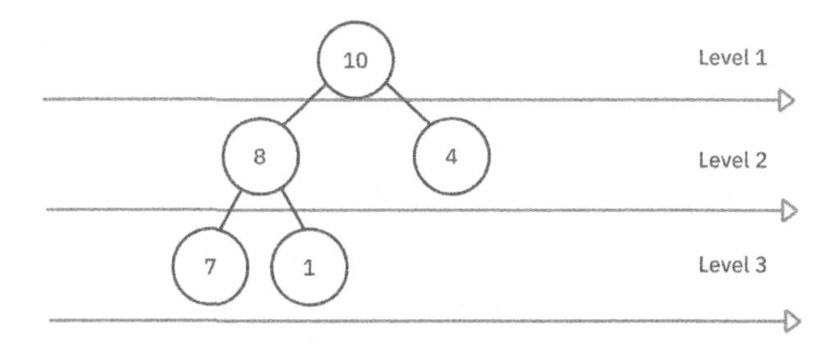

Another essential property of a heap is that it is a nearly **complete** binary tree. This means that every level must be filled, except for the last level. It's like a video game wherein you can't go to the next level until you have completed the current one.

Heap applications

Some practical applications of a heap include:

- Calculating the minimum or maximum element of a collection.
- Heapsort.
- Constructing a priority queue.
- Constructing graph algorithms, like Prim's or Dijkstra's, with a priority queue.

> **Note**: You will learn about priority queues in Chapter 24, heap sort in Chapter 32, and Dijkstra's and Prim's algorithms in Chapter 42 and 44, respectively.

Common heap operations

Open the empty starter playground for this chapter. Start by defining the following basic Heap type:

```
struct Heap<Element: Equatable> {

  var elements: [Element] = []
  let sort: (Element, Element) -> Bool

  init(sort: @escaping (Element, Element) -> Bool) {
    self.sort = sort
  }
}
```

This type contains an array to hold the elements in a heap and a sort function that defines how the heap should be ordered. By passing an appropriate function in the initializer, this type can create both min and max heaps.

How do you represent a heap?

Trees hold nodes that store references to their children. In the case of a binary tree, these are references to a left and right child. Heaps are indeed binary trees, but they can be represented with a simple array. This representation might seem like an unusual way to build a tree. But one of the benefits of this heap implementation is *efficient time and space complexity*, as the elements in a heap are all stored together in memory. You will see later on that **swapping** elements will play a big part in heap operations. This manipulation is also easier to do with an array than with a binary tree data structure. Take a look at how you can represent a heap using an array. Take the following binary heap:

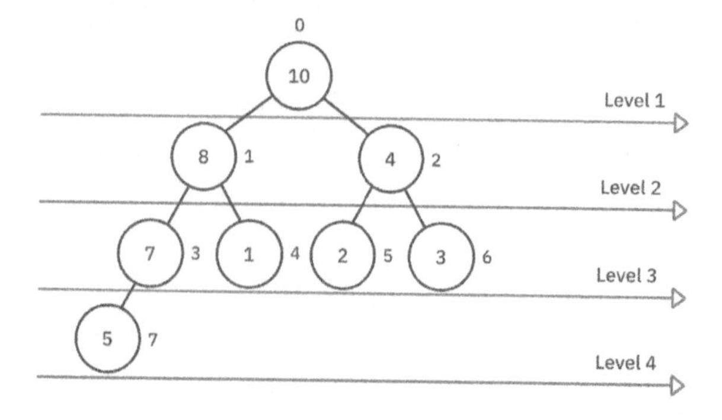

To represent the heap above as an array, you iterate through each element level-by-level from left to right.

Your traversal looks something like this:

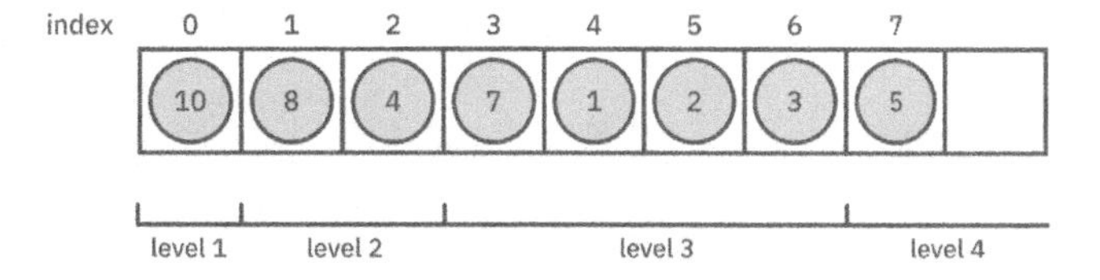

As you go up a level, you'll have twice as many nodes than in the level before.

It's now easy to access any node in the heap. You can compare this to how you'd access elements in an array: Instead of traversing down the left or right branch, you can access the node in your array using simple formulas.

Given a node at a zero-based index `i`:

- The **left child** of this node is at index `2i + 1`.
- The **right child** of this node is at index `2i + 2`.

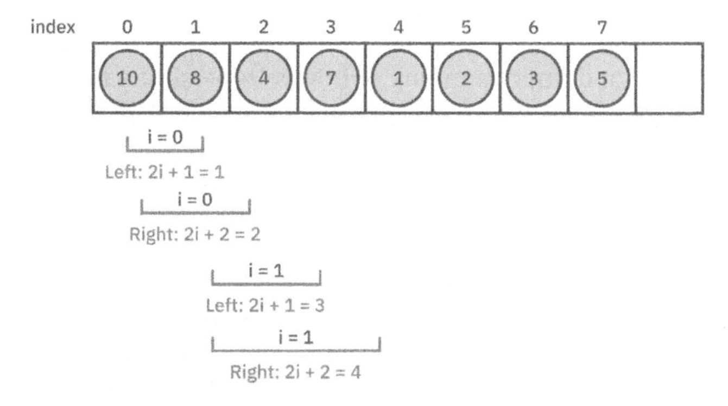

You might want to obtain the parent of a node. You can solve for `i` in this case. Given a child node at index `i`, this child's parent node can be found at index `floor( (i - 1) / 2)`.

> **Note**: Traversing down an actual binary tree to get the left and right child of a node is a *O(log n)* operation. That same operation is just *O*(1) in a random-access data structure, such as an array.

Next, use your new knowledge to add some properties and convenience methods to Heap:

```
var isEmpty: Bool {
  elements.isEmpty
}

var count: Int {
  elements.count
}

func peek() -> Element? {
  elements.first
}

func leftChildIndex(ofParentAt index: Int) -> Int {
  (2 * index) + 1
}

func rightChildIndex(ofParentAt index: Int) -> Int {
  (2 * index) + 2
}

func parentIndex(ofChildAt index: Int) -> Int {
  (index - 1) / 2
}
```

Now that you have a good understanding of how to represent a heap using an array, you'll look at some important operations of a heap.

Removing from a heap

A basic remove operation removes the root node from the heap.

Take the following max heap:

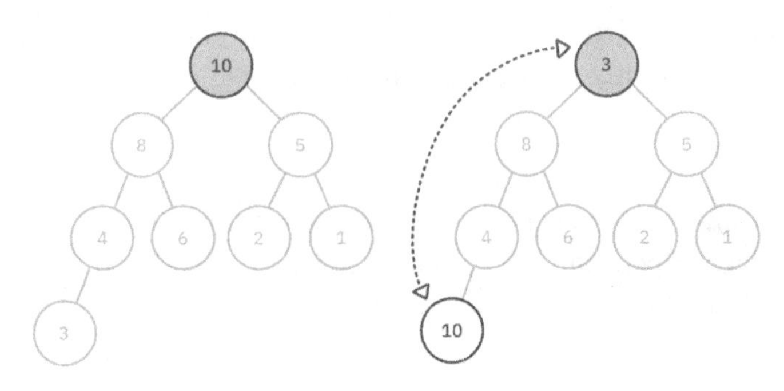

A remove operation will remove the maximum value at the root node. To do so, you must first swap the **root** node with the **last** element in the heap.

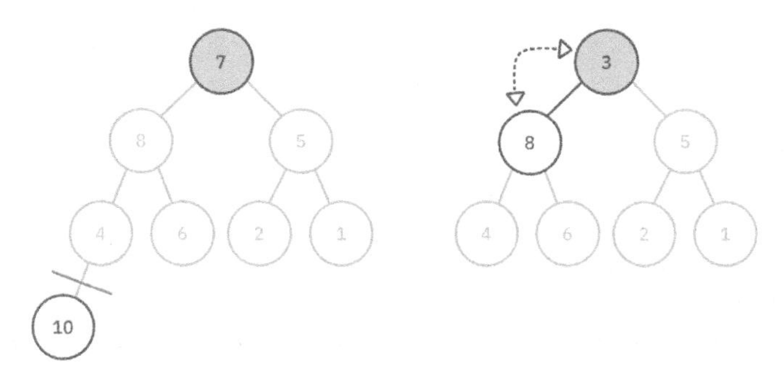

Once you've swapped the two elements, you can remove the last element and store its value so you can later return it.

Now, you must check the max heap's integrity. But first, ask yourself, "Is it still a max heap?"

Remember: The rule for a max heap is that the value of every parent node must be larger than, or equal to, the values of its children. Since the heap no longer follows this rule, you must perform a **sift down**.

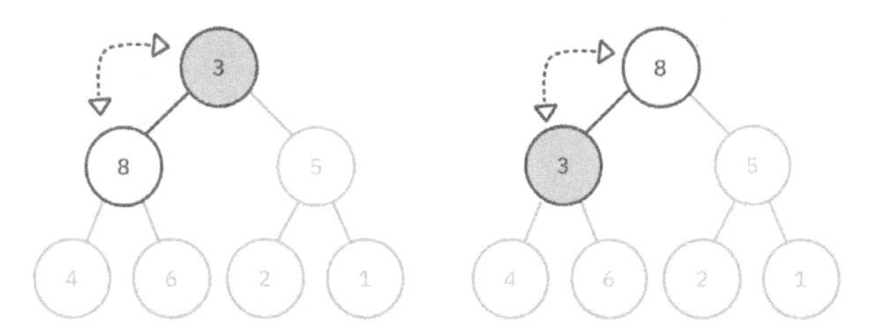

To perform a sift down, you start from the current value **3** and check its left and right child. If one of the children has a value that is greater than the current value, you swap it with the parent. If both children have a greater value, you swap the parent with the child having the greater value.

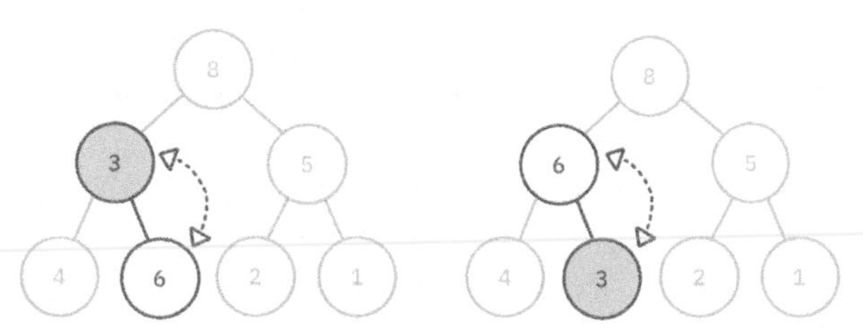

Now, you have to continue to sift down until the node's value is not larger than the values of its children.

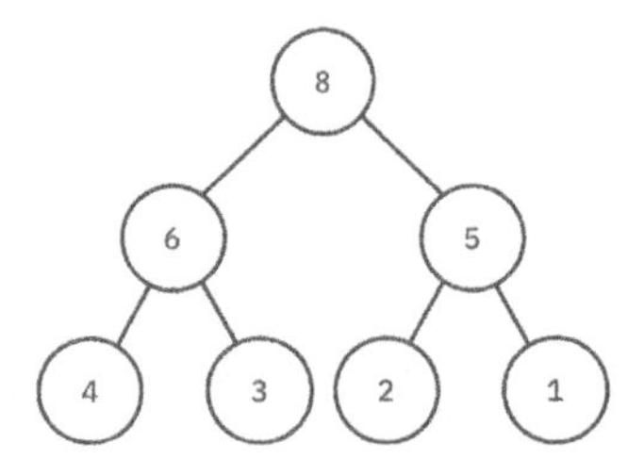

Once you reach the end, you're done, and the max heap's property has been restored!

Implementation of remove

Add the following method to `Heap`:

```
mutating func remove() -> Element? {
  guard !isEmpty else { // 1
    return nil
  }
  elements.swapAt(0, count - 1) // 2
  defer {
    siftDown(from: 0) // 4
  }
  return elements.removeLast() // 3
}
```

Here's how this method works:

1. Check to see if the heap is empty. If it is, return `nil`.
2. Swap the root with the last element in the heap.
3. Remove the last element (the maximum or minimum value) and return it.
4. The heap may not be a max or min heap anymore, so you must perform a sift down to make sure it conforms to the rules.

Now, to see how to sift down nodes, add the following method after `remove()`:

```
mutating func siftDown(from index: Int) {
  var parent = index // 1
  while true { // 2
    let left = leftChildIndex(ofParentAt: parent) // 3
    let right = rightChildIndex(ofParentAt: parent)
    var candidate = parent // 4
```

```
    if left < count && sort(elements[left], elements[candidate])
{
      candidate = left // 5
    }
    if right < count && sort(elements[right],
elements[candidate]) {
      candidate = right // 6
    }
    if candidate == parent {
      return // 7
    }
    elements.swapAt(parent, candidate) // 8
    parent = candidate
  }
}
```

`siftDown(from:)` accepts an arbitrary index. The node in this index will always be treated as the parent node. Here's how the method works:

1. Store the `parent` index.
2. Continue sifting until you `return`.
3. Get the parent's left and right child index.
4. The `candidate` variable is used to keep track of which index to swap with the parent.
5. If there is a left child, and it has a higher priority than its parent, make it the candidate.
6. If there is a right child, and it has an even greater priority, it will become the candidate instead.
7. If `candidate` is still `parent`, you have reached the end, and no more sifting is required.
8. Swap `candidate` with `parent` and set it as the new parent to continue sifting.

> **Complexity**: The overall complexity of `remove()` is $O(log\ n)$. Swapping elements in an array takes only $O(1)$ while sifting down elements in a heap takes $O(log\ n)$ time.

Now how do you *add* to a heap?

Inserting into a heap

Let's say you insert a value of **7** to the heap below:

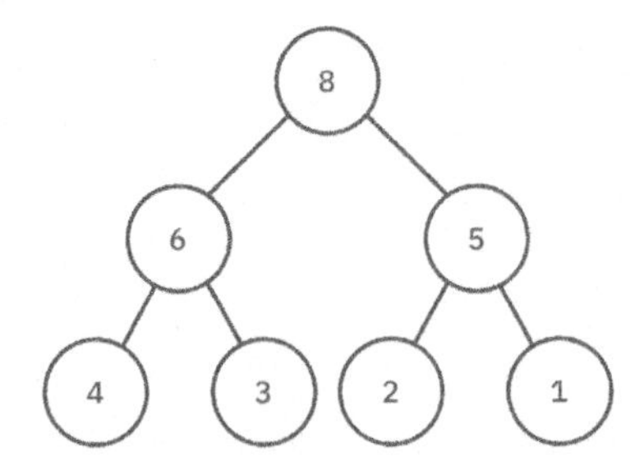

First, you add the value to the end of the heap:

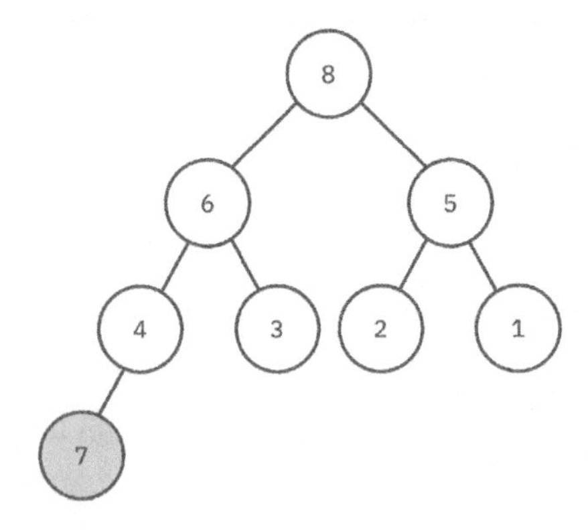

Now, you must check the max heap's property. Instead of sifting down, you must now **sift up** since the node that you just inserted might have a higher priority than its parents. This sifting up works much like sifting down by comparing the current node with its parent and swapping them if needed.

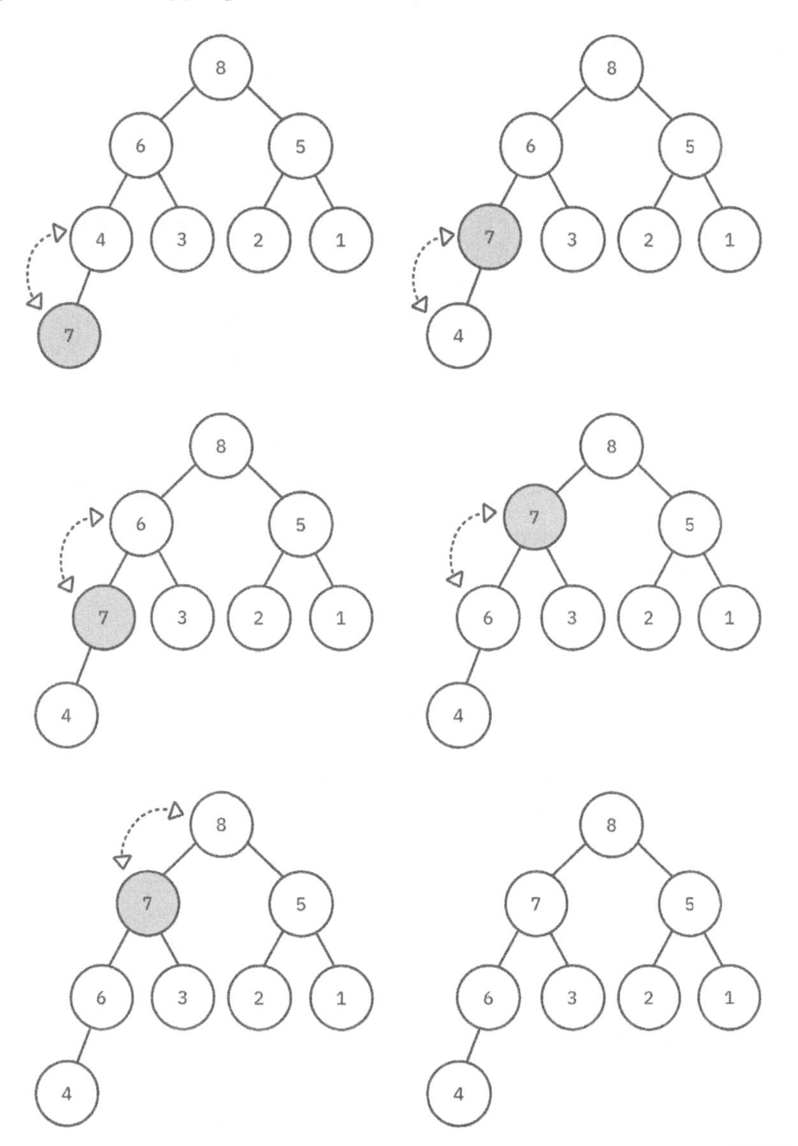

Your heap has now satisfied the max heap property!

Implementation of insert

Add the following method to Heap:

```
mutating func insert(_ element: Element) {
  elements.append(element)
  siftUp(from: elements.count - 1)
}

mutating func siftUp(from index: Int) {
  var child = index
  var parent = parentIndex(ofChildAt: child)
  while child > 0 && sort(elements[child], elements[parent]) {
    elements.swapAt(child, parent)
    child = parent
    parent = parentIndex(ofChildAt: child)
  }
}
```

As you can see, the implementation is pretty straightforward:

- `insert` appends the element to the array and then performs a sift up.
- `siftUp` swaps the current node with its parent, as long as that node has a higher priority than its parent.

> **Complexity**: The overall complexity of `insert(_:)` is *O(log n)*. Appending an element in an array takes only *O(1)* while sifting up elements in a heap takes *O(log n)*.

That's all there is to inserting an element in a heap.

You have so far looked at removing the root element from a heap and inserting into a heap. But what if you wanted to remove any arbitrary element from the heap?

Removing from an arbitrary index

Add the following to Heap:

```
mutating func remove(at index: Int) -> Element? {
  guard index < elements.count else {
    return nil // 1
  }
  if index == elements.count - 1 {
```

```
      return elements.removeLast() // 2
    } else {
      elements.swapAt(index, elements.count - 1) // 3
      defer {
        siftDown(from: index) // 5
        siftUp(from: index)
      }
      return elements.removeLast() // 4
    }
  }
```

To remove any element from the heap, you need an index. Let's go over how this works:

1. Check to see if the index is within the bounds of the array. If not, return `nil`.
2. If you're removing the last element in the heap, you don't need to do anything special. Simply remove and return the element.
3. If you're not removing the last element, first swap the element with the last element.
4. Then, return and remove the last element.
5. Finally, perform a sift down and a sift up to adjust the heap.

But — why do you have to perform *both* a sift down and a sift up?

Assume you are trying to remove **5**. You swap 5 with the last element, which is **8**. You now need to perform a sift up to satisfy the max heap property.

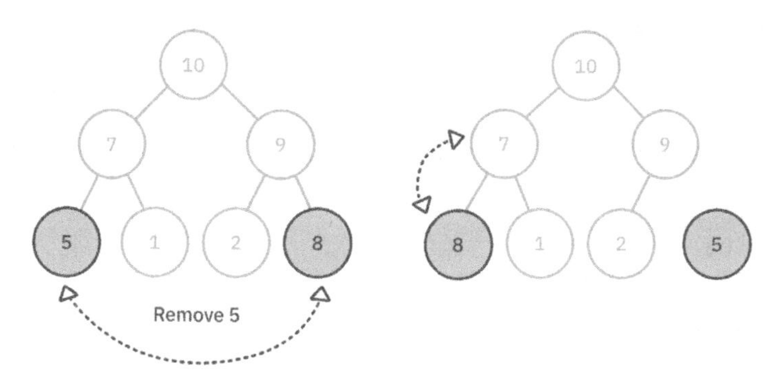

Shifting up case

Now, assume you are trying to remove **7**. You swap 7 with the last element, **1**. You now need to perform a sift down to satisfy the max heap property.

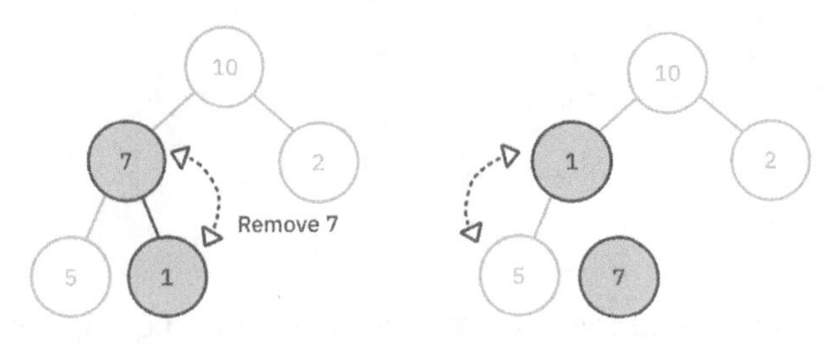

Shifting down case

Removing an arbitrary element from a heap is an *O(log n)* operation. But how do you find the index of the element you wish to delete?

Searching for an element in a heap

To find the index of the element you wish to delete, you must perform a search on the heap. Unfortunately, heaps are not designed for fast searches. With a binary search tree, you can perform a search in *O(log n)* time, but since heaps are built using an array, and the node ordering in an array is different, you can't even perform a binary search.

> **Complexity**: To search for an element in a heap is, in the worst-case, an *O(n)* operation, since you may have to check every element in the array:

```
func index(of element: Element, startingAt i: Int) -> Int? {
  if i >= count {
    return nil // 1
  }
  if sort(element, elements[i]) {
    return nil // 2
  }
  if element == elements[i] {
    return i // 3
  }
  if let j = index(of: element, startingAt:
leftChildIndex(ofParentAt: i)) {
    return j // 4
  }
  if let j = index(of: element, startingAt:
rightChildIndex(ofParentAt: i)) {
```

```
      return j // 5
    }
    return nil // 6
  }
```

Let's go over this implementation:

1. If the index is greater than or equal to the number of elements in the array, the search failed. Return `nil`.
2. Check to see if the element you are looking for has higher priority than the current element at index `i`. If it does, the element you are looking for cannot possibly be lower in the heap.
3. If the element is equal to the element at index `i`, return `i`.
4. Recursively search for the element starting from the left child of `i`.
5. Recursively search for the element starting from the right child of `i`.
6. If both searches failed, the search failed. Return `nil`.

> **Note**: Although searching takes *O*(*n*) time, you have made an effort to optimize searching by taking advantage of the heap's property and checking the element's priority when searching.

Building a heap

You now have all the necessary tools to represent a heap. To wrap up this chapter, you'll build a heap from an existing array of elements and test it out. Update the initializer of `Heap` as follows:

```
init(sort: @escaping (Element, Element) -> Bool,
     elements: [Element] = []) {
  self.sort = sort
  self.elements = elements

  if !elements.isEmpty {
    for i in stride(from: elements.count / 2 - 1, through: 0,
by: -1) {
      siftDown(from: i)
    }
  }
}
```

The initializer now takes an additional parameter. If a non-empty array is provided, you use this as the element for the heap. To satisfy the heap's property, you loop through the array backward, starting from the first non-leaf node, and sift down all parent nodes. You loop through only half of the elements because there is no point in sifting down **leaf** nodes, only parent nodes.

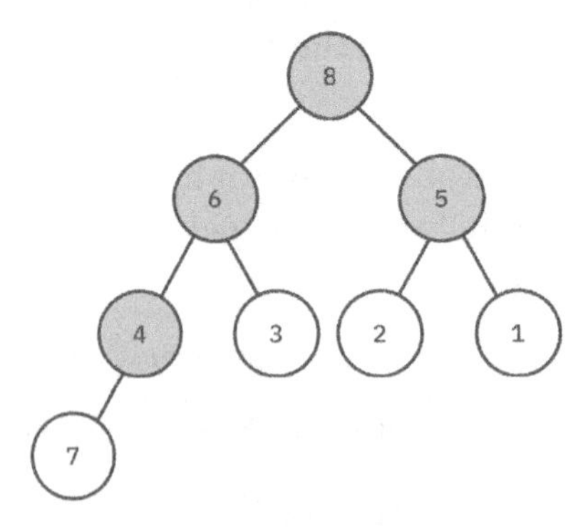

Number of parents = total number of elements /2
4 = 8 / 2

Testing

Time to try it out. Add the following to your playground:

```
var heap = Heap(sort: >, elements: [1,12,3,4,1,6,8,7])

while !heap.isEmpty {
  print(heap.remove()!)
}
```

This loop creates a max heap because > is used as the sorting predicate and removes elements one-by-one until it is empty. Notice that the elements are removed from largest to smallest, and the following numbers are printed to the console.

```
12
8
7
6
4
3
1
1
```

Key points

- Here is a summary of the algorithmic complexity of the heap operations you implemented in this chapter:

Heap Data Structure

Operations	Time Complexity
remove	O(log n)
insert	O(log n)
search	O(n)
peek	O(1)

Heap operation time complexity

- The heap data structure is good for maintaining the highest- or lowest-priority element.
- Elements in a heap are packed into contiguous memory using a simple formula for element lookup.
- Every time you insert or remove items, you must take care to preserve the heap property of the heap.

Chapter 23: Heap Challenges

By Vincent Ngo

Think you have a handle on heaps? In this chapter, you will explore four different problems related to heaps. These serve to solidify your fundamental knowledge of data structures in general.

Challenge 1: Find the nth smallest integer

Write a function to find the `nth` smallest integer in an unsorted array. For example:

```
let integers = [3, 10, 18, 5, 21, 100]
```

If `n = 3`, the result should be `10`.

Challenge 2: Step-by-Step diagram

Given the following array, visually construct a min-heap. Provide a step-by-step diagram of how the min-heap is constructed.

```
[21, 10, 18, 5, 3, 100, 1]
```

Challenge 3: Combining two heaps

Write a method that combines two heaps.

Challenge 4: A Min Heap?

Write a function to check if a given array is a min-heap.

Solutions

Solution to Challenge 1

There are many ways to solve for the `nth` smallest integer in an unsorted array. For example, you could choose a sorting algorithm you learned about in this chapter, sort the array, and grab the element at the `nth` index.

Let's take a look at how you would obtain the `nth` smallest element using a min-heap!

```
func getNthSmallestElement(n: Int, elements: [Int]) -> Int? {
  var heap = Heap(sort: <, elements: elements) // 1
  var current = 1 // 2
  while !heap.isEmpty { // 3
    let element = heap.remove() // 4
    if current == n { // 5
      return element
    }
    current += 1 // 6
  }
  return nil // 7
}
```

Let's go over the solution:

1. Initialize a min-heap with the unsorted array.
2. `current` tracks the `nth` smallest element.
3. As long as the heap is not empty, continue to remove elements.
4. Remove the root element from the heap.
5. Check to see if you reached the `nth` smallest element. If so, return the element.
6. If not, increment `current`.
7. Return `nil` if the heap is empty.

Building a heap takes $O(n)$. Every element removal from the heap takes $O(\log n)$. Keep in mind that you are also doing this `n` times. The overall time complexity is $O(n \log n)$.

Solution to Challenge 2

```
[21, 10, 18, 5, 3, 100, 1]
```

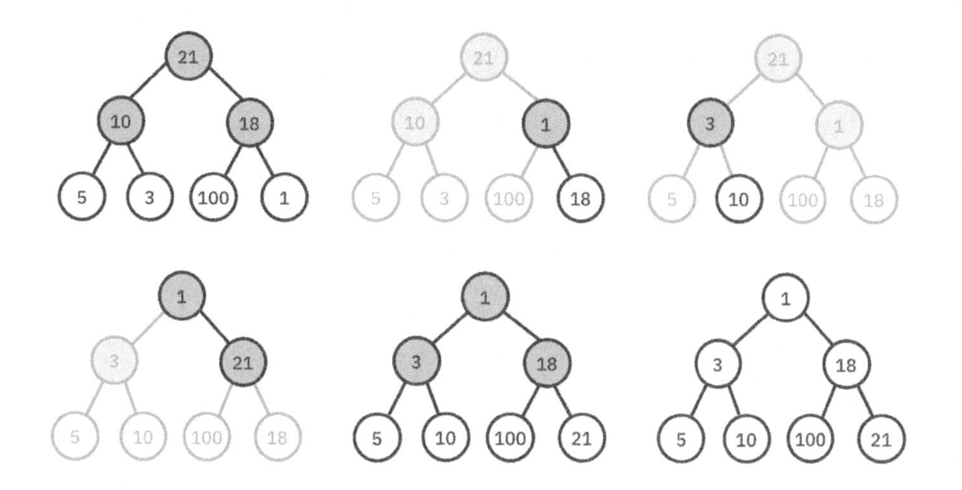

Solution to Challenge 3

Add this as an additional function of **Heap.swift**:

```
mutating public func merge(_ heap: Heap) {
  elements = elements + heap.elements
  buildHeap()
}
```

Merging two heaps is very straightforward. You first combine both arrays, which takes $O(m)$, where `m` is the length of the `heap` you are merging. Building the heap takes $O(n)$. Overall the algorithm runs in $O(n)$.

Solution to Challenge 4

To check if the given array is a min-heap, you only need to go through all the parent nodes of the binary heap. To satisfy the min-heap requirement, every parent node must be less than or equal to its left and right child node.

The following are helper methods to grab the left and right child index for a given parent index.

```
func leftChildIndex(ofParentAt index: Int) -> Int {
  (2 * index) + 1
}

func rightChildIndex(ofParentAt index: Int) -> Int {
  (2 * index) + 2
}
```

Let's now see how you can determine if an array is a min heap:

```
func isMinHeap<Element: Comparable>(elements: [Element]) -> Bool
{
  guard !elements.isEmpty else { // 1
    return true
  }
  // 2
  for i in stride(from: elements.count / 2 - 1, through: 0, by:
-1) {
    let left = leftChildIndex(ofParentAt: i) // 3
    let right = rightChildIndex(ofParentAt: i)
    if elements[left] < elements[i] { // 4
      return false
    }
    if right < elements.count && elements[right] < elements[i]
{ // 5
      return false
    }
  }
  return true // 6
}
```

1. If the array is empty, it is a min-heap!
2. Go through all parent nodes in the array in reverse order.
3. Get the left and right child index.

4. Check to see if the left element is less than the parent.
5. Check to see if the right index is within the array's bounds, and check if the right element is less than the parent.
6. If every parent-child relationship satisfies the min-heap property, return true!

The time complexity of this solution is $O(n)$. This is because you still have to go through every element in the array.

Chapter 24: Priority Queues

By Vincent Ngo

Queues are simply lists that maintain the order of elements using *first-in-first-out* (FIFO) ordering. A priority queue is another version of a queue in which elements are dequeued in priority order instead of using FIFO ordering. For example, a priority queue can either be:

1. **Max-priority**, in which the element at the front is always the largest.
2. **Min-priority**, in which the element at the front is always the smallest.

A priority queue is especially useful when identifying the maximum or minimum value given a list of elements. In this chapter, you will learn the benefits of a priority queue and build one by leveraging the existing queue and heap data structures that you studied in previous chapters.

Applications

Some practical applications of a priority queue include:

- **Dijkstra's algorithm**, which uses a priority queue to calculate the minimum cost.
- **A* pathfinding algorithm**, which uses a priority queue to track the unexplored routes that will produce the path with the shortest length.
- **Heap sort**, which can be implemented using a priority queue.
- **Huffman coding** that builds a compression tree. A min-priority queue is used to repeatedly find two nodes with the smallest frequency that do not yet have a parent node.

These are just some of the use cases, but priority queues have many more applications as well.

Common operations

In Chapter 8, Queues, you established the following protocol for queues:

```
public protocol Queue {
  associatedtype Element
  mutating func enqueue(_ element: Element) -> Bool
  mutating func dequeue() -> Element?
  var isEmpty: Bool { get }
  var peek: Element? { get }
}
```

A priority queue has the same operations as a regular queue, so only the implementation will differ.

The priority queue will conform to the `Queue` protocol and implement the common operations:

- **enqueue**: Inserts an element into the queue. Returns `true` if the operation was successful.
- **dequeue**: Removes the element with the highest priority and returns it. Returns `nil` if the queue was empty.

- **isEmpty**: Checks if the queue is empty.
- **peek**: Returns the element with the highest priority without removing it. Returns `nil` if the queue was empty.

Let's look at different ways to implement a priority queue.

Implementation

You can create a priority queue in the following ways:

1. **Sorted array**: This is useful to obtain the maximum or minimum value of an element in $O(1)$ time. However, insertion is slow and will require $O(n)$ since you have to insert it in order.
2. **Balanced binary search tree**: This is useful in creating a double-ended priority queue, which features getting both the minimum and maximum value in $O(\log n)$ time. Insertion is better than a sorted array, also in $O(\log n)$.
3. **Heap**: This is a natural choice for a priority queue. A heap is more efficient than a sorted array because a heap only needs to be partially sorted. All heap operations are $O(\log n)$ except extracting the min value from a min priority heap is a lightning-fast $O(1)$. Likewise, extracting the max value from a max priority heap is also $O(1)$.

Next, you will look at how to use a heap to create a priority queue. Open up the starter playground to get started. In the **Sources** folder, you will notice the following files:

1. **Heap.swift**: The heap data structure (from the previous chapter) you will use to implement the priority queue.
2. **Queue.swift**: Contains the protocol that defines a queue.

In the main playground page, add the following:

```
struct PriorityQueue<Element: Equatable>: Queue { // 1

  private var heap: Heap<Element> // 2

  init(sort: @escaping (Element, Element) -> Bool,
       elements: [Element] = []) { // 3
    heap = Heap(sort: sort, elements: elements)
  }
```

```
  // more to come ...
}
```

Let's go over this code:

1. `PriorityQueue` will conform to the `Queue` protocol. The generic parameter `Element` must conform to `Equatable` as you need to compare elements.
2. You will use this heap to implement the priority queue.
3. By passing an appropriate function into this initializer, `PriorityQueue` can be used to create both min and max priority queues.

To conform to the `Queue` protocol, add the following right after the `init(sort:elements:)` initializer:

```
var isEmpty: Bool {
  heap.isEmpty
}

var peek: Element? {
  heap.peek()
}

mutating func enqueue(_ element: Element) -> Bool { // 1
  heap.insert(element)
  return true
}

mutating func dequeue() -> Element? { // 2
  heap.remove()
}
```

The heap is a perfect candidate for a priority queue. You need to call various methods of a heap to implement the operations of a priority queue!

1. From the previous chapter, you should understand that, by calling `enqueue(_:)`, you insert into the heap, and the heap will sift up to validate itself. The overall complexity of `enqueue(_:)` is $O(\log n)$.
2. By calling `dequeue(_:)`, you remove the root element from the heap by replacing it with the last element in the heap and then sift down to validate the heap. The overall complexity of `dequeue()` is $O(\log n)$.

Testing

Add the following to your playground:

```
var priorityQueue = PriorityQueue(sort: >, elements:
[1,12,3,4,1,6,8,7])
while !priorityQueue.isEmpty {
  print(priorityQueue.dequeue()!)
}
```

You'll notice that a priority queue has the same interface as a regular queue. The previous code creates a max priority queue. Notice that the elements are removed from largest to smallest. The following numbers are printed to the console:

```
12
8
7
6
4
3
1
1
```

Key points

- A priority queue is often used to find the element in **priority order**.
- It creates a layer of abstraction by focusing on key operations of a queue and leaving out additional functionality provided by the heap data structure.
- This makes the priority queue's intent clear and concise. Its only job is to enqueue and dequeue elements, nothing else!
- Composition for the win!

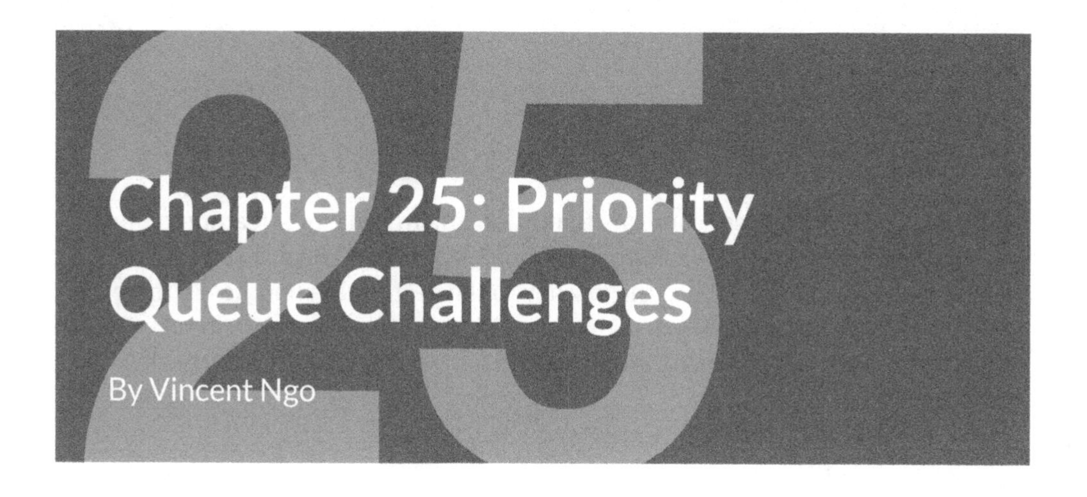

Chapter 25: Priority Queue Challenges

By Vincent Ngo

Challenge 1: Array-based priority queue

You have learned to use a heap to construct a priority queue by conforming to the `Queue` protocol. Now, construct a priority queue using an `Array`.

```
public protocol Queue {
  associatedtype Element
  mutating func enqueue(_ element: Element) -> Bool
  mutating func dequeue() -> Element?
  var isEmpty: Bool { get }
  var peek: Element? { get }
}
```

Challenge 2: Prioritize a waitlist

Your favorite T-Swift concert was sold out. Fortunately, there is a waitlist for people who still want to go! However, ticket sales will first prioritize someone with a military background, followed by seniority. Write a `sort` function that will return the list of people on the waitlist by the priority mentioned. The `Person` struct is defined below:

```
public struct Person: Equatable {
  let name: String
  let age: Int
  let isMilitary: Bool
}
```

Challenge 3: Minimize recharge stops

Swift-la is a new electric car company that is looking to add a new feature to their vehicles. They want to add the ability for their customers to check if the car can reach a given destination. Since the journey to the destination may be far, there are charging stations that the car can recharge at. The company wants to find the **minimum number of charging stops** needed for the vehicle to reach its destination.

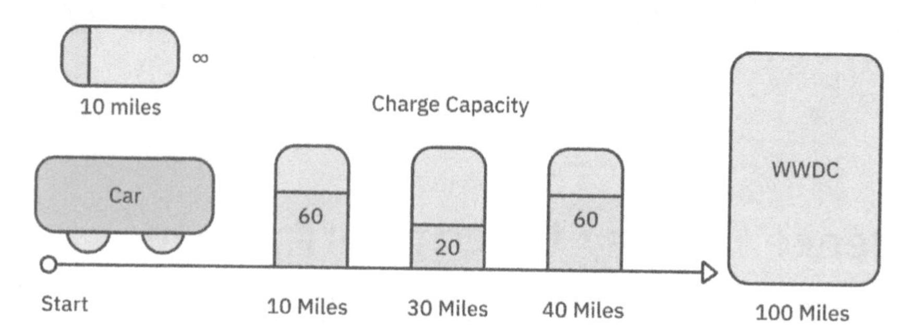

You're given the following information:

- The `target` distance the vehicle needs to travel.
- The `startCharge`, how much charge the car has to begin the journey.
- An ordered list of `stations` that the car can potentially stop at to charge along the way.

Each `ChargingStation` has a `distance` from the start location and a `chargeCapacity`. This capacity is the amount of charge a station can add to the car.

You may assume the following:

1. An electric car has an **infinite** charge capacity.
2. One charge capacity is equivalent to one mile.
3. The list of `stations` is sorted by distance from the start location:

```
stations[0].distance < stations[1].distance <
stations[k].distance
```

To get you started, objects and functions are provided. Open **25-priorityqueue-challenge/projects/starter/PriorityQueueChallenge.playground** and navigate to **Minimum Recharge Stops** playground page.

Solutions

Solution to Challenge 1

Recall that a priority queue dequeues elements in priority order. It could either be a min or max priority queue. You have been given the following protocol:

```
public protocol Queue {
  associatedtype Element
  mutating func enqueue(_ element: Element) -> Bool
  mutating func dequeue() -> Element?
  var isEmpty: Bool { get }
  var peek: Element? { get }
}
```

To make an array-based priority queue, all you have to do is conform to the `Queue` protocol. Instead of using a heap, you use an array data structure!

First, add the following:

```
public struct PriorityQueueArray<T: Equatable>: Queue {

  private var elements: [T] = []
  let sort: (Element, Element) -> Bool

}
```

Within the `PriorityQueueArray`, you store an array of elements and the given `sort` function.

The `sort` function helps prioritize the elements in the queue.

Next add the following initializer:

```
public init(sort: @escaping (Element, Element) -> Bool,
            elements: [Element] = []) {
  self.sort = sort
  self.elements = elements
  self.elements.sort(by: sort)
}
```

The initializer takes a `sort` function and an array of `elements`. Within the `init` method, you leverage the array's `sort` function. According to Apple, the sort function takes $O(n \log n)$ time.

> Swift's sort function uses **introsort**, a combination of insertion sort and heap sort. Check it out here: https://github.com/apple/swift/blob/master/stdlib/public/core/Sort.swift

Next, you should conform to the `Queue` protocol. Add the following methods:

```
public var isEmpty: Bool {
  elements.isEmpty
}

public var peek: T? {
  elements.first
}
```

Fairly straightforward. To check if the queue is empty, check if the array is empty.

To peek at what's at the start of the queue, return the first element of the array.

Next, add the enqueue method:

```
public mutating func enqueue(_ element: T) -> Bool {
  for (index, otherElement) in elements.enumerated() { // 1
    if sort(element, otherElement) { // 2
      elements.insert(element, at: index) // 3
      return true
    }
  }
  elements.append(element) // 4
  return true
}
```

To enqueue an element into an array-based priority queue, do the following:

1. For every element in the queue.
2. Check to see if the element you are adding has a higher priority.
3. If it does, insert it at the current `index`.
4. If the element does not have a higher priority than any element in the queue, append the element to the end.

This method has overall $O(n)$ time complexity since you have to go through every element to check the priority against the new element you are adding. Also, if you are inserting in between elements in the array, you have to shift elements to the right by one.

Next add the dequeue method:

```
public mutating func dequeue() -> T? {
  isEmpty ? nil : elements.removeFirst()
}
```

Here you check to see if the queue is empty before removing the first element from the array. This method is an $O(n)$ operation since you must shift the existing elements to the left by one.

Finally, let's print out the priority queue in a friendly format. Add the following:

```
extension PriorityQueueArray: CustomStringConvertible {

  public var description: String {
    String(describing: elements)
  }
}
```

There you have it! An array-based priority queue!

To test out the priority queue add the following:

```
var priorityQueue = PriorityQueueArray(sort: >, elements:
[1,12,3,4,1,6,8,7])
priorityQueue.enqueue(5)
priorityQueue.enqueue(0)
priorityQueue.enqueue(10)
while !priorityQueue.isEmpty {
  print(priorityQueue.dequeue()!)
}
```

Solution to Challenge 2

You are given the following `Person` type:

```
public struct Person: Equatable {
  let name: String
  let age: Int
  let isMilitary: Bool
}
```

Given a list of people on the waitlist, you would like to prioritize the people in the following order:

1. Military background
2. Seniority, by age

One solution to this problem is using a priority queue data structure and build a proper sort function to address the priority!

Add the following sort function below:

```
func tswiftSort(person1: Person, person2: Person) -> Bool {
  if person1.isMilitary == person2.isMilitary {
    return person1.age > person2.age
  }

  return person1.isMilitary
}
```

`tswiftSort` takes two people and checks to see if both of them have or don't have a military background. If so, you check their age, and if not, you give priority to whoever has a military background.

To test your priority sort function out, let's try a sample data set by adding the following:

```
let p1 = Person(name: "Josh", age: 21, isMilitary: true)
let p2 = Person(name: "Jake", age: 22, isMilitary: true)
let p3 = Person(name: "Clay", age: 28, isMilitary: false)
let p4 = Person(name: "Cindy", age: 28, isMilitary: false)
let p5 = Person(name: "Sabrina", age: 30, isMilitary: false)

let waitlist = [p1, p2, p3, p4, p5]

var priorityQueue = PriorityQueue(sort: tswiftSort, elements:
waitlist)
while !priorityQueue.isEmpty {
  print(priorityQueue.dequeue()!)
}
```

Solution to Challenge 3

The question provides two entities to get you started:

The first is `ChargingStation`:

```
struct ChargingStation {
  /// Distance from start location.
  let distance: Int
  /// The amount of electricity the station has to charge a car.
  /// 1 capacity = 1 mile
  let chargeCapacity: Int
}
```

The second is `DestinationResult`:

```
enum DestinationResult {
  /// Able to reach your destination with the minimum number of
stops.
  case reachable(rechargeStops: Int)
  /// Unable to reach your destination.
  case unreachable
}
```

`DestinationResult` describes whether the vehicle can complete its journey.

Lastly, the question provides a `minRechargeStops(_:)` function with three parameters.

- `target`: the distance in miles the vehicle needs to travel.
- `startCharge`: the starting charge you have to start the journey.
- `stations`: the `ChargingStations` along the way, sorted by distance.

To find the minimum number of charging stations to stop at, one solution is to leverage a priority queue.

Add the following in `minRechargeStops(_:)`:

```
func minRechargeStops(target: Int, startCharge: Int, stations:
[ChargingStation]) -> DestinationResult {
  // 1
  guard startCharge <= target else {
    return .reachable(rechargeStops: 0)
  }

  // 2
  var minStops = -1
```

```
  // 3
  var currentCharge = 0
  // 4
  var currentStation = 0
  // 5
  var chargePriority = PriorityQueue(sort: >, elements:
[startCharge])
}
```

Going over the initial setup:

1. If the starting charge of the electric vehicle is greater than or equal to the target destination, it is `.reachable` with zero stops.
2. `minStops` keeps track of the minimum number of stops needed to reach `target`.
3. `currentCharge` keeps track of the vehicle's current charge on the journey.
4. `currentStation` tracks the number of stations passed.
5. `chargePriority` is a priority queue that holds all the reachable charging stations. It is responsible for providing the station with the highest charging capacity. The priority queue is also initialized with the vehicle's `startCharge`.

Next add the following to `minRechargeStops`:

```
// 1
while !chargePriority.isEmpty {
  // 2
  guard let charge = chargePriority.dequeue() else {
    return .unreachable
  }
  // 3
  currentCharge += charge
  // 4
  minStops += 1

  // 5
  if currentCharge >= target {
    return .reachable(rechargeStops: minStops)
  }

  // 6
  while currentStation < stations.count &&
        currentCharge >= stations[currentStation].distance {
    let distance = stations[currentStation].chargeCapacity
    _ = chargePriority.enqueue(distance)
    currentStation += 1
  }
}
```

```
// 7
return .unreachable
```

Recall: The priority queue `chargePriority` will give us the station with the highest charge capacity.

This loop is a greedy algorithm in that the priority queue will always give us the reachable station with the highest capacity to charge the vehicle.

1. If the `chargePriority` queue is not empty, this means that there are reachable charging stations the car can charge at.
2. `chargePriority` queue removes the station with the highest charge capacity.
3. Charge the vehicle by adding the `charge` to `currentCharge`.
4. Every time you dequeue from the priority queue, you must increment `minStops`, since you've stopped at a station.
5. Check to see if the `currentCharge` can reach the `target`. If it can reach the target, return `.reachable` with the minimum stops.
6. Our current charge can't reach our destination, but we have not exhausted all charging stations, and the car's `currentCharge` can reach the next `currentStation`. Let's add the station's `chargeCapacity` to the `chargePriority` queue.
7. We are unable to reach the destination.

That's it! Let's test this new feature out for electric car company Swift-la!

```
let stations = [ChargingStation(distance: 10, chargeCapacity:
60),
                ChargingStation(distance: 20, chargeCapacity:
30),
                ChargingStation(distance: 30, chargeCapacity:
30),
                ChargingStation(distance: 60, chargeCapacity:
40)]

minRechargeStops(target: 100, startCharge: 10, stations:
stations)
```

This goal should be reachable with two minimum stops!

Section IV: Sorting Algorithms

Putting lists in order is a classical computational problem. Sorting has been studied since the days of vacuum tubes and perhaps even before that. Although you may never need to write your own sorting algorithm using the highly optimized standard library, studying sorting has many benefits. You'll learn, for example, about the all-important technique of divide-and-conquer, stability, and best and worst case timings.

This section will follow the same structure of introducing you to a concept with a chapter, followed by a Challenge chapter to practice the skills you are acquiring.

Studying sorting may seem a bit academic and disconnected from the "real world" of app development, but understanding the tradeoffs for these simple cases will lead you to a better understanding and let you analyze any algorithm.

$O(n^2)$ time complexity is not great performance, but the sorting algorithms in this category are easy to understand and useful in some scenarios. These algorithms are space-efficient; they only require constant $O(1)$ additional memory space. For small data sets, these sorts compare very favorably against more complex sorts.

In this chapter, you'll be looking at the following sorting algorithms:

- Bubble sort
- Selection sort
- Insertion sort

All of these are **comparison-based** sorting methods. They rely on a comparison method, such as the less-than operator, to order the elements. The number of times this comparison gets called is how you can measure a sorting technique's general performance.

Bubble sort

One of the most straightforward sorts is the bubble sort, which repeatedly compares adjacent values and swaps them, if needed, to perform the sort. Therefore, the larger values in the set will "bubble up" to the end of the collection.

Example

Consider the following hand of cards:

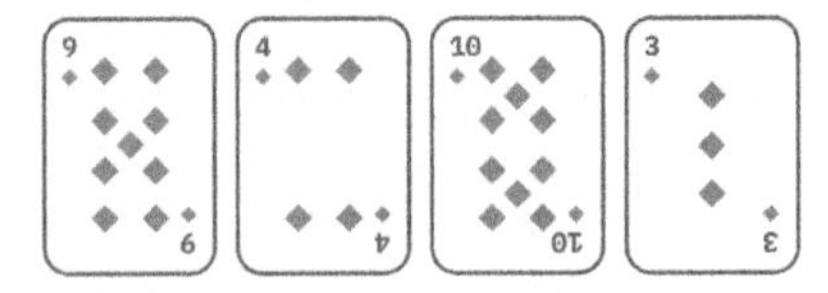

A single pass of the bubble-sort algorithm would consist of the following steps:

- Start at the beginning of the collection. Compare 9 and 4. These values need to be swapped. The collection then becomes `[4, 9, 10, 3]`.
- Move to the next index in the collection. Compare 9 and 10. These are in order.
- Move to the next index in the collection. Compare 10 and 3. These values need to be swapped. The collection then becomes `[4, 9, 3, 10]`.

A single pass of the algorithm will seldom result in a complete ordering, which is true for this collection. It will, however, cause the largest value — 10 — to bubble up to the end of the collection.

Subsequent passes through the collection will do the same for 9 and 4, respectively:

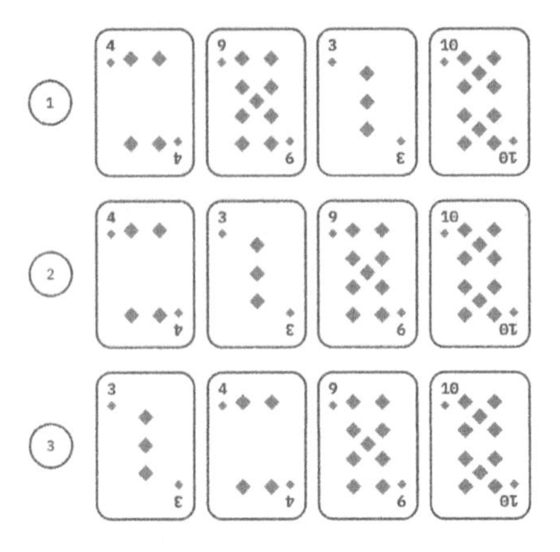

The sort is only complete when you can perform a full pass over the collection without swapping any values. At worst, this will require n-1 passes, where n is the count of members in the collection.

Implementation

Open up the Swift playground for this chapter to get started. In the **Sources** directory of your playground, create a new file named **BubbleSort.swift**. Write the following inside the file:

```
public func bubbleSort<Element>(_ array: inout [Element])
    where Element: Comparable {
  // 1
  guard array.count >= 2 else {
    return
  }
  // 2
  for end in (1..<array.count).reversed() {
    var swapped = false
    // 3
    for current in 0..<end {
      if array[current] > array[current + 1] {
        array.swapAt(current, current + 1)
        swapped = true
      }
    }
    // 4
    if !swapped {
      return
    }
  }
}
```

Here's the play-by-play:

1. There is no need to sort the collection if it has less than two elements.
2. A single-pass bubbles the largest value to the end of the collection. Every pass needs to compare one less value than in the previous pass, so you essentially shorten the array by one with each pass.
3. This loop performs a single pass; it compares adjacent values and swaps them if needed.
4. If no values were swapped this pass, the collection must be sorted, and you can exit early.

Try it out! Head back into the main playground page and write the following:

```
example(of: "bubble sort") {
  var array = [9, 4, 10, 3]
  print("Original: \(array)")
  bubbleSort(&array)
  print("Bubble sorted: \(array)")
}
```

You should see the following output:

```
---Example of bubble sort---
Original: [9, 4, 10, 3]
Bubble sorted: [3, 4, 9, 10]
```

Bubble sort has a *best* time complexity of $O(n)$ if it's already sorted, and a *worst* and *average* time complexity of $O(n^2)$, making it one of the *least* appealing sorts in the known universe.

Selection sort

Selection sort follows the basic idea of bubble sort but improves this algorithm by reducing the number of swapAt operations. Selection sort will only swap at the end of each pass. You'll see how that works in the following example and implementation.

Example

Assume you have the following hand of cards:

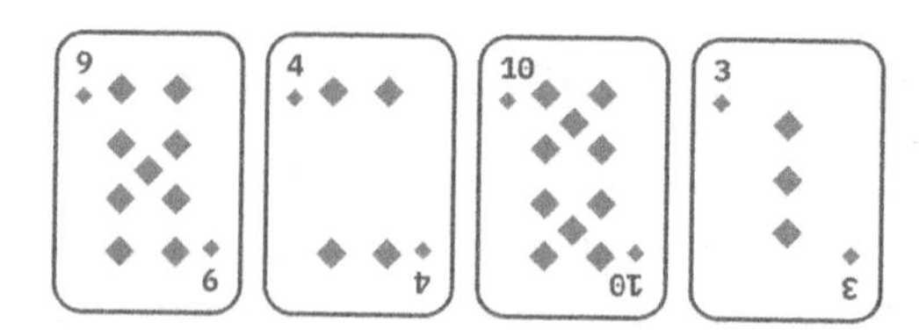

During each pass, selection sort will find the lowest unsorted value and swap it into place:

1. First, 3 is found as the lowest value. It is swapped with 9.
2. The next lowest value is 4. It's already in the right place.
3. Finally, 9 is swapped with 10.

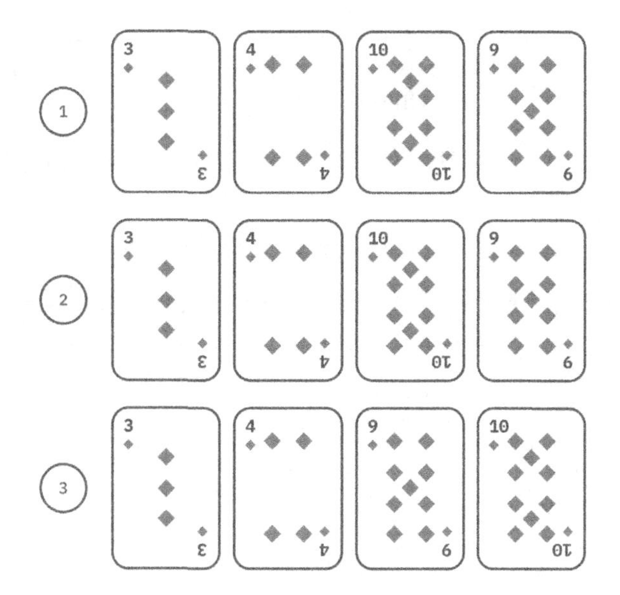

Implementation

In the **Sources** directory of your playground, create a new file named **SelectionSort.swift**. Write the following inside the file:

```
public func selectionSort<Element>(_ array: inout [Element])
    where Element: Comparable {
  guard array.count >= 2 else {
    return
  }
  // 1
  for current in 0..<(array.count - 1) {
    var lowest = current
    // 2
    for other in (current + 1)..<array.count {
      if array[lowest] > array[other] {
        lowest = other
      }
    }
```

```
      // 3
      if lowest != current {
        array.swapAt(lowest, current)
      }
    }
  }
```

Here's what's going on:

1. You perform a pass for every element in the collection, except for the last one. There is no need to include the last element since if all other elements are in their correct order, the last one will be as well.
2. In every pass, you go through the remainder of the collection to find the element with the lowest value.
3. If that element is not the current element, swap them.

Try it out! Head back to the main playground page and add the following:

```
example(of: "selection sort") {
  var array = [9, 4, 10, 3]
  print("Original: \(array)")
  selectionSort(&array)
  print("Selection sorted: \(array)")
}
```

You should see the following output in your console:

```
---Example of selection sort---
Original: [9, 4, 10, 3]
Selection sorted: [3, 4, 9, 10]
```

Just like bubble sort, selection sort has a *best*, *worst* and *average* time complexity of $O(n^2)$, which is fairly dismal. It's a simple one to understand, though, and it does perform better than bubble sort!

Insertion sort

Insertion sort is a more useful algorithm. Like bubble sort and selection sort, insertion sort has an *average* time complexity of $O(n^2)$, but the performance of insertion sort can vary. The more the data is already sorted, the less work it needs to do. Insertion sort has a *best* time complexity of $O(n)$ if the data is already sorted. The Swift standard library sort algorithm uses a hybrid of sorting approaches, with insertion sort being used for small (<20 element) unsorted partitions.

Example

The idea of insertion sort is similar to how you'd sort a hand of cards. Consider the following hand:

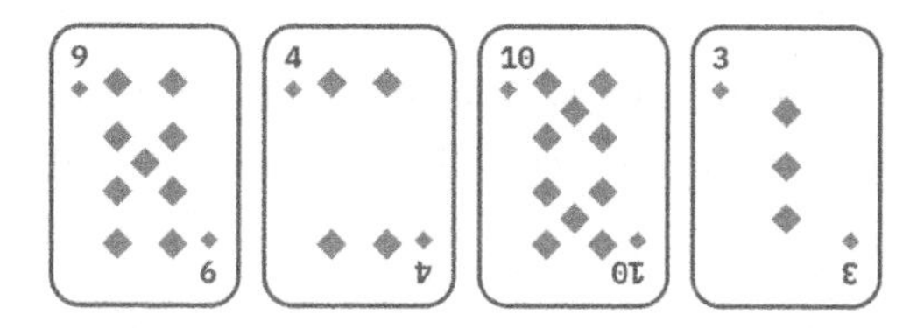

Insertion sort will iterate *once* through the cards, from left to right. Each card is shifted to the left until it reaches its correct position.

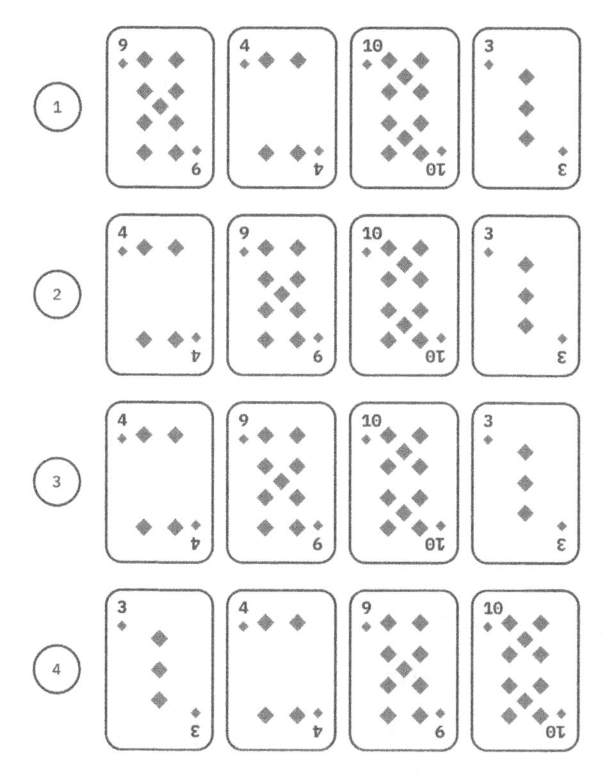

1. You can ignore the first card, as there are no previous cards to compare it with.
2. Next, you compare 4 with 9 and shift 4 to the left by swapping positions with 9.

3. 10 doesn't need to shift, as it's in the correct position compared to the previous card.
4. Finally, 3 is shifted all the way to the front by comparing and swapping it with 10, 9 and 4, respectively.

It's worth pointing out that the best-case scenario for insertion sort occurs when the sequence of values is already in sorted order, and no left shifting is necessary.

Implementation

In the **Sources** directory of your playground, create a new file named **InsertionSort.swift**. Write the following inside the file:

```
public func insertionSort<Element>(_ array: inout [Element])
    where Element: Comparable {
  guard array.count >= 2 else {
    return
  }
  // 1
  for current in 1..<array.count {
    // 2
    for shifting in (1...current).reversed() {
      // 3
      if array[shifting] < array[shifting - 1] {
        array.swapAt(shifting, shifting - 1)
      } else {
        break
      }
    }
  }
}
```

Here's what you did above:

1. Insertion sort requires you to iterate from left to right once. This loop does that.
2. Here, you run backward from the current index so you can shift left as needed.
3. Keep shifting the element left as long as necessary. As soon as the element is in position, break the inner loop and start with the next element.

Head back to the main playground page and write the following at the bottom:

```
example(of: "insertion sort") {
  var array = [9, 4, 10, 3]
  print("Original: \(array)")
  insertionSort(&array)
  print("Insertion sorted: \(array)")
}
```

You should see the following console output:

```
---Example of insertion sort---
Original: [9, 4, 10, 3]
Insertion sorted: [3, 4, 9, 10]
```

Insertion sort is one of the fastest sorting algorithms if the data is already sorted. That might sound obvious, but it isn't true for *all* sorting algorithms. In practice, many data collections will already be largely — if not entirely — sorted, and insertion sort will perform exceptionally well in those scenarios.

Generalization

In this section, you'll generalize these sorting algorithms for collection types other than `Array`. Exactly *which* collection types, though, depends on the algorithm:

- Insertion sort traverses the collection backward when shifting elements. As such, the collection must be of type `BidirectionalCollection`.
- Bubble sort and selection sort only traverse the collection front to back so that they can handle any `Collection`.
- In any case, the collection must be a `MutableCollection` as you need to be able to swap elements.

Head back to **BubbleSort.swift** and update the function to the following:

```
public func bubbleSort<T>(_ collection: inout T)
    where T: MutableCollection, T.Element: Comparable {
  guard collection.count >= 2 else {
      return
  }
  for end in collection.indices.reversed() {
    var swapped = false
    var current = collection.startIndex
    while current < end {
      let next = collection.index(after: current)
      if collection[current] > collection[next] {
        collection.swapAt(current, next)
        swapped = true
      }
      current = next
    }
    if !swapped {
      return
    }
  }
}
```

The algorithm stays the same; you update the loop to use the collection's indices. Head back to the main playground page to verify that bubble sort still works the way it should.

Selection sort can be updated as follows:

```
public func selectionSort<T>(_ collection: inout T)
    where T: MutableCollection, T.Element: Comparable {
  guard collection.count >= 2 else {
    return
  }
  for current in collection.indices {
    var lowest = current
    var other = collection.index(after: current)
    while other < collection.endIndex {
      if collection[lowest] > collection[other] {
        lowest = other
      }
      other = collection.index(after: other)
    }
    if lowest != current {
      collection.swapAt(lowest, current)
    }
  }
}
```

And insertion sort becomes:

```
public func insertionSort<T>(_ collection: inout T)
    where T: BidirectionalCollection & MutableCollection,
          T.Element: Comparable {
  guard collection.count >= 2 else {
    return
  }
  for current in collection.indices {
    var shifting = current
    while shifting > collection.startIndex {
      let previous = collection.index(before: shifting)
      if collection[shifting] < collection[previous] {
        collection.swapAt(shifting, previous)
      } else {
        break
      }
      shifting = previous
    }
  }
}
```

With just a bit of practice, generalizing these algorithms becomes a somewhat mechanical process.

In the following chapters, you'll take a look at sorting algorithms that perform better than $O(n^2)$. Next is a sorting algorithm that uses a classical approach known as **divide and conquer** — merge sort!

Key points

- n^2 algorithms often have a terrible reputation. Still, some of these algorithms usually have some redeeming points. Insertion sort can sort in $O(n)$ time if the collection is already in sorted order and gradually scales down to $O(n^2)$.
- Insertion sort is one of the best sorts in situations wherein you know that your data is mostly in sorted order ahead of time.

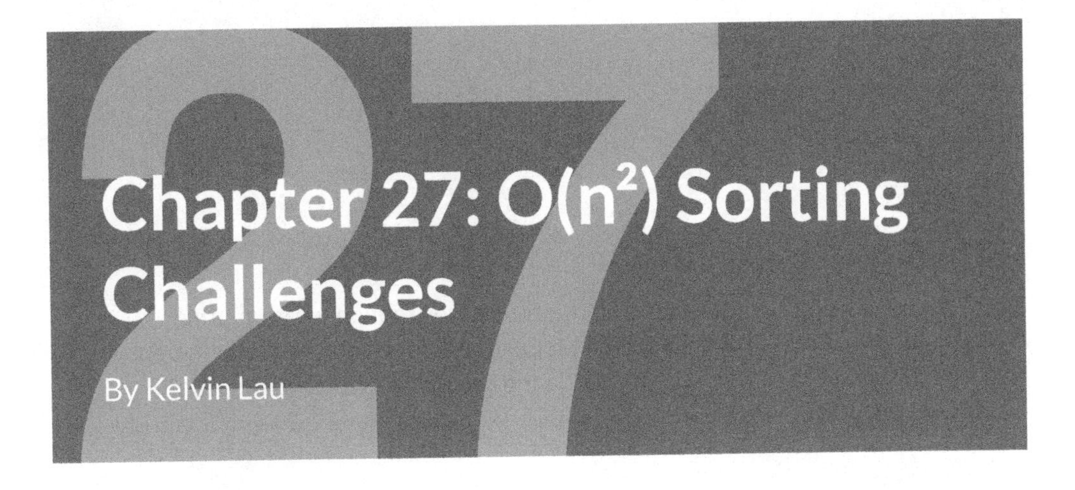

Chapter 27: O(n^2) Sorting Challenges

By Kelvin Lau

Challenge 1: Group elements

Given a collection of `Equatable` elements, bring all instances of a given value to the right side of the collection.

Challenge 2: Find a duplicate

Given a collection of `Equatable` (and `Hashable`) elements, return the first element that is a duplicate in the collection.

Challenge 3: Reverse a collection

Reverse a collection of elements by hand using `swapAt()`. Do not rely on the `reverse` or `reversed` methods.

Solutions

Solution to Challenge 1

The trick to this problem is to control two references to manage swapping operations. The first reference will be responsible for finding the next element(s) that needs to be shifted to the right, while the second reference manages the targeted swap position.

```
extension MutableCollection
  where Self: BidirectionalCollection, Element: Equatable {

  mutating func rightAlign(value: Element) {
    var left = startIndex
    var right = index(before: endIndex)

    while left < right {
      while self[right] == value {
        formIndex(before: &right)
      }
      while self[left] != value {
        formIndex(after: &left)
      }

      guard left < right else {
        return
      }
      swapAt(left, right)
    }
  }
}
```

The tricky part here is to understand what sort of capabilities you need. Since you need to change the underlying storage, this function is only available to `MutableCollection` types.

To complete this algorithm efficiently, you need backward index traversal, which is why you also constrain against the `BidirectionalCollection` protocol.

Finally, you also need the elements to be `Equatable` to target the appropriate values.

The time complexity of this solution is $O(n)$.

Solution to Challenge 2

Finding the first duplicated element is relatively straightforward. You use a `Set` to keep track of the elements you've encountered so far.

```
extension Sequence where Element: Hashable {

  var firstDuplicate: Element? {
    var found: Set<Element> = []
    for value in self {
      if found.contains(value) {
        return value
      } else {
        found.insert(value)
      }
    }
    return nil
  }
}
```

This solution is generalized to `Sequence` since it only relies on iterating the elements. Each element must also be `Hashable` so that you can store it in a set.

The time complexity of this solution is $O(n)$.

Solution to Challenge 3

Reversing a collection is also relatively straightforward. Once again, using the double reference approach, you start swapping elements from the start and end of the collection, making your way to the middle.

Once you've hit the middle, you're done swapping, and the collection is reversed.

```
extension MutableCollection
  where Self: BidirectionalCollection {

  mutating func reverse() {
    var left = startIndex
    var right = index(before: endIndex)

    while left < right {
      swapAt(left, right)
      formIndex(after: &left)
      formIndex(before: &right)
    }
  }
}
```

This solution requires capabilities fromMutableCollection since you need to mutate the collection to reverse.

You also constrain against BidirectionalCollection to utilize backward index traversal.

The time complexity of this solution is *O(n)*.

Chapter 28: Merge Sort

By Kelvin Lau

Merge sort is one of the most efficient sorting algorithms. With a time complexity of $O(n \log n)$, it's one of the fastest of all general-purpose sorting algorithms. The idea behind merge sort is *divide and conquer* — to break up a big problem into several smaller, easier-to-solve problems and then combine those solutions into a final result. The merge sort mantra is to *split first* and *merge after*. In this chapter, you'll implement merge sort from scratch. Let's start with an example.

Example

Assume that you're given a pile of unsorted playing cards:

The merge sort algorithm works as follows:

1. First, split the pile in half. You now have two unsorted piles:

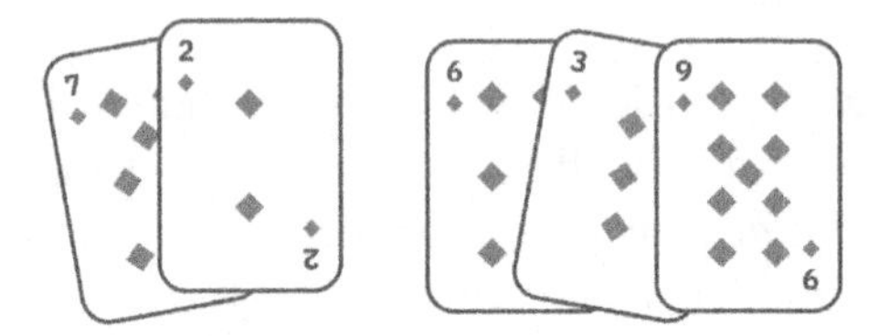

2. Now, keep splitting the resulting piles until you can't split anymore. In the end, you will have one (sorted!) card in each pile:

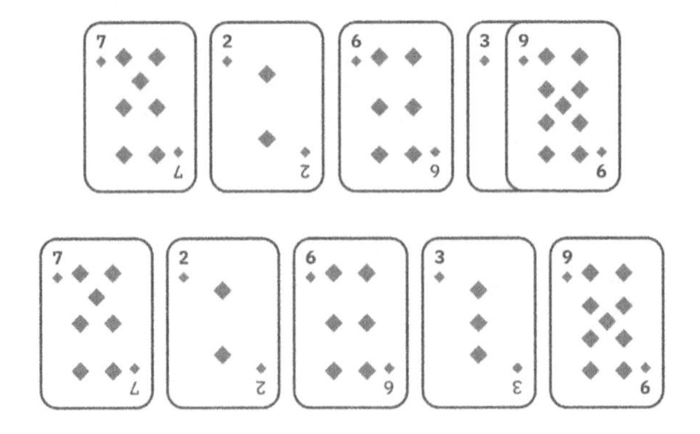

3. Finally, merge the piles in the reverse order in which you split them. During each merge, you put the contents in sorted order. This process is easy because each pile is already sorted:

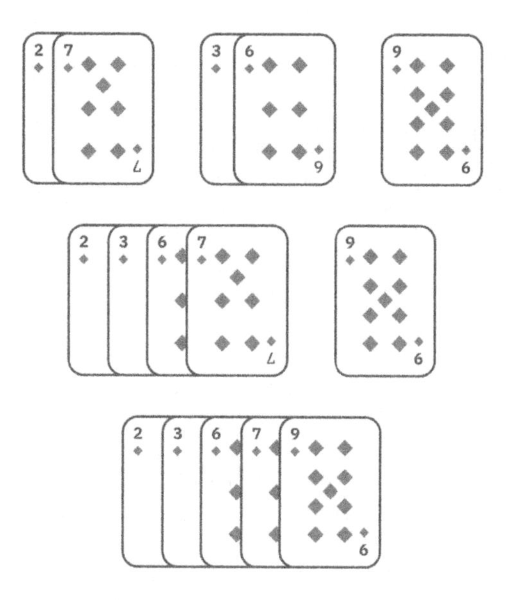

Implementation

Open up the starter playground to get started.

Split

In the **Sources** folder in your playground, create a new file named **MergeSort.swift**. Write the following inside the file:

```
public func mergeSort<Element>(_ array: [Element])
    -> [Element] where Element: Comparable {
  let middle = array.count / 2
  let left = Array(array[..<middle])
  let right = Array(array[middle...])
  // ... more to come
}
```

Here, you split the array into halves. Splitting once isn't enough. However, you have to keep splitting recursively until you can't split any more, which is when each subdivision contains just one element.

To do this, update mergeSort as follows:

```
public func mergeSort<Element>(_ array: [Element])
    -> [Element] where Element: Comparable {
  // 1
  guard array.count > 1 else {
    return array
  }
  let middle = array.count / 2
  // 2
  let left = mergeSort(Array(array[..<middle]))
  let right = mergeSort(Array(array[middle...]))
  // ... more to come
}
```

You've made two changes here:

1. Recursion needs a **base case**, which you can also think of as an "exit condition." In this case, the base case is when the array only has one element.

2. You're now calling mergeSort on the left and right halves of the original array. As soon as you've split the array in half, you'll try to split again.

There's still more work to do before your code compiles. Now that you've accomplished the splitting part, it's time to focus on merging.

Merge

Your final step is to merge the left and right arrays. To keep things clean, you will create a separate merge function for this.

The sole responsibility of the merging function is to take in two sorted arrays and combine them while retaining the sort order. Add the following just below the mergeSort function:

```
private func merge<Element>(_ left: [Element], _ right:
[Element])
    -> [Element] where Element: Comparable {
  // 1
  var leftIndex = 0
  var rightIndex = 0
  // 2
  var result: [Element] = []
  // 3
  while leftIndex < left.count && rightIndex < right.count {
    let leftElement = left[leftIndex]
    let rightElement = right[rightIndex]
    // 4
```

```
      if leftElement < rightElement {
        result.append(leftElement)
        leftIndex += 1
      } else if leftElement > rightElement {
        result.append(rightElement)
        rightIndex += 1
      } else {
        result.append(leftElement)
        leftIndex += 1
        result.append(rightElement)
        rightIndex += 1
      }
    }
    // 5
    if leftIndex < left.count {
      result.append(contentsOf: left[leftIndex...])
    }
    if rightIndex < right.count {
      result.append(contentsOf: right[rightIndex...])
    }
    return result
  }
```

Here's what's going on:

1. The `leftIndex` and `rightIndex` variables track your progress as you parse through the two arrays.
2. The `result` array will house the combined array.
3. Starting from the beginning, you sequentially compare the elements in the `left` and `right` arrays. If you've reached the end of either array, there's nothing else to compare.
4. The smaller of the two elements go into the `result` array. If the elements were equal, they can both be added.
5. The first loop guarantees that either `left` or `right` is empty. Since both arrays are sorted, this ensures that the leftover elements are greater than or equal to the ones currently in `result`. In this scenario, you can append the rest of the elements without comparison.

Finishing up

Complete the `mergeSort` function by calling `merge`. Because you call `mergeSort` recursively, the algorithm will split and sort both halves before merging them.

```
public func mergeSort<Element>(_ array: [Element])
    -> [Element] where Element: Comparable {
  guard array.count > 1 else {
    return array
  }
  let middle = array.count / 2
  let left = mergeSort(Array(array[..< middle]))
  let right = mergeSort(Array(array[middle...]))
  return merge(left, right)
}
```

This code is the final version of the merge sort algorithm. Here's a summary of the key procedures of merge sort:

1. The strategy of merge sort is to *divide and conquer* so that you solve many small problems instead of one big problem.
2. It has two core responsibilities: a method to divide the initial array recursively and a method to merge two arrays.
3. The merging function should take two sorted arrays and produce a single sorted array.

Finally — time to see this in action. Head back to the main playground page and test your merge sort with the following:

```
example(of: "merge sort") {
  let array = [7, 2, 6, 3, 9]
  print("Original: \(array)")
  print("Merge sorted: \(mergeSort(array))")
}
```

This outputs:

```
---Example of merge sort---
Original: [7, 2, 6, 3, 9]
Merge sorted: [2, 3, 6, 7, 9]
```

Performance

The best, worst and average time complexity of merge sort is $O(n \log n)$, which isn't too bad. If you're struggling to understand where $n \log n$ comes from, think about how the recursion works:

- In general, if you have an array of size n, the number of levels is $\log2(n)$. As you recurse, you split a single array into two smaller arrays. This means an array of size two will need one recursion level, an array of size four will need two levels, an array of size eight will need three levels, and so on. If you had an array of 1,024 elements, it would take ten levels of recursively splitting in two to get down to 1024 single element arrays.

- The cost of a single recursion is $O(n)$. A single recursion level will merge n elements. It doesn't matter if there are many small merges or one large one; the number of elements merged will still be n at each level.

This brings the total cost to $O(\log n) \times O(n) = O(n \log n)$.

The previous chapter's sort algorithms were **in-place** and used `swapAt` to move elements around. Merge sort, by contrast, allocates additional memory to do its work. How much? There are $\log2(n)$ levels of recursion, and at each level, n elements are used. That makes the total $O(n \log n)$ in space complexity. Merge sort is one of the hallmark sorting algorithms. It's relatively simple to understand and serves as a great introduction to how divide-and-conquer algorithms work. Merge sort is $O(n \log n)$, and this implementation requires $O(n \log n)$ of space. If you are clever with your bookkeeping, you can reduce the memory required to $O(n)$ by discarding the memory that is not actively being used.

Key points

- Merge sort is in the category of the **divide-and-conquer** algorithms.

- There are many implementations of merge sort, and you can have different performance characteristics depending on the implementation.

Chapter 29: Merge Sort Challenges

By Kelvin Lau

Challenge 1: Speeding up appends

Consider the following code:

```
let size = 1024
var values: [Int] = []
// 1
for i in 0 ..< size {
  values.append(i)
}
```

This code will result in almost a dozen reallocations. Add a statement at `// 1` that reduces it to a single allocation.

> **Hint:** `reserveCapacity` is your friend. ;]

Challenge 2: Merge two sequences

Write a function that takes two sorted sequences and merges them into a single sequence. Here's the function signature to start off:

```
func merge<T: Sequence>(first: T, second: T)
  -> AnySequence<T.Element> where T.Element: Comparable {}
```

`AnySequence` is a type eraser that abstracts away the concrete implementation details.

Solutions

Solution to Challenge 1

```
let size = 1024
var values: [Int] = []
values.reserveCapacity(size)
for i in 0 ..< size {
  values.append(i)
}
```

Using `reserveCapacity` is a great way to speed up your appends.

Solution to Challenge 2

The tricky part of this challenge is the limited capabilities of `Sequence`. Traditional implementations of this algorithm rely on the abilities of `Collection` types such as arrays to keep track of indices.

Since `Sequence` types have no notion of indices, you'll make use of their iterator.

Open the starter project to begin. Update its contents to the following:

```
func merge<T: Sequence>(first: T, second: T)
  -> AnySequence<T.Element> where T.Element: Comparable {

  // 1
  var result: [T.Element] = []

  // 2
  var firstIterator = first.makeIterator()
  var secondIterator = second.makeIterator()

  // 3
  var firstNextValue = firstIterator.next()
  var secondNextValue = secondIterator.next()

  // ...
}
```

Setting up the algorithm involves the following steps:

1. Create a new container to store the merged sequences.
2. Grab the iterators of the first and second sequences. Iterators sequentially dispense values of the sequence via the `next` method.
3. Create two variables that are initialized as the first and second iterator's first value. `next` returns an optional element of the sequence, and a `nil` return value suggests the iterator has dispensed all elements in the sequence.

Using the iterators, you'll decide which element should be appended into the `result` array by comparing the first and second next values. Write the following at the end of the `merge` function:

```
while let first = firstNextValue,
      let second = secondNextValue {

  if first < second { // 1
    result.append(first)
    firstNextValue = firstIterator.next()
  } else if second < first { // 2
    result.append(second)
    secondNextValue = secondIterator.next()
  } else { // 3
    result.append(first)
    result.append(second)
    firstNextValue = firstIterator.next()
    secondNextValue = secondIterator.next()
  }
}
```

This code is the main component of the merging algorithm. Using `while let`, you check to see if it's necessary to compare which values are to be inserted into the `result` array.

1. If the first value is less than the second one, you'll append the first value in `result` and seed the next value to be compared with by invoking `next` on the first iterator.

2. If the second value is less than the first, you'll do the opposite. You seed the next value to be compared by invoking `next` on the second iterator.

3. You append both the `first` and `second` values and seed both next values if they are equal.

This process will continue until one of the iterators run out of elements to dispense. In that scenario, it means the iterator with elements left has elements equal to or greater than the current values in `result`.

To add the rest of those values, write the following at the end of the `merge` function:

```
while let first = firstNextValue {
  result.append(first)
  firstNextValue = firstIterator.next()
}

while let second = secondNextValue {
  result.append(second)
  secondNextValue = secondIterator.next()
}

return AnySequence<T.Element>(result)
```

Confirm that this function works by writing the following:

```
var array1 = [1, 2, 3, 4, 5, 6, 7, 8]
var array2 = [1, 3, 4, 5, 5, 6, 7, 7]

for element in merge(first: array1, second: array2) {
  print(element)
}
```

You should see the following console output:

```
1
1
2
3
3
4
4
5
5
5
6
6
7
7
7
8
```

Chapter 30: Radix Sort

By Kelvin Lau

In this chapter, you'll look at a completely different model of sorting. So far, you've been relying on comparisons to determine the sorting order.

Radix sort is a non-comparative algorithm for sorting integers in linear time. There are multiple implementations of radix sort that focus on different problems.

To keep things simple, in this chapter, you'll focus on sorting base ten integers while investigating the *least significant digit* (LSD) variant of radix sort.

Example

To show how radix sort works, you'll sort the following array:

```
var array = [88, 410, 1772, 20]
```

Radix sort relies on the positional notation of integers, as shown here:

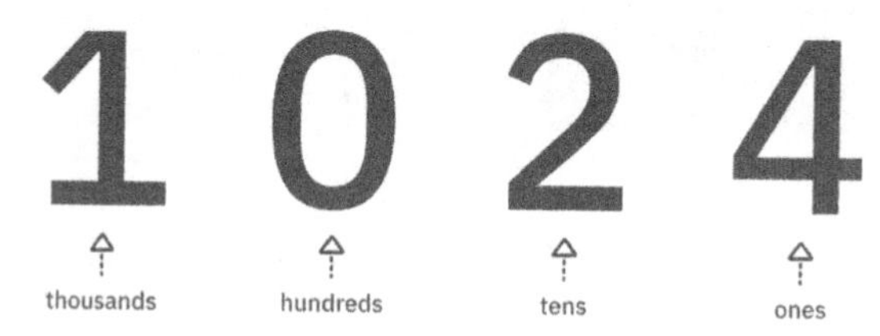

First, the array is divided into buckets based on the value of the least significant digit: the **ones** digit.

0 - 410, 20

2 - 1772

8 - 88

These buckets are then emptied in order, resulting in the following partially sorted array:

```
array = [410, 20, 1772, 88]
```

Next, repeat this procedure for the **tens** digit:

1 - 410

2 - 20

7 - 1772

8 - 88

The relative order of the elements didn't change this time, but you've still got more digits to inspect.

The next digit to consider is the **hundreds** digit:

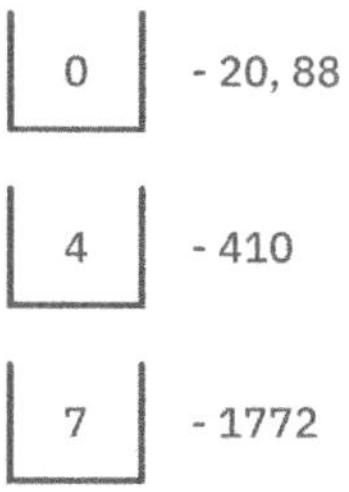

0 - 20, 88

4 - 410

7 - 1772

For values with no hundreds position (or any other position without a value), the digit will be assumed to be **zero**.

Reassembling the array based on these buckets gives the following:

```
array = [20, 88, 410, 1772]
```

Finally, you need to consider the **thousands** digit:

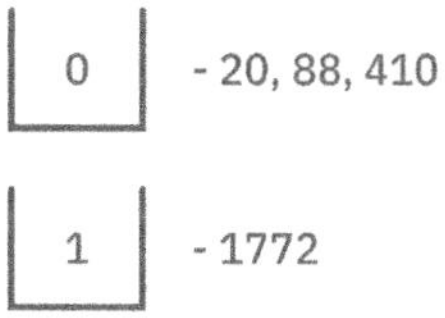

0 - 20, 88, 410

1 - 1772

Reassembling the array from these buckets leads to the final sorted array:

```
array = [20, 88, 410, 1772]
```

When multiple numbers end up in the same bucket, their relative ordering doesn't change. For example, in the zero bucket for the hundreds position, 20 comes before 88. This is because the previous step put 20 in a lower bucket than 80, so 20 ended up before 88 in the array.

Implementation

Open up the starter project for this chapter. In the **Sources** directory, create a new file named **RadixSort.swift**.

Add the following to the file:

```
extension Array where Element == Int {

  public mutating func radixSort() {

  }
}
```

Here, you've added a `radixSort` method to arrays of integers via an extension. Start implementing the `radixSort` method using the following:

```
public mutating func radixSort() {
  // 1
  let base = 10
  // 2
  var done = false
  var digits = 1
  while !done {

  }
}
```

This bit is relatively straightforward:

1. You're sorting base ten integers in this instance. Since you'll use this value multiple times in the algorithm, you store it in a constant `base`.
2. You declare two variables to track your progress. Radix sort works in multiple passes, so `done` serves as a flag that determines whether the sort is complete. The `digits` variable keeps track of the current digit you're looking at.

Next, you'll write the logic that sorts each element into buckets (also known as **Bucket sort**).

Bucket Sort

Write the following **inside** the `while` loop:

```
// 1
var buckets: [[Int]] = .init(repeating: [], count: base)
// 2
forEach {
  number in
  let remainingPart = number / digits
  let digit = remainingPart % base
  buckets[digit].append(number)
}
// 3
digits *= base
self = buckets.flatMap { $0 }
```

Here's what you've written:

1. You instantiate the buckets using a two-dimensional array. Because you're using base 10, you need ten buckets.
2. You place each number in the correct bucket.
3. You update `digits` to the next digit you wish to inspect and update the array using the contents of `buckets`. `flatMap` will flatten the two-dimensional array to a one-dimensional array, as if you're emptying the buckets into the array.

When do you stop?

Your `while` loop currently runs forever, so you'll need a terminating condition somewhere. You'll do that as follows:

1. At the beginning of the `while` loop, add `done = true`.
2. Inside the closure of `forEach`, add the following:

```
if remainingPart > 0 {
  done = false
}
```

Since `forEach` iterates over all the integers, as long as one of the integers still has unsorted digits, you'll need to continue sorting.

With that, you've learned about your first non-comparative sorting algorithm! Head back to the playground page and write the following to try out your code:

```
example(of: "radix sort") {
  var array = [88, 410, 1772, 20]
  print("Original array: \(array)")
  array.radixSort()
  print("Radix sorted: \(array)")
}
```

You should see the following console output:

```
---Example of: radix sort---
Original: [88, 410, 1772, 20]
Radix sorted: [20, 88, 410, 1772]
```

Radix sort is one of the fastest sorting algorithms. The average time complexity of radix sort is $O(k \times n)$, where k is the number of significant digits of the largest number, and n is the number of integers in the array.

Radix sort works best when k is constant, which occurs when all numbers in the array have the same count of significant digits. Its time complexity then becomes $O(n)$. Radix sort also incurs an $O(n)$ space complexity, as you need space to store each bucket.

Key points

- Unlike other searches you've been working on in the previous chapter, radix sort is non-comparative and doesn't rely on comparing two values. Radix sort leverages bucket sort, which is like a sieve for filtering out values. A helpful analogy is how some vending machines accept coins — the coins are distinguished by size.
- Radix sort can be one of the fastest sorting algorithms for sorting values with positional notation.
- This chapter covered the **least significant digit** radix sort. Another way to implement radix sort is the **most significant digit** form. This form sorts by prioritizing the most significant digits over the lesser ones and is best illustrated by the sorting behavior of the `String` type.

Chapter 31: Radix Sort Challenges

By Kelvin Lau

Challenge 1: Most significant digit

Open the starter playground for this chapter to begin.

The implementation discussed in the chapter used a *least significant digit* radix sort. Your task is to implement a *most significant digit* radix sort.

This sorting behavior is called **lexicographical sorting** and is also used for `String` sorting.

For example:

```
var array = [500, 1345, 13, 459, 44, 999]
array.lexicographicalSort()
print(array) // outputs [13, 1345, 44, 459, 500, 999]
```

Solution to Challenge 1

MSD radix sort is closely related to LSD radix sort in that both utilize bucket sort. The difference is that MSD radix sort needs to carefully curate subsequent passes of the bucket sort. In LSD radix sort, bucket sort ran repeatedly using the whole array for every pass. In MSD radix sort, you run bucket sort with the whole array only once. Subsequent passes will sort each bucket recursively.

You'll implement MSD radix sort piece-by-piece, starting with the components it depends on.

Digits

Add the following inside your playground page:

```
extension Int {

  var digits: Int {
    var count = 0
    var num = self
    while num != 0 {
      count += 1
      num /= 10
    }
    return count
  }

  func digit(atPosition position: Int) -> Int? {
    guard position < digits else {
      return nil
    }
    var num = self
    let correctedPosition = Double(position + 1)
    while num / Int(pow(10.0, correctedPosition)) != 0 {
      num /= 10
    }
    return num % 10
  }
}
```

`digits` is a computed property that returns the number of digits the `Int` has. For example, the value 1024 has four digits.

`digit(atPosition:)` returns the digit at a given position. Like arrays, the leftmost position is zero. Thus, the digit for position zero of the value 1024 is **1**. The digit for position 3 is **4**. Since there are only four digits, the digit for position five will return `nil`.

The implementation of `digit(atPosition:)` works by repeatedly chopping a digit off the end of the number until the requested digit is at the end. It is then extracted using the remainder operator.

Lexicographical sort

With the helper methods, you're now equipped to deal with MSD radix sort. Write the following at the bottom of the playground:

```
extension Array where Element == Int {

  mutating func lexicographicalSort() {
    self = msdRadixSorted(self, 0)
  }

  private func msdRadixSorted(_ array: [Int], _ position: Int)
-> [Int] {
    // more to come...
  }
}
```

`lexicographicalSort` is the user-facing API for MSD radix sort. `msdRadixSorted` is the meat of the algorithm and will be used to apply MSD radix sort to the array recursively.

Update `msdRadixSorted` to the following:

```
private func msdRadixSorted(_ array: [Int], _ position: Int) ->
[Int] {

  // 1
  var buckets: [[Int]] = .init(repeating: [], count: 10)
  // 2
  var priorityBucket: [Int] = []

  // 3
  array.forEach { number in
    guard let digit = number.digit(atPosition: position) else {
      priorityBucket.append(number)
      return
    }
    buckets[digit].append(number)
  }
```

```
  // more to come...
}
```

1. Similar to LSD radix sort, you instantiate a two-dimensional array for the buckets.
2. The `priorityBucket` is a special bucket that stores values with fewer digits than the current position. Values that go in the `priorityBucket` will be sorted first.
3. For every number in the array, you find the digit of the current position and place the number in the appropriate bucket.

Next, you need to recursively apply MSD radix sort for each of the individual buckets. Write the following at the end of `msdRadixSorted`:

```
priorityBucket.append(contentsOf: buckets.reduce(into: []) {
  result, bucket in
  guard !bucket.isEmpty else {
    return
  }
  result.append(contentsOf: msdRadixSorted(bucket, position + 1)
})

return priorityBucket
```

This statement calls `reduce(into:)` to collect the results of the recursive sorts and appends them to the `priorityBucket`. That way, the elements in the `priorityBucket` always go first. You're almost done!

Base case

As with all recursive operations, you need to set a terminating condition that stops the recursion. Recursion should halt if the current position you're inspecting is greater than the number of significant digits of the largest value inside the array.

At the top of the `Array` extension, write the following:

```
private var maxDigits: Int {
  self.max()?.digits ?? 0
}
```

Next, add the following at the top of `msdRadixSorted`:

```
guard position < array.maxDigits else {
  return array
}
```

This check ensures that if the position is equal or greater than the array's `maxDigits`, you'll terminate the recursion.

Let's take it out for a spin! Add the following at the bottom of the playground to test the code:

```
var array: [Int] = (0...10).map { _ in Int(arc4random()) }
array.lexicographicalSort()
print(array)
```

You should see an array of random numbers similar to this:

```
[1350975449, 1412970969, 1727253826, 2003696829, 2281464743,
2603566662, 3012182591, 3552993620, 3665442670, 4167824072,
465277276]
```

Since the numbers are random, you won't get an identical array. The important thing to note is the lexicographical ordering of the values.

Chapter 32: Heapsort

By Vincent Ngo

Heapsort is another comparison-based algorithm that sorts an array in ascending order using a heap. This chapter builds on the heap concepts presented in Chapter 22, "Heaps".

Heapsort takes advantage of a heap being, by definition, a partially sorted binary tree with the following qualities:

1. In a max heap, all parent nodes are larger than their children.
2. In a min heap, all parent nodes are smaller than their children.

The diagram below shows a heap with parent node values underlined:

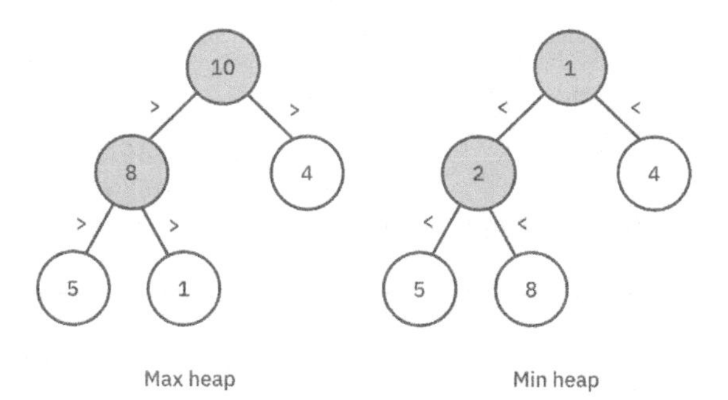

Getting started

Open up the starter playground. This playground already contains an implementation of a max heap. Your goal is to extend `Heap` so it can also sort. Before you get started, let's look at a visual example of how heap sort works.

Example

For any given unsorted array, to sort from lowest to highest, heap sort must first convert this array into a max heap:

6	12	2	26	8	18	21	9	5

This conversion is done by sifting down all the parent nodes to end up in the right spot. The resulting max heap is:

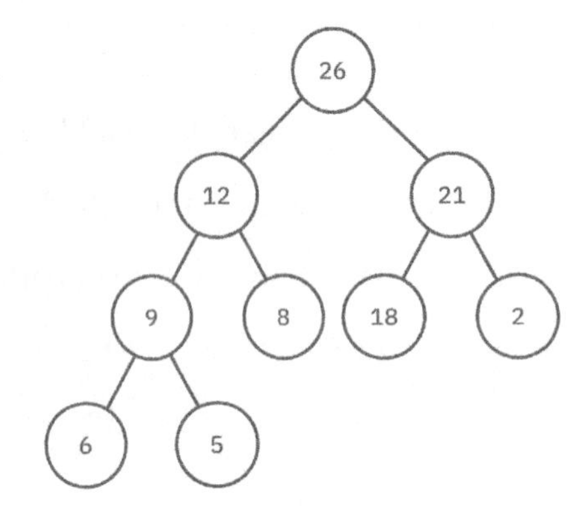

This corresponds with the following array:

26	12	21	9	8	18	2	6	5

Because the time complexity of a single sift-down operation is $O(\log n)$, the total time complexity of building a heap is $O(n \log n)$.

Let's look at how to sort this array in ascending order.

Because the largest element in a max heap is always at the root, you start by swapping the first element at index **0** with the last element at index ***n* - 1**. After the swap, the last element of the array is in the correct spot but invalidates the heap. The next step is, thus, to sift down the new root note **5** until it lands in its correct position.

5	12	21	9	8	18	2	6	26
21	12	18	9	8	5	2	6	26

Note that you exclude the last element of the heap as you no longer consider it part of the heap but of the sorted array.

As a result of sifting down **5**, the second largest element **21** becomes the new root. You can now repeat the previous steps, swapping **21** with the last element **6**, shrinking the heap and sifting down **6**.

6	12	18	9	8	5	2	21	26
18	12	6	9	8	5	2	21	26

Are you starting to see a pattern? Heapsort is very straightforward. As you swap the first and last elements, the larger elements make their way to the back of the array in the correct order. You repeat the swapping and sifting steps until you reach a heap of size 1.

The array is then fully sorted.

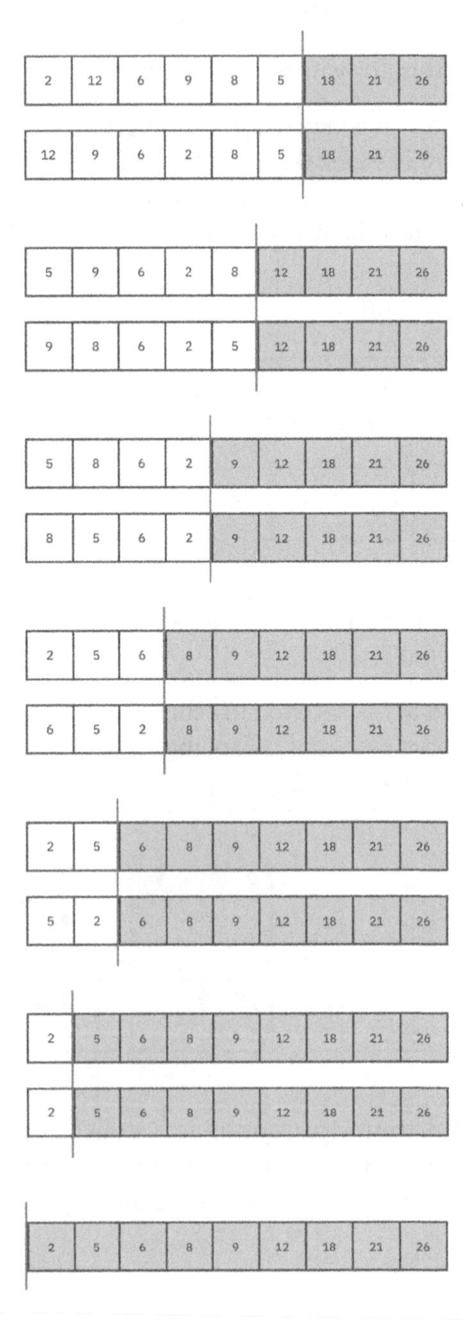

> **Note**: This sorting process is very similar to selection sort from **Chapter 26**.

Implementation

Next, you'll implement this sorting algorithm. The actual implementation is very simple, as the heavy lifting is already done by the `siftDown` method:

```
extension Heap {
  func sorted() -> [Element] {
    var heap = Heap(sort: sort, elements: elements) // 1
    for index in heap.elements.indices.reversed() { // 2
      heap.elements.swapAt(0, index) // 3
      heap.siftDown(from: 0, upTo: index) // 4
    }
    return heap.elements
  }
}
```

Here's what's going on:

1. You first make a copy of the heap. After heap sort sorts the `elements` array, it is no longer a valid heap. By working on a copy of the heap, you ensure the heap remains valid.

2. You loop through the array, starting from the last element.

3. You swap the first element and the last element. This swap moves the largest unsorted element to its correct spot.

4. Because the heap is now invalid, you must sift down the new root node. As a result, the next largest element will become the new root.

> **Note**: To support heap sort, you've added the `upTo` parameter to the `siftDown` method. This way, the sift down only uses the unsorted part of the array, which shrinks with every loop iteration.

Finally, give your new method a try:

```
let heap = Heap(sort: >, elements: [6, 12, 2, 26, 8, 18, 21, 9,
5])
print(heap.sorted())
```

This code should print:

```
[2, 5, 6, 8, 9, 12, 18, 21, 26]
```

Performance

Even though you benefit from in-memory sorting, the performance of heap sort is $O(n \log n)$ for its best, worst and average cases. This uniformity in performance is because you have to traverse the whole list once and, every time you swap elements, you must perform a sift down, which is an $O(\log n)$ operation.

Heapsort is also not a stable sort because it depends on how the elements are laid out and put into the heap. If you were heap sorting a deck of cards by their rank, for example, you might see their suite change order compared to the original deck.

Key points

- Heapsort leverages the max heap data structure to sort elements in an array.
- Heapsort sorts its elements by following a simple pattern:

1. Swap the first and last element.
2. Perform a `sift-down` from the root to satisfy the requirement of being a heap.
3. Decrease the array size by one since the element at the end will be the largest element.
4. Repeat these steps till you reach the start of the array.

Chapter 33: Heapsort Challenges

By Vincent Ngo

Challenge 1: Add heap sort to Array

Add a `heapSort()` method to `Array`. This method should sort the array in ascending order. A starting template is in the starter playground.

Challenge 2: Theory

When performing heapsort in ascending order, which of these starting arrays requires the fewest comparisons?

- `[1,2,3,4,5]`
- `[5,4,3,2,1]`

Challenge 3: Descending order

The current implementation of heapsort in Chapter 32 sorts the elements in **ascending** order. How would you sort in **descending** order?

Solutions

Solution to Challenge 1

To add heap sort to `Array`, you must create an `extension`, where the elements in the array must be `Comparable`. Everything else is straightforward as the implementation is similar to the `Heap` in Chapter 32.

You are now referencing the internal properties of the `Array`.

```
extension Array where Element: Comparable {

  func leftChildIndex(ofParentAt index: Int) -> Int {
    (2 * index) + 1
  }

  func rightChildIndex(ofParentAt index: Int) -> Int {
    (2 * index) + 2
  }

  mutating func siftDown(from index: Int, upTo size: Int) {
    var parent = index
    while true {
      let left = leftChildIndex(ofParentAt: parent)
      let right = rightChildIndex(ofParentAt: parent)
      var candidate = parent

      if (left < size) && (self[left] > self[candidate]) {
        candidate = left
      }
      if (right < size) && (self[right] > self[candidate]) {
        candidate = right
      }
      if candidate == parent {
        return
      }
      swapAt(parent, candidate)
      parent = candidate
    }
  }

  mutating func heapSort() {
    // Build Heap
    if !isEmpty {
      for i in stride(from: count / 2 - 1, through: 0, by: -1) {
        siftDown(from: i, upTo: count)
      }
    }
```

```
    // Perform Heap Sort.
    for index in indices.reversed() {
      swapAt(0, index)
      siftDown(from: 0, upTo: index)
    }
  }
}
```

Solution to Challenge 2

When sorting elements in ascending order using heap sort, you first need a max heap. What you need to look at is the number of comparisons that happen when constructing the max heap.

`[5,4,3,2,1]` will yield the fewest number of comparisons since it's already a max heap and no swaps take place.

When building a max heap, you only look at the parent nodes. In this case, there are two parent nodes with two comparisons.

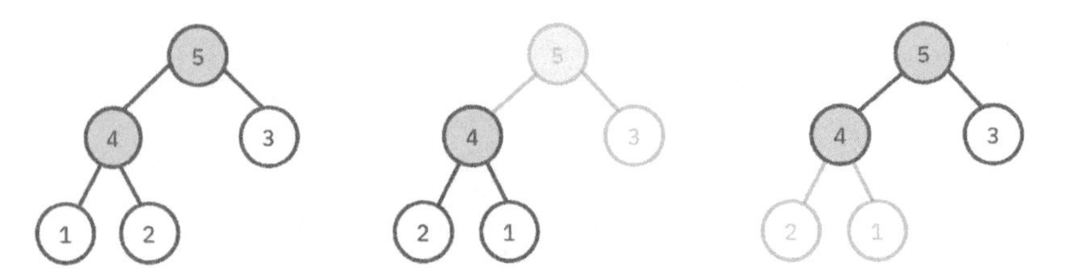

`[1,2,3,4,5]` will yield the most number of comparisons. There are two parent nodes, but you have to perform three comparisons:

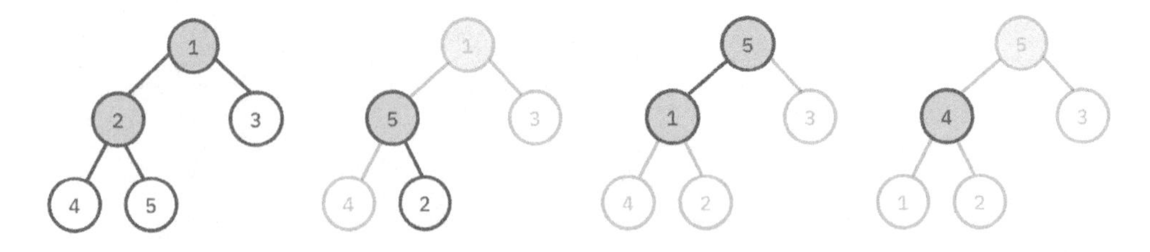

Solution to Challenge 3

Simply use a min heap instead of a max heap before sorting:

```
let heap = Heap(sort: <, elements: [6, 12, 2, 26, 8, 18, 21, 9,
5])
print(heap.sorted())
```

Chapter 34: Quicksort

By Vincent Ngo

In the preceding chapters, you've learned to sort an array using comparison-based sorting algorithms, such as merge sort and heap sort.

Quicksort is another comparison-based sorting algorithm. Much like merge sort, it uses the same strategy of **divide and conquer**. One important feature of quicksort is choosing a **pivot** point. The pivot divides the array into three partitions:

```
[ elements < pivot | pivot | elements > pivot ]
```

In this chapter, you will implement quicksort and look at various partitioning strategies to get the most out of this sorting algorithm.

Example

Open up the starter playground. A naïve implementation of quicksort is provided in **quicksortNaive.swift**:

```
public func quicksortNaive<T: Comparable>(_ a: [T]) -> [T] {
  guard a.count > 1 else { // 1
    return a
  }
  let pivot = a[a.count / 2] // 2
  let less = a.filter { $0 < pivot } // 3
  let equal = a.filter { $0 == pivot }
  let greater = a.filter { $0 > pivot }
  return quicksortNaive(less) + equal +
quicksortNaive(greater) // 4
}
```

The implementation above recursively filters the array into three partitions. Let's look at how it works:

1. There must be more than one element in the array. If not, the array is considered sorted.
2. Pick the **middle** element of the array as your pivot.
3. Using the pivot, split the original array into three partitions. Elements **less than**, **equal to** or **greater than** the pivot go into different buckets.
4. Recursively sort the partitions and then combine them.

Let's now visualize the code above. Given the **unsorted** array below:

```
[12, 0, 3, 9, 2, 18, 8, 27, 1, 5, 8, -1, 21]
                     *
```

Your partition strategy in this implementation is to always select the **middle** element as the pivot. In this case, the element is **8**. Partitioning the array using this pivot results in the following partitions:

```
less: [0, 3, 2, 1, 5, -1]
equal: [8, 8]
greater: [12, 9, 18, 27, 21]
```

Notice that the three partitions aren't completely sorted yet. Quicksort will recursively divide these partitions into even smaller ones. The recursion will only halt when all partitions have either zero or one element.

Here's an overview of all the partitioning steps:

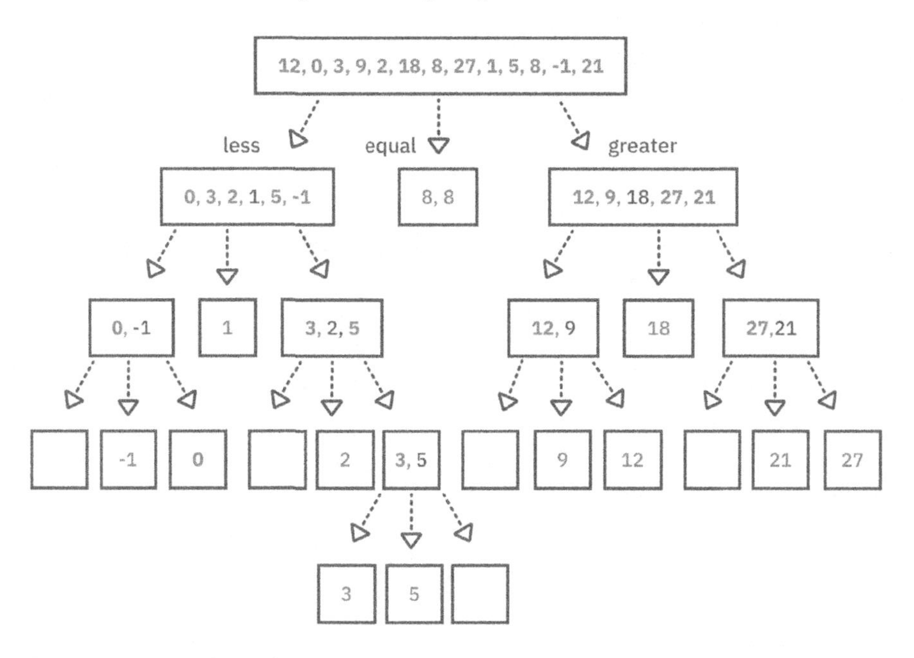

Each level corresponds with a recursive call to quicksort. Once recursion stops, the leafs are combined again, resulting in a fully sorted array:

```
[-1, 1, 2, 3, 5, 8, 8, 9, 12, 18, 21, 27]
```

While this naïve implementation is easy to understand, it raises some issues and questions:

- Calling `filter` three times on the same array is not efficient.
- Creating a new array for every partition isn't space-efficient. Could you possibly sort in place?
- Is picking the middle element the best pivot strategy? What pivot strategy should you adopt?

Partitioning strategies

In this section, you will look at partitioning strategies and ways to make this quicksort implementation more efficient. The first partitioning algorithm you will look at is **Lomuto's algorithm**.

Lomuto's partitioning

Lomuto's partitioning algorithm always chooses the **last** element as the pivot. Let's look at how this works in code.

In your playground, create a file called **quicksortLomuto.swift** and add the following function declaration:

```
public func partitionLomuto<T: Comparable>(_ a: inout [T],
                                           low: Int,
                                           high: Int) -> Int {
}
```

This function takes three arguments:

- a is the array you are partitioning.
- `low` and `high` set the range within the array you will partition. This range will get smaller and smaller with every recursion.

The function returns the index of the pivot.

Now, implement the function as follows:

```
let pivot = a[high] // 1

var i = low // 2
for j in low..<high { // 3
  if a[j] <= pivot { // 4
    a.swapAt(i, j) // 5
    i += 1
  }
}

a.swapAt(i, high) // 6
return i // 7
```

Here's what this code does:

1. Set the pivot. Lomuto always chooses the last element as the pivot.
2. The variable `i` indicates how many elements are **less** than the pivot. When you encounter an element less than the pivot, swap it with the element at index `i` and increase `i`.
3. Loop through all the elements from `low` to `high`, but not including `high` since it's the pivot.
4. Check to see if the current element is less than or equal to the pivot.
5. If it is, swap it with the element at index `i` and increase `i`.
6. Once done with the loop, swap the element at `i` with the pivot. The pivot always sits between the **less** and **greater** partitions.
7. Return the index of the pivot.

While this algorithm loops through the array, it divides the array into four regions:

1. `a[low..<i]` contains all elements <= `pivot`.
2. `a[i...j-1]` contains all elements > `pivot`.
3. `a[j...high-1]` are elements you have not compared yet.
4. `a[high]` is the pivot element.

```
[ values <= pivot | values > pivot | not compared yet | pivot ]
  low         i-1   i          j-1   j          high-1   high
```

Step-by-step

Look at a few steps of the algorithm to get a clear understanding of how it works. Given the **unsorted** array below:

```
[12, 0, 3, 9, 2, 21, 18, 27, 1, 5, 8, -1, 8]
```

First, the last element **8** is selected as the pivot:

```
  0   1  2  3  4  5   6   7   8  9  10  11     12
[ 12, 0, 3, 9, 2, 21, 18, 27, 1, 5, 8, -1, |  8  ]
  low                                         high
  i
  j
```

Then, the first element, **12**, is compared to the pivot. It is not smaller than the pivot, so the algorithm continues to the next element:

```
   0  1  2  3  4  5   6   7   8  9  10  11    12
 [ 12, 0, 3, 9, 2, 21, 18, 27, 1, 5, 8, -1, |  8  ]
   low                                        high
   i
        j
```

The second element **0** *is* smaller than the pivot, so it is swapped with the element currently at index `i` (**12**) and `i` is increased:

```
  0    1  2  3  4  5   6   7   8  9  10  11    12
 [ 0, 12, 3, 9, 2, 21, 18, 27, 1, 5, 8, -1, |  8  ]
  low                                         high
       i
           j
```

The third element **3** is again smaller than the pivot, so another swap occurs:

```
  0    1  2  3  4  5   6   7   8  9  10  11    12
 [ 0, 3, 12, 9, 2, 21, 18, 27, 1, 5, 8, -1, |  8  ]
  low                                         high
           i
               j
```

These steps continue until all but the pivot element have been compared. The resulting array is:

```
  0    1  2  3  4  5   6   7   8  9  10  11    12
 [ 0, 3, 2, 1, 5, 8, -1, 27, 9, 12, 21, 18, |  8  ]
  low                                         high
                          i
```

Finally, the pivot element is swapped with the element currently at index `i`:

```
  0    1  2  3  4  5   6   7   8  9  10  11     12
 [ 0, 3, 2, 1, 5, 8, -1 | 8 | 9, 12, 21, 18, |  27  ]
  low                                           high
                          i
```

Lomuto's partitioning is now complete. Notice how the pivot is between the two regions of elements less than or equal to the pivot and elements greater than the pivot.

In the naïve implementation of quicksort, you created three new arrays and filtered the unsorted array three times. Lomuto's algorithm performs the partitioning in place. That's much more efficient!

With your partitioning algorithm in place, you can now implement quicksort:

```
public func quicksortLomuto<T: Comparable>(_ a: inout [T],
                                            low: Int, high: Int)
{
  if low < high {
    let pivot = partitionLomuto(&a, low: low, high: high)
    quicksortLomuto(&a, low: low, high: pivot - 1)
    quicksortLomuto(&a, low: pivot + 1, high: high)
  }
}
```

Here, you apply Lomuto's algorithm to partition the array into two regions; then, you recursively sort these regions. The recursion ends once a region has less than two elements.

You can try out Lomuto's quicksort by adding the following to your playground:

```
var list = [12, 0, 3, 9, 2, 21, 18, 27, 1, 5, 8, -1, 8]
quicksortLomuto(&list, low: 0, high: list.count - 1)
print(list)
```

Hoare's partitioning

Hoare's partitioning algorithm always chooses the **first** element as the pivot. Let's look at how this works in code.

In your playground, create a file named **quicksortHoare.swift** and add the following function:

```
public func partitionHoare<T: Comparable>(_ a: inout [T],
                                           low: Int, high: Int)
-> Int {
  let pivot = a[low] // 1
  var i = low - 1 // 2
  var j = high + 1

  while true {
    repeat { j -= 1 } while a[j] > pivot // 3
    repeat { i += 1 } while a[i] < pivot // 4

    if i < j { // 5
      a.swapAt(i, j)
    } else {
      return j // 6
    }
  }
}
```

Let's go over these steps:

1. Select the first element as the pivot.
2. Indexes `i` and `j` define two regions. Every index before `i` will be **less than or equal to** the pivot. Every index after `j` will be **greater than or equal to** the pivot.
3. Decrease `j` until it reaches an element that is not greater than the pivot.
4. Increase `i` until it reaches an element that is not less than the pivot.
5. If `i` and `j` have not overlapped, swap the elements.
6. Return the index that separates both regions.

> **Note**: The index returned from the partition does not necessarily have to be the index of the pivot element.

Step-by-step

Given the **unsorted** array below:

```
[ 12, 0, 3, 9, 2, 21, 18, 27, 1, 5, 8, -1, 8  ]
```

First, **12** is set as the pivot. Then `i` and `j` will start running through the array, looking for elements that are not less than (in the case of `i`) or greater than (in the case of `j`) the pivot. `i` will stop at element **12** and `j` will stop at element **8**:

```
[ 12, 0, 3, 9, 2, 21, 18, 27, 1, 5, 8, -1,  8  ]
  p
  i                                         j
```

These elements are then swapped:

```
[ 8, 0, 3, 9, 2, 21, 18, 27, 1, 5, 8, -1, 12 ]
  i                                       j
```

`i` and `j` now continue moving, this time stopping at **21** and **-1**:

```
[ 8, 0, 3, 9, 2, 21, 18, 27, 1, 5, 8, -1, 12 ]
                 i                     j
```

Which are then swapped:

```
[ 8, 0, 3, 9, 2, -1, 18, 27, 1, 5, 8, 21, 12 ]
                 i                     j
```

Next, **18** and **8** are swapped, followed by **27** and **5**.

After this swap, the array and indices are as follows:

```
[ 8, 0, 3, 9, 2, -1, 8, 5, 1, 27, 18, 21, 12 ]
                        i     j
```

The next time you move `i` and `j`, they will overlap:

```
[ 8, 0, 3, 9, 2, -1, 8, 5, 1, 27, 18, 21, 12 ]
                           j  i
```

Hoare's algorithm is now complete, and index `j` is returned as the separation between the two regions. There are far fewer swaps here compared to Lomuto's algorithm. Isn't that nice?

You can now implement a `quicksortHoare` function:

```
public func quicksortHoare<T: Comparable>(_ a: inout [T],
                                          low: Int, high: Int) {
  if low < high {
    let p = partitionHoare(&a, low: low, high: high)
    quicksortHoare(&a, low: low, high: p)
    quicksortHoare(&a, low: p + 1, high: high)
  }
}
```

Try it out by adding the following in your playground:

```
var list2 = [12, 0, 3, 9, 2, 21, 18, 27, 1, 5, 8, -1, 8]
quicksortHoare(&list2, low: 0, high: list.count - 1)
print(list2)
```

Effects of a bad pivot choice

The most crucial part of implementing quicksort is choosing the right partitioning strategy.

You have looked at three different partitioning strategies:

1. Choosing the middle element as a pivot.
2. **Lomuto**, or choosing the last element as a pivot.
3. **Hoare**, or choosing the first element as a pivot.

What are the implications of choosing a bad pivot?

Let's start with the following unsorted array:

```
[8, 7, 6, 5, 4, 3, 2, 1]
```

If you use Lomuto's algorithm, the pivot will be the last element, 1. This results in the following partitions:

```
less: [ ]
equal: [1]
greater: [8, 7, 6, 5, 4, 3, 2]
```

An ideal pivot would split the elements evenly between the **less than** and **greater than** partitions. Choosing the first or last element of an already sorted array as a pivot makes quicksort perform much like **insertion sort**, which results in a worst-case performance of $O(n^2)$. One way to address this problem is by using the **median of three** pivot selection strategy. Here, you find the median of the first, middle and last element in the array and use that as a pivot. This selection strategy prevents you from picking the highest or lowest element in the array.

Let's look at an implementation. Create a new file named **quicksortMedian.swift** and add the following function:

```
public func medianOfThree<T: Comparable>(_ a: inout [T],
                                         low: Int, high: Int) ->
Int {
  let center = (low + high) / 2
  if a[low] > a[center] {
    a.swapAt(low, center)
  }
  if a[low] > a[high] {
    a.swapAt(low, high)
  }
```

```
  if a[center] > a[high] {
    a.swapAt(center, high)
  }
  return center
}
```

Here, you find the median of `a[low]`, `a[center]` and `a[high]` by sorting them. The median will end up at index `center`, which is what the function returns.

Next, let's implement a variant of Quicksort using this median of three:

```
public func quickSortMedian<T: Comparable>(_ a: inout [T],
                                            low: Int, high: Int)
{
  if low < high {
    let pivotIndex = medianOfThree(&a, low: low, high: high)
    a.swapAt(pivotIndex, high)
    let pivot = partitionLomuto(&a, low: low, high: high)
    quicksortLomuto(&a, low: low, high: pivot - 1)
    quicksortLomuto(&a, low: pivot + 1, high: high)
  }
}
```

This code is simply a variation on `quicksortLomuto` that chooses the median of the three elements as a first step.

Try this out by adding the following in your playground:

```
var list3 = [12, 0, 3, 9, 2, 21, 18, 27, 1, 5, 8, -1, 8]
quickSortMedian(&list3, low: 0, high: list3.count - 1)
print(list3)
```

This strategy is an improvement, but can we do better?

Dutch national flag partitioning

A problem with Lomuto's and Hoare's algorithms is that they don't handle duplicates well. With Lomuto's algorithm, duplicates end up in the *less than* partition and aren't grouped together. With Hoare's algorithm, the situation is even worse as duplicates can be all over the place.

A solution to organize duplicate elements is using **Dutch national flag partitioning**. This technique is named after the Dutch flag, which has three bands of colors: red, white and blue and is similar to how you create three partitions. Dutch national flag partitioning is an excellent technique to use if you have a lot of duplicate elements.

Let's look at how it's implemented. Create a file named **quicksortDutchFlag.swift** and add the following function:

```
public func partitionDutchFlag<T: Comparable>(_ a: inout [T],
                                               low: Int, high:
Int,
                                               pivotIndex: Int)
                                               -> (Int, Int) {
  let pivot = a[pivotIndex]
  var smaller = low // 1
  var equal = low // 2
  var larger = high // 3
  while equal <= larger { // 4
    if a[equal] < pivot {
      a.swapAt(smaller, equal)
      smaller += 1
      equal += 1
    } else if a[equal] == pivot {
      equal += 1
    } else {
      a.swapAt(equal, larger)
      larger -= 1
    }
  }
  return (smaller, larger) // 5
}
```

You will adopt the same strategy as Lomuto's partition by choosing the last element as the `pivotIndex`. Let's go over how it works:

1. Whenever you encounter an element less than the pivot, move it to index `smaller`. This rule means that all elements that come before this index are less than the pivot.
2. Index `equal` points to the next element to compare. Elements that are equal to the pivot are skipped, which means that all elements between `smaller` and `equal` are equal to the pivot.
3. Whenever you encounter an element greater than the pivot, move it to index `larger`. This rule means that all elements that come after this index are greater than the pivot.
4. The main loop compares elements and swaps them if needed. This process continues until index `equal` moves past index `larger`, meaning all elements have been moved to their correct partition.
5. The algorithm returns indices `smaller` and `larger`. These point to the first and last elements of the middle partition.

Step-by-step

Let's go over an example using the **unsorted** array below:

```
[ 12, 0, 3, 9, 2, 21, 18, 27, 1, 5, 8, -1, 8 ]
```

Since this algorithm is independent of a pivot selection strategy, adopt Lomuto and pick the last element **8**.

> **Note**: For practice, try a different strategy, such as median of three.

Next, you set up the indices `smaller`, `equal` and `larger`:

```
[12, 0, 3, 9, 2, 21, 18, 27, 1, 5, 8, -1, 8]
  s
  e
                                           l
```

The first element to be compared is **12**. Since it is larger than the pivot, it is swapped with the element at index `larger`, and this index is decremented.

Note that index `equal` is not incremented, so the element that was swapped in (**8**) is compared next:

```
[8, 0, 3, 9, 2, 21, 18, 27, 1, 5, 8, -1, 12]
 s
 e
                                     l
```

Remember that the pivot you selected is still **8**. **8** is equal to the pivot, so you increment `equal`:

```
[8, 0, 3, 9, 2, 21, 18, 27, 1, 5, 8, -1, 12]
 s
    e
                                     l
```

0 is smaller than the pivot, so you swap the elements at `equal` and `smaller` and increase both pointers:

```
[0, 8, 3, 9, 2, 21, 18, 27, 1, 5, 8, -1, 12]
    s
       e
                                     l
```

And so on.

Note how `smaller`, `equal` and `larger` partition the array:

- Elements in `[low..<smaller]` are smaller than the pivot.
- Elements in `[smaller..<equal]` are equal to the pivot.
- Elements in `[larger>..high]` are larger than the pivot.
- Elements in `[equal...larger]` haven't been compared yet.

To understand how and when the algorithm ends, let's continue from the second-to-last step:

```
[0, 3, -1, 2, 5, 8, 8, 27, 1, 18, 21, 9, 12]
                 s
                       e
                           l
```

Here, **27** is being compared. It is greater than the pivot, so it is swapped with **1** and index `larger` is decremented:

```
[0, 3, -1, 2, 5, 8, 8, 1, 27, 18, 21, 9, 12]
                 s
                       e
                       l
```

Even though `equal` is now equal to `larger`, the algorithm isn't complete.

The element currently at `equal` hasn't been compared yet. It is smaller than the pivot, so it is swapped with **8**, and both indices `smaller` and equal are incremented:

```
[0, 3, -1, 2, 5, 1, 8, 8, 27, 18, 21, 9, 12]
                    s
                          e
                       l
```

Indices `smaller` and `larger` now point to the first and last elements of the middle partition. By returning them, the function marks the boundaries of the three partitions.

You're now ready to implement a new version of quicksort using Dutch national flag partitioning:

```
public func quicksortDutchFlag<T: Comparable>(_ a: inout [T],
                                              low: Int, high:
Int) {
```

```
  if low < high {
    let (middleFirst, middleLast) =
      partitionDutchFlag(&a, low: low, high: high, pivotIndex:
high)
    quicksortDutchFlag(&a, low: low, high: middleFirst - 1)
    quicksortDutchFlag(&a, low: middleLast + 1, high: high)
  }
}
```

Notice how recursion uses the `middleFirst` and `middleLast` indices to determine the partitions that need to be sorted recursively. Because the elements equal to the pivot are grouped together, they can be excluded from the recursion.

Try out your new quicksort by adding the following in your playground:

```
var list4 = [12, 0, 3, 9, 2, 21, 18, 27, 1, 5, 8, -1, 8]
quicksortDutchFlag(&list4, low: 0, high: list4.count - 1)
print(list4)
```

That's it!

Key points

- The naïve partitioning creates a new array on every filter function; this is inefficient. All other strategies sort in place.
- **Lomuto's** partitioning chooses the last element as the pivot.
- **Hoare's** partitioning chooses the first element as its pivot.
- An ideal pivot would split the elements evenly between partitions.
- Choosing a bad pivot can cause quicksort to perform in $O(n^2)$.
- **Median of three** finds the pivot by taking the median of the first, middle and last element.
- **Dutch national flag** partitioning strategy helps to organize duplicate elements more efficiently.

Chapter 35: Quicksort Challenges

By Vincent Ngo

Here are a couple of quicksort challenges to make sure you have the topic down. Make sure to try them out yourself before looking at the solutions.

Challenge 1: Iterative Quicksort

In this chapter, you learned how to implement Quicksort recursively. Your challenge here is to implement it iteratively. Choose any partition strategy you learned in this chapter.

Challenge 2: Merge sort or Quicksort

Explain when and why you would use merge sort over Quicksort.

Challenge 3: Partitioning with Swift standard library

Implement Quicksort using the `partition(by:)` function that is part of the Swift standard library.

> For more information refer to Apple's documentation here: https://developer.apple.com/documentation/swift/array/3017524-partition

Solutions

Solution to Challenge 1

In Chapter 34, you implemented Quicksort recursively. Let's look at how you might do it iteratively. This solution uses Lomuto's partition strategy.

This function takes in an array and the range between `low` and `high`. You will leverage the stack to store pairs of `start` and end values.

```
public func quicksortIterativeLomuto<T: Comparable>(_ a: inout
[T],
                                                  low: Int,
                                                  high: Int) {
  var stack = Stack<Int>() // 1
  stack.push(low) // 2
  stack.push(high)

  while !stack.isEmpty { // 3
    // 4
    guard let end = stack.pop(),
          let start = stack.pop() else {
      continue
    }

    let p = partitionLomuto(&a, low: start, high: end) // 5

    // 6
    if (p - 1) > start {
      stack.push(start)
      stack.push(p - 1)
    }

    // 7
    if (p + 1) < end {
      stack.push(p + 1)
      stack.push(end)
    }
  }

}
```

Let's go over the solution:

1. Create a stack that stores indices.
2. Push the starting `low` and `high` boundaries on the stack to initiate the algorithm.
3. As long as the stack is not empty, Quicksort is not complete.
4. Get the pair of `start` and `end` indices from the stack.
5. Perform Lomuto's partitioning with the current `start` and `end` index. Recall that Lomuto picks the last element as the pivot and splits the partitions into three parts: elements that are less than the pivot, the pivot, and finally, elements that are greater than the pivot.
6. Once the partitioning is complete, check and add the lower bound's `start` and `end` indices to partition the lower half later.
7. Similarly, check and add the upper bound's `start` and `end` indices to partition the upper half later.

You use the stack to store a pair of `start` and `end` indices to perform the partitions.

Let's check to see if your iterative version of quicksort works:

```
var list = [12, 0, 3, 9, 2, 21, 18, 27, 1, 5, 8, -1, 8]
quicksortIterativeLomuto(&list, low: 0, high: list.count - 1)
print(list)
```

Solution to Challenge 2

- Merge sort is preferable over Quicksort when you need stability. Merge sort is stable and guarantees $O(n \log n)$. These characteristics are not the case with Quicksort, which isn't stable and can perform as bad as $O(n^2)$.
- Merge sort works better for larger data structures or data structures where elements are scattered throughout memory. Quicksort works best when elements are stored in a contiguous block.

Solution to Challenge 3

To perform Quicksort on a `Collection`, the following must hold:

- The collection must be a `MutableCollection`. This gives you the ability to change the value of elements in a collection.
- The collection must be a `BidirectionalCollection`. This gives you the ability to traverse the collection forwards and backward. Quicksort depends on the first and last index of a collection.
- The elements in the collection must be `Comparable`.

First, add the following extension:

```
extension MutableCollection where Self: BidirectionalCollection,
                                  Element: Comparable {
  mutating func quicksort() {
    quicksortLumuto(low: startIndex, high: index(before:
endIndex))
  }

  private mutating func quicksortLumuto(low: Index, high: Index)
{

  }
}
```

Here you define a function called `quicksort()`. This function internally calls a `quicksortLumuto(_:)` that takes in the `low` and `high` indexes to start the sorting algorithm.

Next add the following in `quicksortLumuto(_:)`:

```
private mutating func quicksortLumuto(low: Index, high: Index) {
  if low <= high { // 1
    let pivotValue = self[high] // 2
    var p = self.partition { $0 > pivotValue } // 3

    if p == endIndex { // 4
      p = index(before: p)
    }
    // 5
    self[..<p].quicksortLumuto(low: low, high: index(before: p))
    // 6
    self[p...].quicksortLumuto(low: index(after: p), high: high)
  }
}
```

1. Continue to perform Quicksort on the collection till the start and end indexes overlap each other.

2. Lumuto's partition always takes the last element in the collection to perform the partition.

3. `partition` the elements in the collection and return the first index `p` satisfying the condition where elements are greater than the `pivotValue`. Elements before index `p` represent elements that don't satisfy the predicate, and elements after `p` represent elements that satisfy the condition.

4. Handle the base case. If `p` is the last index, move to the index before. Consider the following case:

```
[8 3 2 8]
       p
```

If `p` was the last index, and you perform a partition, the partition would still be the same!

Remember that elements before `p` do not satisfy the partition. You would go in a recursive loop till you run out of memory! The first partition you perform in **step 5** would have the same number of elements as the previous partition.

5. Perform Quicksort on the first partition that is made up of elements **not greater than** the `pivotValue`.

6. Perform Quicksort on the second partition that is made up of elements **greater than** the `pivotValue`.

To test it out, add the following:

```
var numbers = [12, 0, 3, 9, 2, 21, 18, 27, 1, 5, 8, -1, 8]
print(numbers)
numbers.quicksort()
print(numbers)
```

Fun Fact: If you look at the implementation of `partition(by:)`, you'll notice `_partitionImpl(by:)` adopts a similar strategy as Hoare's partition. Check it out here: http://bit.ly/partitionimpl

Section V: Graphs

Graphs are an instrumental data structure that can model a wide range of things: webpages on the internet, the migration patterns of birds, protons in the nucleus of an atom. This section gets you thinking deeply (and broadly) about using graphs and graph algorithms to solve real-world problems.

The chapters that follow will give the foundation you need to understand graph data structures. Like previous sections, every other chapter will serve as a Challenge chapter so you can practice what you've learned.

After completing this section, you will have powerful tools at your disposal to model and solve important real-life problems using graphs. Let's get started!

Chapter 36: Graphs

By Vincent Ngo

What do social networks have in common with booking cheap flights around the world? You can represent both of these real-world models as **graphs**!

A graph is a data structure that captures relationships between objects. It is made up of **vertices** connected by **edges**.

Circles in the graph below represent the vertices, and the edges are the lines that connect them.

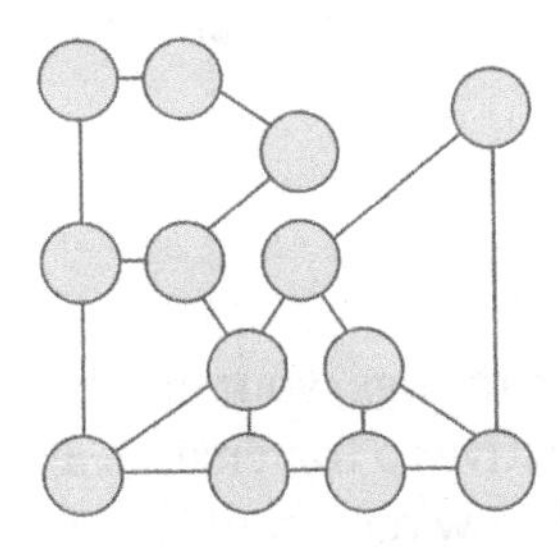

Weighted graphs

In a **weighted graph**, every edge has a weight associated with it that represents the cost of using this edge. These weights let you choose the cheapest or shortest path between two vertices.

Take the airline industry as an example and think of a network with varying flight paths:

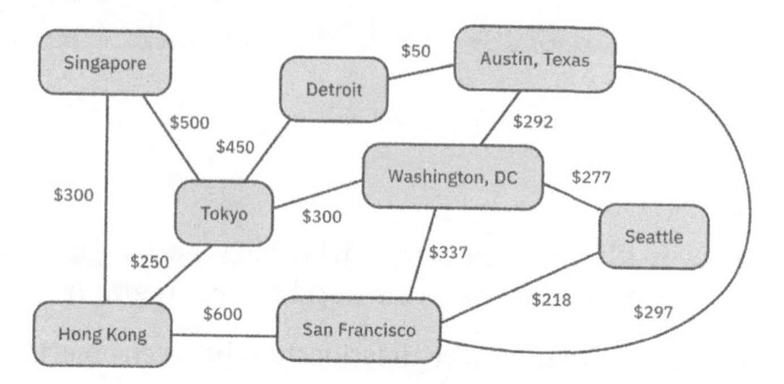

In this example, the vertices represent a state or country, while the edges represent a route from one place to another. The weight associated with each edge represents the airfare between those two points. Using this network, you can determine the cheapest flights from San Francisco to Singapore for all those budget-minded digital nomads out there!

Directed graphs

As well as assigning a weight to an edge, your graphs can also have **direction**. Directed graphs are more restrictive to traverse, as an edge may only permit traversal in one direction. The diagram below represents a directed graph.

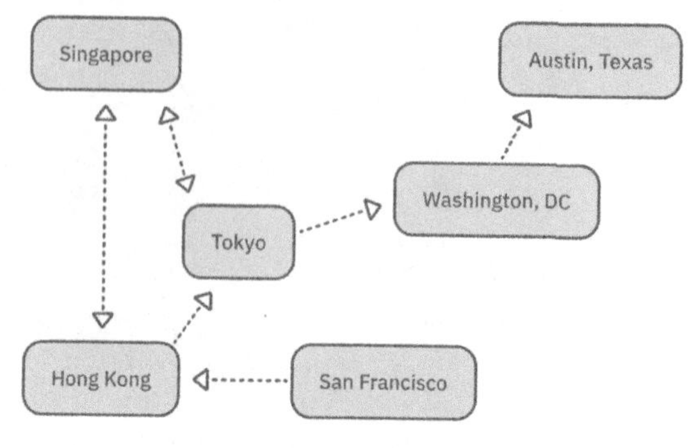

A directed graph

You can tell a lot from this diagram:

- There is a flight from Hong Kong to Tokyo.
- There is no direct flight from San Francisco to Tokyo.
- You can buy a roundtrip ticket between Singapore and Tokyo.
- There is no way to get from Tokyo to San Francisco.

Undirected graphs

You can think of an undirected graph as a directed graph where all edges are bi-directional.

In an undirected graph:

- Two connected vertices have edges going back and forth.
- The weight of an edge applies to both directions.

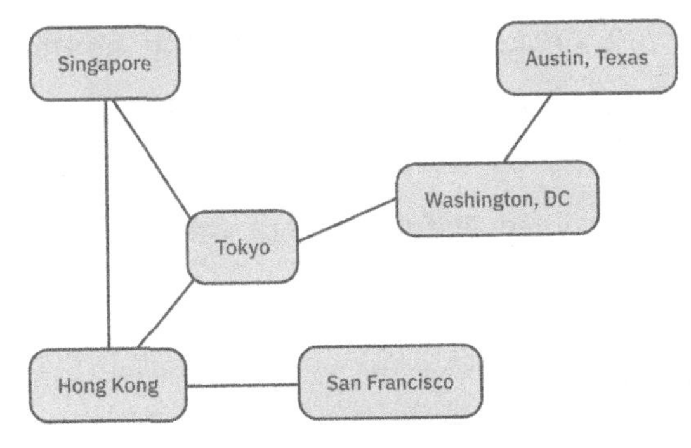

An undirected graph

Common operations

Let's establish a protocol for graphs.

Open up the starter project for this chapter. Create a new file named **Graph.swift** and add the following inside the file:

```
public enum EdgeType {

  case directed
  case undirected
```

```
}

public protocol Graph {

  associatedtype Element

  func createVertex(data: Element) -> Vertex<Element>
  func addDirectedEdge(from source: Vertex<Element>,
                       to destination: Vertex<Element>,
                       weight: Double?)
  func addUndirectedEdge(between source: Vertex<Element>,
                         and destination: Vertex<Element>,
                         weight: Double?)
  func add(_ edge: EdgeType, from source: Vertex<Element>,
                             to destination: Vertex<Element>,
                             weight: Double?)
  func edges(from source: Vertex<Element>) -> [Edge<Element>]
  func weight(from source: Vertex<Element>,
              to destination: Vertex<Element>) -> Double?
}
```

This protocol describes the common operations for a graph:

- `createVertex(data:)`: Creates a vertex and adds it to the graph.
- `addDirectedEdge(from:to:weight:)`: Adds a directed edge between two vertices.
- `addUndirectedEdge(between:and:weight:)`: Adds an undirected (or bi-directional) edge between two vertices.
- `add(from:to:)`: Uses `EdgeType` to add either a directed or undirected edge between two vertices.
- `edges(from:)`: Returns a list of outgoing edges from a specific vertex.
- `weight(from:to:)`: Returns the weight of the edge between two vertices.

In the following sections, you'll implement this protocol in two ways:

- Using an adjacency list.
- Using an adjacency matrix.

Before you can do that, you must first build types to represent vertices and edges.

Defining a vertex

A collection of vertices — not yet a graph

Create a new file named **Vertex.swift** and add the following inside the file:

```
public struct Vertex<T> {

  public let index: Int
  public let data: T
}
```

Here, you've defined a generic `Vertex` struct. A vertex has a unique index within its graph and holds a piece of data.

You'll use `Vertex` as the key type for a dictionary, so you need to conform to `Hashable`. Add the following extension to implement the requirements for `Hashable`:

```
extension Vertex: Hashable where T: Hashable {}
extension Vertex: Equatable where T: Equatable {}
```

The `Hashable` protocol inherits from `Equatable`, so you must also satisfy this protocol's requirement. The compiler can synthesize conformance to both protocols, which is why the extensions above are empty.

Finally, you want to provide a custom string representation of `Vertex`. Add the following right after:

```
extension Vertex: CustomStringConvertible {

  public var description: String {
    "\(index): \(data)"
  }
}
```

Defining an edge

To connect two vertices, there must be an edge between them!

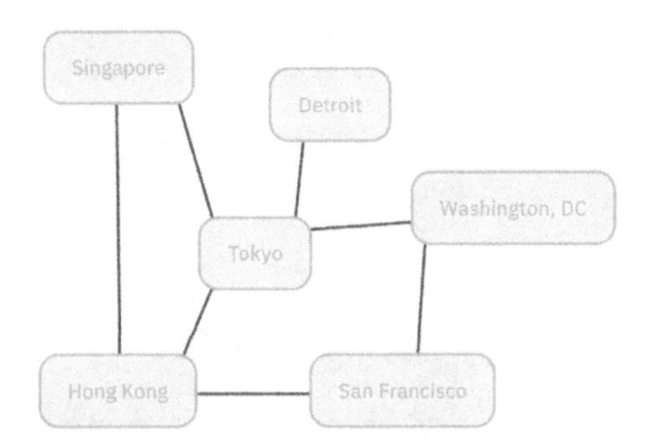

Edges added to the collection of vertices

Create a new file named **Edge.swift** and add the following inside the file:

```
public struct Edge<T> {

  public let source: Vertex<T>
  public let destination: Vertex<T>
  public let weight: Double?
}
```

An Edge connects two vertices and has an optional weight. Simple, isn't it?

Adjacency list

The first graph implementation that you'll learn uses an **adjacency list**. For every vertex in the graph, the graph stores a list of outgoing edges.

Take as an example the following network:

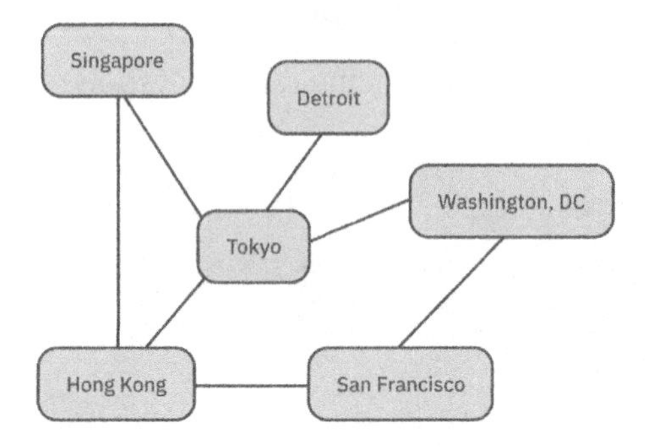

The adjacency list below describes the network of flights depicted above:

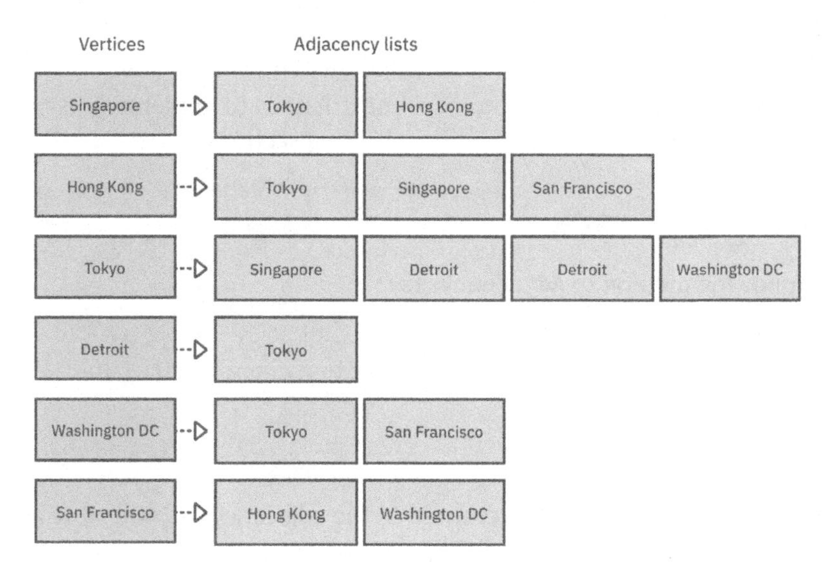

There is a lot you can learn from this adjacency list:

1. Singapore's vertex has two outgoing edges. There is a flight from Singapore to Tokyo and Hong Kong.
2. Detroit has the smallest number of outgoing traffic.
3. Tokyo is the busiest airport, with the most outgoing flights.

In the next section, you will create an adjacency list by storing a **dictionary of arrays**. Each key in the dictionary is a vertex, and in every vertex, the dictionary holds a corresponding array of edges.

Implementation

Create a new file named **AdjacencyList.swift** and add the following:

```
public class AdjacencyList<T: Hashable>: Graph {

  private var adjacencies: [Vertex<T>: [Edge<T>]] = [:]

  public init() {}

  // more to come ...
}
```

Here, you've defined an `AdjacencyList` that uses a dictionary to store the edges. Notice that the generic parameter `T` must be `Hashable` because it is used as a key in a dictionary.

You've already adopted the `Graph` protocol but still need to implement its requirements. That's what you'll do in the following sections.

Creating a vertex

Add the following method to `AdjacencyList`:

```
public func createVertex(data: T) -> Vertex<T> {
  let vertex = Vertex(index: adjacencies.count, data: data)
  adjacencies[vertex] = []
  return vertex
}
```

Here, you create a new vertex and return it. In the adjacency list, you store an empty array of edges for this new vertex.

Creating a directed edge

Recall that there are **directed** and **undirected** graphs.

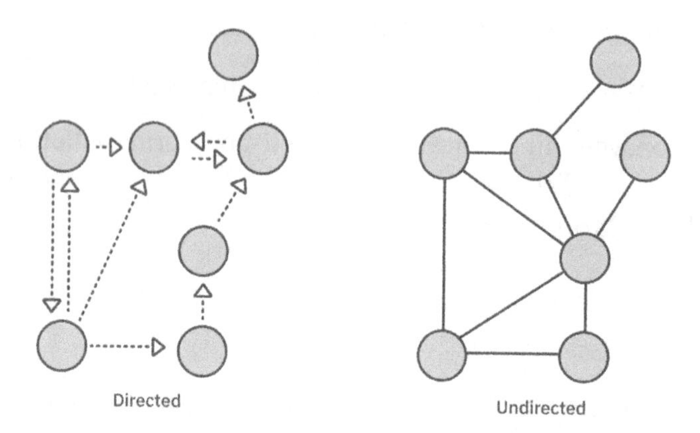

Start by implementing the `addDirectedEdge` requirement. Add the following method:

```
public func addDirectedEdge(from source: Vertex<T>,
                            to destination: Vertex<T>,
                            weight: Double?) {
  let edge = Edge(source: source,
                  destination: destination,
```

```
                    weight: weight)
  adjacencies[source]?.append(edge)
}
```

This method creates a new edge and stores it in the adjacency list.

Creating an undirected edge

You just created a method to add a directed edge between two vertices. How would you create an undirected edge between two vertices?

Remember that an undirected graph can be viewed as a bidirectional graph. Every edge in an undirected graph can be traversed in both directions. This is why you'll implement `addUndirectedEdge` on top of `addDirectedEdge`. Because this implementation is reusable, you'll add it as a protocol extension on `Graph`.

In **Graph.swift**, add the following extension:

```
extension Graph {

  public func addUndirectedEdge(between source: Vertex<Element>,
                                 and destination:
Vertex<Element>,
                                 weight: Double?) {
    addDirectedEdge(from: source, to: destination, weight:
weight)
    addDirectedEdge(from: destination, to: source, weight:
weight)
  }
}
```

Adding an undirected edge is the same as adding two directed edges.

Now that you've implemented both `addDirectedEdge` and `addUndirectedEdge`, you can implement `add` by delegating to one of these methods. In the same protocol extension, add:

```
public func add(_ edge: EdgeType, from source: Vertex<Element>,
                                  to destination:
Vertex<Element>,
                                  weight: Double?) {
  switch edge {
  case .directed:
    addDirectedEdge(from: source, to: destination, weight:
weight)
  case .undirected:
    addUndirectedEdge(between: source, and: destination, weight:
weight)
```

```
  }
}
```

The add method is a convenient helper method that creates either a directed or undirected edge. This is where protocols can become very powerful!

Anyone that adopts the Graph protocol only needs to implement addDirectedEdge to get addUndirectedEdge and add for free!

Retrieving the outgoing edges from a vertex

Back in **AdjacencyList.swift**, continue your work on conforming to Graph by adding the following method:

```
public func edges(from source: Vertex<T>) -> [Edge<T>] {
  adjacencies[source] ?? []
}
```

This code is a straightforward implementation: You either return the stored edges or an empty array if the source vertex is unknown.

Retrieving the weight of an edge

How much is the flight from Singapore to Tokyo?

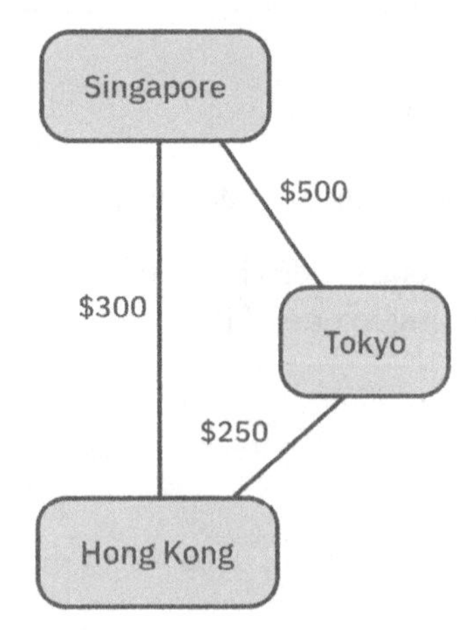

Add the following right after `edges(from:)`:

```
public func weight(from source: Vertex<T>,
                   to destination: Vertex<T>) -> Double? {
  edges(from: source)
    .first { $0.destination == destination }?
    .weight
}
```

Here, you find the first edge from `source` to `destination`; if there is one, you return its weight.

Visualizing the adjacency list

Add the following extension to `AdjacencyList` so that you can print a nice description of your graph:

```
extension AdjacencyList: CustomStringConvertible {

  public var description: String {
    var result = ""
    for (vertex, edges) in adjacencies { // 1
      var edgeString = ""
      for (index, edge) in edges.enumerated() { // 2
        if index != edges.count - 1 {
          edgeString.append("\(edge.destination), ")
        } else {
          edgeString.append("\(edge.destination)")
        }
      }
      result.append("\(vertex) ---> [ \(edgeString) ]\n") // 3
    }
    return result
  }
}
```

Here's what's going on in the code above:

1. You loop through every key-value pair in `adjacencies`.
2. For every vertex, you loop through all its outgoing edges and add an appropriate string to the output.
3. Finally, for every vertex, you print both the vertex itself and its outgoing edges.

You have finally completed your first graph! Let's now try it out by building a network.

Building a network

Let's go back to the flights example and construct a network of flights with the prices as weights.

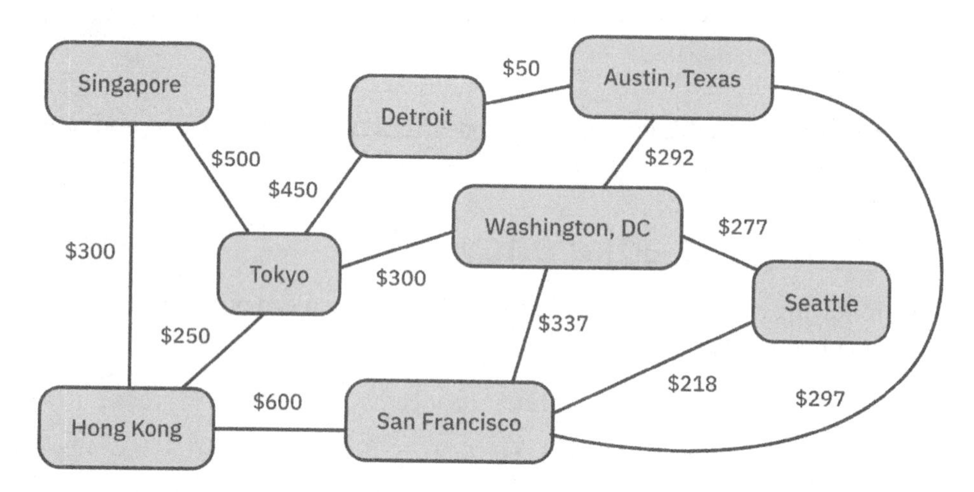

Within the main playground page, add the following code:

```
let graph = AdjacencyList<String>()

let singapore = graph.createVertex(data: "Singapore")
let tokyo = graph.createVertex(data: "Tokyo")
let hongKong = graph.createVertex(data: "Hong Kong")
let detroit = graph.createVertex(data: "Detroit")
let sanFrancisco = graph.createVertex(data: "San Francisco")
let washingtonDC = graph.createVertex(data: "Washington DC")
let austinTexas = graph.createVertex(data: "Austin Texas")
let seattle = graph.createVertex(data: "Seattle")

graph.add(.undirected, from: singapore, to: hongKong, weight:
300)
graph.add(.undirected, from: singapore, to: tokyo, weight: 500)
graph.add(.undirected, from: hongKong, to: tokyo, weight: 250)
graph.add(.undirected, from: tokyo, to: detroit, weight: 450)
graph.add(.undirected, from: tokyo, to: washingtonDC, weight:
300)
graph.add(.undirected, from: hongKong, to: sanFrancisco, weight:
600)
graph.add(.undirected, from: detroit, to: austinTexas, weight:
50)
graph.add(.undirected, from: austinTexas, to: washingtonDC,
weight: 292)
graph.add(.undirected, from: sanFrancisco, to: washingtonDC,
weight: 337)
```

```
graph.add(.undirected, from: washingtonDC, to: seattle, weight:
277)
graph.add(.undirected, from: sanFrancisco, to: seattle, weight:
218)
graph.add(.undirected, from: austinTexas, to: sanFrancisco,
weight: 297)

print(graph)
```

You should get the following output in your playground:

```
2: Hong Kong ---> [ 0: Singapore, 1: Tokyo, 4: San Francisco ]
4: San Francisco ---> [ 2: Hong Kong, 5: Washington DC, 7:
Seattle, 6: Austin Texas ]
5: Washington DC ---> [ 1: Tokyo, 6: Austin Texas, 4: San
Francisco, 7: Seattle ]
6: Austin Texas ---> [ 3: Detroit, 5: Washington DC, 4: San
Francisco ]
7: Seattle ---> [ 5: Washington DC, 4: San Francisco ]
0: Singapore ---> [ 2: Hong Kong, 1: Tokyo ]
1: Tokyo ---> [ 0: Singapore, 2: Hong Kong, 3: Detroit, 5:
Washington DC ]
3: Detroit ---> [ 1: Tokyo, 6: Austin Texas ]
```

This output shows a visual description of an adjacency list. You can see all the outbound flights from any place! Pretty cool, huh?

You can also obtain other helpful information such as:

- How much is a flight from Singapore to Tokyo?

```
graph.weight(from: singapore, to: tokyo)
```

- What are all the outgoing flights from San Francisco?

```
print("San Francisco Outgoing Flights:")
print("--------------------------------")
for edge in graph.edges(from: sanFrancisco) {
  print("from: \(edge.source) to: \(edge.destination)")
}
```

You have just created a graph using an adjacency list, wherein you used a dictionary to store the outgoing edges for every vertex. Let's take a look at a different approach to how to store vertices and edges.

Adjacency matrix

An **adjacency matrix** uses a square matrix to represent a graph. This matrix is a two-dimensional array wherein the value of `matrix[row][column]` is the weight of the edge between the vertices at `row` and `column`.

Below is an example of a directed graph that depicts a flight network traveling to different places. The weight represents the cost of the airfare.

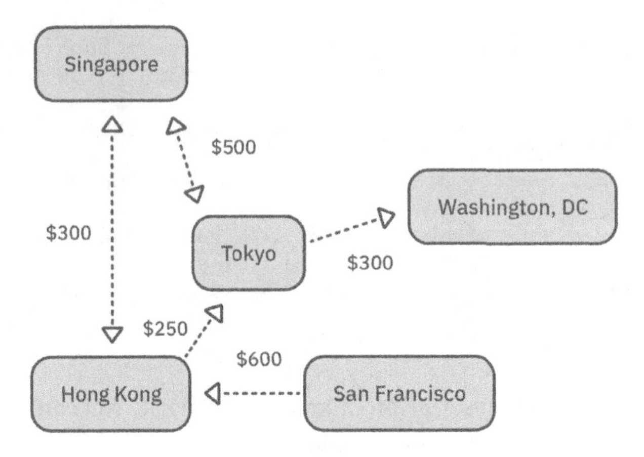

The following adjacency matrix describes the network for the flights depicted above.

Edges that don't exist have a weight of 0.

Vertices

0	Singapore
1	Hong Kong
2	Tokyo
3	Washington DC
4	San Francisco

Columns / Rows

Rows	0	1	2	3	4
0	0	$300	$500	0	0
1	$300	0	$250	0	0
2	$500	0	0	$300	0
3	0	0	0	0	0
4	0	$600	0	0	0

Compared to an adjacency list, this matrix is a little harder to read. Using the array of vertices on the left, you can learn a lot from the matrix. For example:

- `[0][1]` is 300, so there is a flight from Singapore to Hong Kong for $300.
- `[2][1]` is 0, so there is no flight from Tokyo to Hong Kong.
- `[1][2]` is 250, so there is a flight from Hong Kong to Tokyo for $250.
- `[2][2]` is 0, so there is no flight from Tokyo to Tokyo!

> **Note**: There is a pink line in the middle of the matrix. When the row and column are equal, this represents an edge between a vertex and itself, which is not allowed.

Implementation

Create a new file named **AdjacencyMatrix.swift** and add the following to it:

```
public class AdjacencyMatrix<T>: Graph {

  private var vertices: [Vertex<T>] = []
  private var weights: [[Double?]] = []

  public init() {}

  // more to come ...
}
```

Here, you've defined an `AdjacencyMatrix` that contains an array of vertices and an adjacency matrix to keep track of the edges and their weights.

Just as before, you've already declared conformance to `Graph` but still need to implement the requirements.

Creating a Vertex

Add the following method to `AdjacencyMatrix`:

```
public func createVertex(data: T) -> Vertex<T> {
  let vertex = Vertex(index: vertices.count, data: data)
  vertices.append(vertex) // 1
  for i in 0..<weights.count { // 2
    weights[i].append(nil)
  }
  let row = [Double?](repeating: nil, count: vertices.count) //
3
  weights.append(row)
  return vertex
}
```

To create a vertex in an adjacency matrix, you:

1. Add a new vertex to the array.
2. Append a `nil` weight to every row in the matrix, as none of the current vertices have an edge to the new vertex.

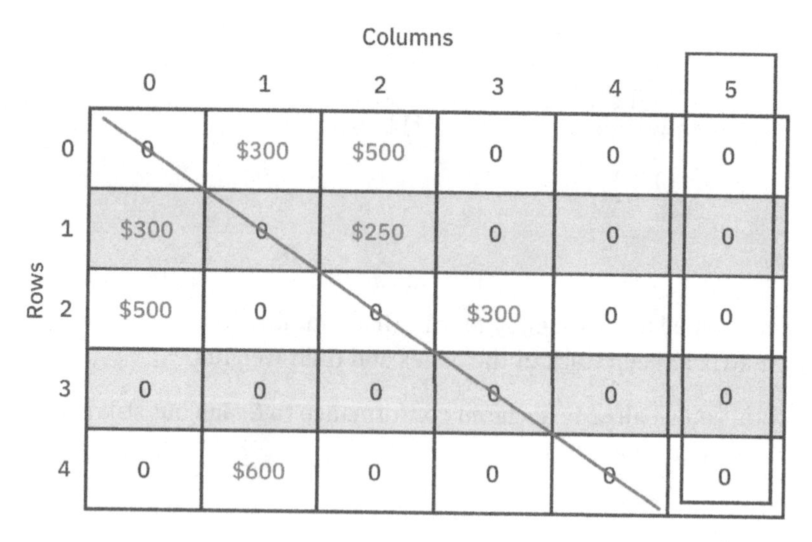

3. Add a new row to the matrix. This row holds the outgoing edges for the new vertex.

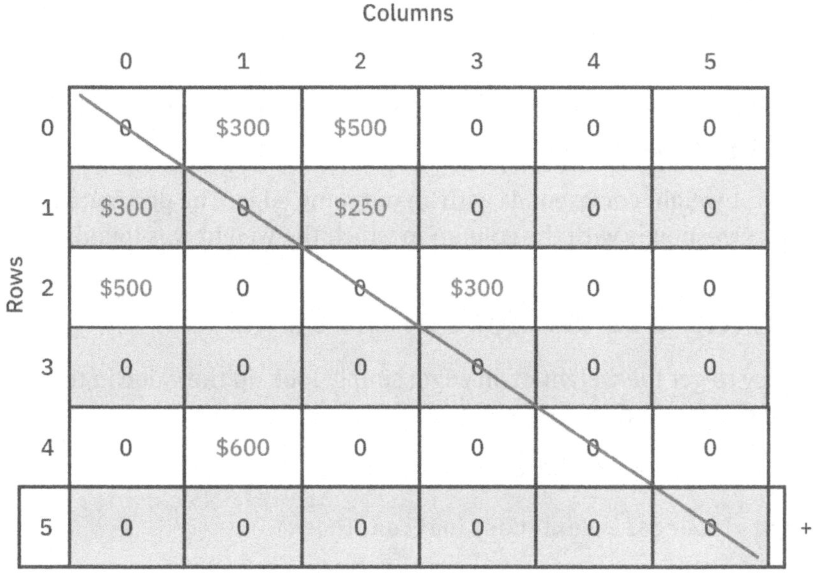

Columns

Rows	0	1	2	3	4	5
0	0	$300	$500	0	0	0
1	$300	0	$250	0	0	0
2	$500	0	0	$300	0	0
3	0	0	0	0	0	0
4	0	$600	0	0	0	0
5	0	0	0	0	0	0

+

Creating edges

Creating edges is as simple as filling in the matrix. Add the following method:

```
public func addDirectedEdge(from source: Vertex<T>,
                            to destination: Vertex<T>, weight:
Double?) {
  weights[source.index][destination.index] = weight
}
```

Remember that `addUndirectedEdge` and `add` have a default implementation in the protocol extension, so this is all you need to do!

Retrieving the outgoing edges from a vertex

Add the following method:

```
public func edges(from source: Vertex<T>) -> [Edge<T>] {
  var edges: [Edge<T>] = []
  for column in 0..<weights.count {
    if let weight = weights[source.index][column] {
      edges.append(Edge(source: source,
```

```
                          destination: vertices[column],
                          weight: weight))
    }
  }
  return edges
}
```

To retrieve the outgoing edges for a vertex, search the row for this vertex in the matrix for weights that are not `nil`.

Every non-`nil` weight corresponds with an outgoing edge. The destination is the vertex that corresponds with the column in which the weight was found.

Retrieving the weight of an edge

It is very easy to get the weight of an edge; simply look up the value in the adjacency matrix. Add this method:

```
public func weight(from source: Vertex<T>,
                   to destination: Vertex<T>) -> Double? {
  weights[source.index][destination.index]
}
```

Visualize an adjacency matrix

Finally, add the following extension so you can print out a nice, readable description of your graph:

```
extension AdjacencyMatrix: CustomStringConvertible {

  public var description: String {
    // 1
    let verticesDescription = vertices.map { "\($0)" }
                                      .joined(separator: "\n")
    // 2
    var grid: [String] = []
    for i in 0..<weights.count {
      var row = ""
      for j in 0..<weights.count {
        if let value = weights[i][j] {
          row += "\(value)\t"
        } else {
          row += "ø\t\t"
        }
      }
      grid.append(row)
    }
```

```
        let edgesDescription = grid.joined(separator: "\n")
        // 3
        return "\(verticesDescription)\n\n\(edgesDescription)"
    }
}
```

Here are the steps:

1. You first create a list of the vertices.
2. Then, you build up a grid of weights, row by row.
3. Finally, you join both descriptions together and return them.

Building a network

You will reuse the same example from `AdjacencyList`:

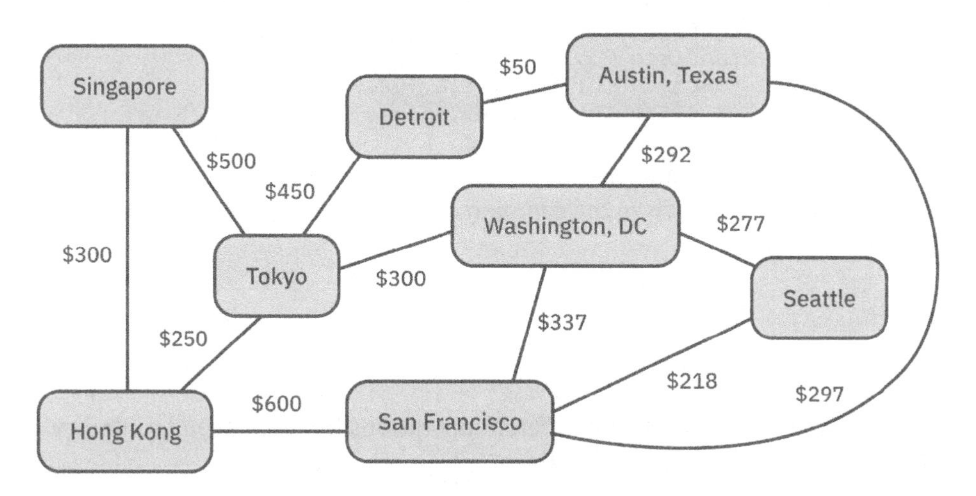

Go to the main playground page and replace:

```
let graph = AdjacencyList<String>()
```

With:

```
let graph = AdjacencyMatrix<String>()
```

`AdjacencyMatrix` and `AdjacencyList` conform to the same protocol `Graph`, so the rest of the code stays the same.

You should get the following output in your playground:

```
0: Singapore
1: Tokyo
2: Hong Kong
3: Detroit
4: San Francisco
5: Washington DC
6: Austin Texas
7: Seattle
ø    500.0 300.0 ø    ø    ø    ø    ø
500.0 ø    250.0 450.0 ø    300.0 ø    ø
300.0 250.0 ø    ø    600.0 ø    ø    ø
ø    450.0 ø    ø    ø    ø    50.0 ø
ø    ø    600.0 ø    ø    337.0 297.0 218.0
ø    300.0 ø    ø    337.0 ø    292.0 277.0
ø    ø    ø    50.0 297.0 292.0 ø    ø
ø    ø    ø    ø    218.0 277.0 ø    ø
San Francisco Outgoing Flights:
--------------------------------
from: 4: San Francisco to: 2: Hong Kong
from: 4: San Francisco to: 5: Washington DC
from: 4: San Francisco to: 6: Austin Texas
from: 4: San Francisco to: 7: Seattle
```

In terms of visual beauty, an adjacency list is a lot easier to follow and trace than an adjacency matrix. Let's analyze the common operations of these two approaches and see how they perform.

Graph analysis

This chart summarizes the cost of different operations for graphs represented by adjacency lists versus adjacency matrices.

Operations	Adjacency List	Adjacency Matrix
Storage Space	O(V + E)	O(V²)
Add Vertex	O(1)	O(V²)
Add Edge	O(1)	O(1)
Finding Edges and Weight	O(V)	O(1)

V represents vertices, and **E** represents edges.

An adjacency list takes less storage space than an adjacency matrix. An adjacency list simply stores the number of vertices and edges needed. As for an adjacency matrix, recall that the number of rows and columns equals the number of vertices. This explains the quadratic space complexity of $O(V^2)$.

Adding a vertex is efficient in an adjacency list: Simply create a vertex and set its key-value pair in the dictionary. It is amortized as $O(1)$. When adding a vertex to an adjacency matrix, you must add a column to every row and create a new row for the new vertex. This is at least $O(V)$, and if you choose to represent your matrix with a contiguous block of memory, it can be $O(V^2)$.

Adding an edge is efficient in both data structures, as they are both constant time. The adjacency list appends to the array of outgoing edges. The adjacency matrix simply sets the value in the two-dimensional array.

Adjacency list loses out when trying to find a particular edge or weight. To find an edge in an adjacency list, you must obtain the list of outgoing edges and loop through every edge to find a matching destination. This happens in $O(V)$ time. With an adjacency matrix, finding an edge or weight is constant time access to retrieve the value from the two-dimensional array.

Which data structure should you choose to construct your graph?

If there are few edges in your graph, it is considered a **sparse** graph, and an adjacency list would be a good fit. An adjacency matrix would be a bad choice for a sparse graph because a lot of memory will be wasted since there aren't many edges.

If your graph has lots of edges, it's considered a **dense graph**, and an adjacency matrix would be a better fit as you'd be able to access your weights and edges far more quickly.

Key points

- You can represent real-world relationships through **vertices** and **edges**.
- Think of **vertices** as objects and **edges** as the relationship between the objects.
- Weighted graphs associate a weight with every edge.
- Directed graphs have edges that traverse in one direction.
- Undirected graphs have edges that point both ways.
- Adjacency list stores a list of outgoing edges for every vertex.
- Adjacency matrix uses a square matrix to represent a graph.
- Adjacency list is generally good for **sparse graphs** when your graph has the least amount of edges.
- Adjacency matrix is generally suitable for **dense graphs** when your graph has lots of edges.

Challenge 1: Count the number of paths

Write a method to count the number of paths between two vertices in a directed graph. The example graph below has five paths from **A** to **E**:

Challenge 2: Graph your friends

Vincent has three friends, Chesley, Ruiz and Patrick. Ruiz has friends as well: Ray, Sun, and a mutual friend of Vincent's. Patrick is friends with Cole and Kerry. Cole is friends with Ruiz and Vincent. Create an adjacency list that represents this friendship graph. Which mutual friend do Ruiz and Vincent share?

Solutions

Solution to Challenge 1

The goal is to write a function that finds the number of paths between two vertices in a graph. One solution is to perform a depth-first traversal and keep track of the visited vertices.

```
extension Graph where Element: Hashable {
  public func numberOfPaths(from source: Vertex<Element>,
                            to destination: Vertex<Element>) ->
Int {
    var numberOfPaths = 0 // 1
    var visited: Set<Vertex<Element>> = [] // 2
    paths(from: source,
          to: destination,
          visited: &visited,
          pathCount: &numberOfPaths) // 3
    return numberOfPaths
  }

}
```

Here you do the following:

1. `numberOfPaths` keeps track of the number of paths found between the `source` and `destination`.
2. `visited` is a `Set` that keeps track of all the vertices visited.
3. `paths` is a recursive helper function that takes in four parameters. The first two parameters are the `source` and `destination` vertex. The last two parameters, `visited`, tracks the vertices visited, and `numberOfPaths` tracks the number of paths found. The last two parameters are modified within `paths`.

Add the following right after the `numberOfPaths` function:

```
func paths(from source: Vertex<Element>,
           to destination: Vertex<Element>,
           visited: inout Set<Vertex<Element>>,
           pathCount: inout Int) {
  visited.insert(source) // 1
  if source == destination { // 2
    pathCount += 1
  } else {
    let neighbors = edges(from: source) // 3
    for edge in neighbors { // 4
```

```
        if !visited.contains(edge.destination) {
          paths(from: edge.destination,
                to: destination,
                visited: &visited,
                pathCount: &pathCount)
        }
      }
    }
    // 5
    visited.remove(source)
  }
```

To get the paths from the `source` to `destination`:

1. Initiate the algorithm by marking the `source` vertex as visited.
2. Check to see if the `source` is the `destination`. If it is, you have found a path, increment the count by one.
3. If it is not, get all the edges adjacent to the `source` vertex.
4. For every edge, if it has not been visited before, recursively traverse the neighboring vertices to find a path to the `destination` vertex.
5. Remove the `source` vertex from the visited set, so you can continue to find other paths to that node.

You are doing a depth-first graph traversal. You recursively dive down one path till you reach the destination and back-track by popping off the stack. The time-complexity is $O(V + E)$.

Solution to Challenge 2

This solution uses the AdjacencyList API you built in the last chapter. You can use any non-nil weight, but a good default is 1.

```
let graph = AdjacencyList<String>()

let vincent = graph.createVertex(data: "vincent")
let chesley = graph.createVertex(data: "chesley")
let ruiz = graph.createVertex(data: "ruiz")
let patrick = graph.createVertex(data: "patrick")
let ray = graph.createVertex(data: "ray")
let sun = graph.createVertex(data: "sun")
let cole = graph.createVertex(data: "cole")
let kerry = graph.createVertex(data: "kerry")

graph.add(.undirected, from: vincent, to: chesley, weight: 1)
graph.add(.undirected, from: vincent, to: ruiz, weight: 1)
graph.add(.undirected, from: vincent, to: patrick, weight: 1)
graph.add(.undirected, from: ruiz, to: ray, weight: 1)
graph.add(.undirected, from: ruiz, to: sun, weight: 1)
graph.add(.undirected, from: patrick, to: cole, weight: 1)
graph.add(.undirected, from: patrick, to: kerry, weight: 1)
graph.add(.undirected, from: cole, to: ruiz, weight: 1)
graph.add(.undirected, from: cole, to: vincent, weight: 1)
print(graph)
```

You can simply look at the graph to find the common friend.

```
print("Ruiz and Vincent both share a friend name Cole")
```

If you want to solve it with a program, you can use the fact that elements are `Hashable` and find the intersection of the `Set` of Ruiz's and Vincent's friends.

```
let vincentsFriends = Set(graph.edges(from: vincent).map
{ $0.destination.data })
let mutual = vincentsFriends.intersection(graph.edges(from:
ruiz).map { $0.destination.data })
print(mutual)
```

In the previous chapter, you explored using graphs to capture relationships between objects. Remember that objects are just vertices, and edges represent the relationships between them.

Several algorithms exist to traverse or search through a graph's vertices. One such algorithm is the **breadth-first search** (BFS) algorithm.

BFS can be used to solve a wide variety of problems:

1. Generating a minimum-spanning tree.
2. Finding potential paths between vertices.
3. Finding the shortest path between two vertices.

Example

BFS starts by selecting any vertex in a graph. The algorithm then explores all neighbors of this vertex before traversing the neighbors of said neighbors and so forth. As the name suggests, this algorithm takes a **breadth-first** approach.

Going through a BFS example using the following undirected graph:

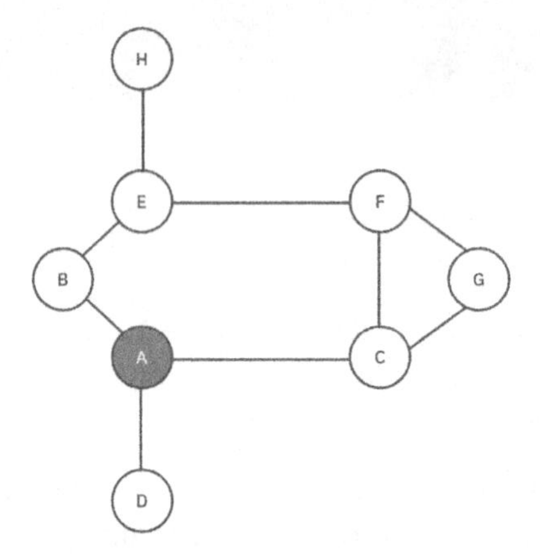

> **Note**: Highlighted vertices represent visited vertices.

You will use a **queue** to keep track of which vertices to visit next. The **first-in-first-out** approach of the queue guarantees that all of a vertex's neighbors are visited before you traverse one level deeper.

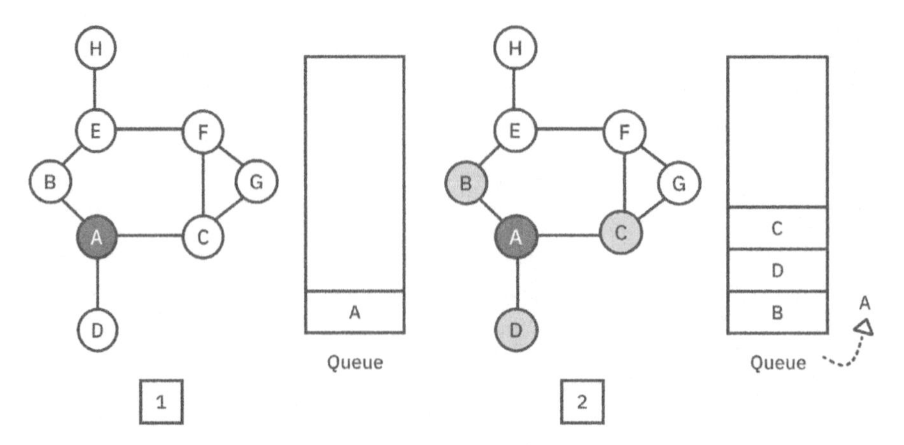

1. To begin, you pick a source vertex to start from. Here, you have chosen A, which is added to the queue.

2. As long as the queue is not empty, you dequeue and visit the next vertex, in this case, A. Next, you add all of A's neighboring vertices [B, D, C] to the queue.

> **Note**: It's important to note that you only add a vertex to the queue when it has not yet been visited and is not already in the queue.

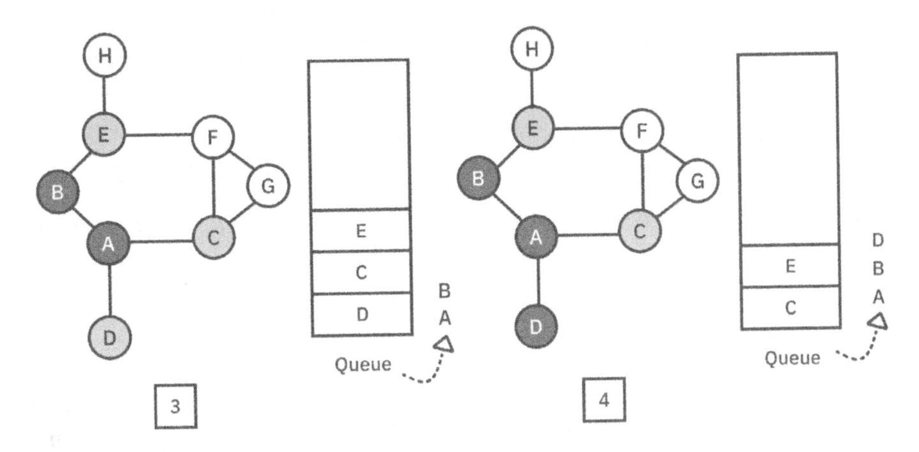

3. The queue is not empty, so you dequeue and visit the next vertex, B. You then add B's neighbor E to the queue. A is already visited, so it does not get added. The queue now has [D, C, E].

4. The next vertex to be dequeued is `D`. `D` does not have any neighbors that aren't visited. The queue now has `[C, E]`.

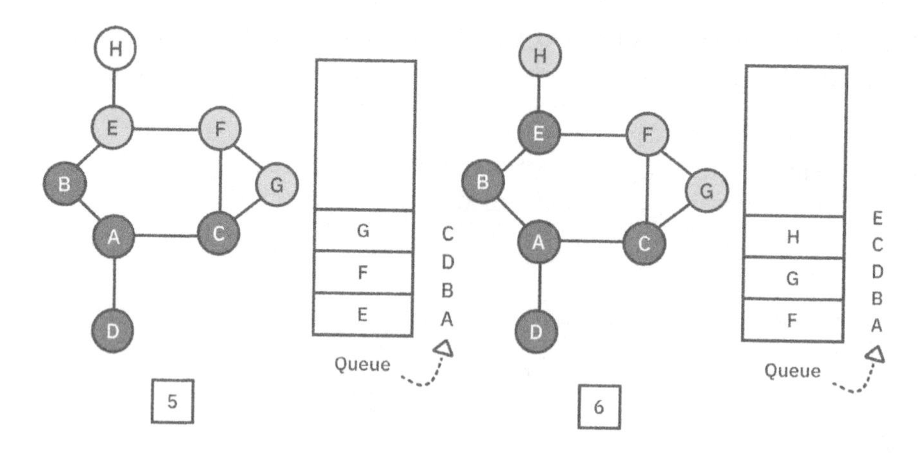

5. Next, you dequeue `C` and add its neighbors `[F, G]` to the queue. The queue now has `[E, F, G]`.

Note that you have now visited all of `A`'s neighbors! BFS now moves on to the second level of neighbors.

6. You dequeue `E` and add `H` to the queue. The queue now has `[F, G, H]`. You don't add `B` or `F` to the queue because `B` is already visited and `F` is already in the queue.

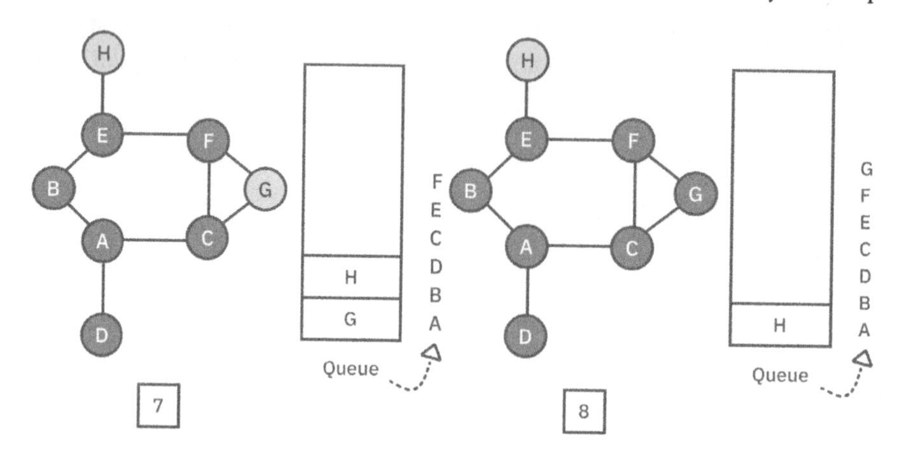

7. You dequeue `F`, and since all its neighbors are already in the queue or visited, you don't add anything to the queue.

8. Like the previous step, you dequeue G and don't add anything to the queue.

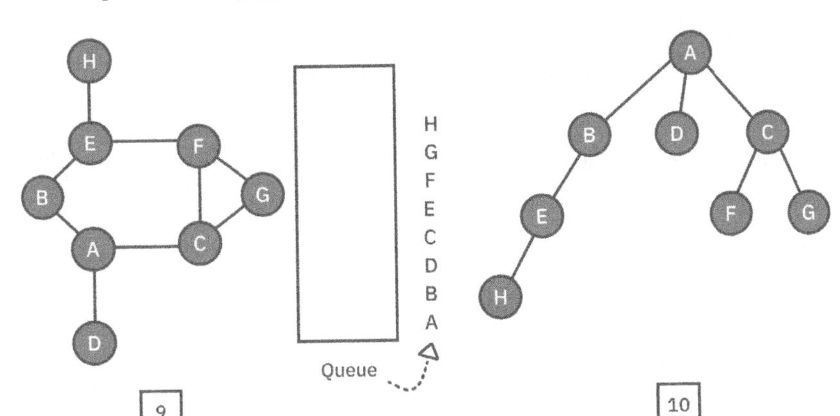

9. Finally, you dequeue H. The breadth-first search is complete since the queue is now empty!

10. When exploring the vertices, you can construct a tree-like structure, showing the vertices at each level: first the vertex you started from, then its neighbors, then its neighbors' neighbors and so on.

Implementation

Open up the starter playground for this chapter. This playground contains an implementation of a graph you built in the previous chapter. It also includes a stack-based queue implementation, which you will use to implement BFS.

In your main playground file, you will notice a pre-built sample graph. Add the below code:

```
extension Graph where Element: Hashable {

  func breadthFirstSearch(from source: Vertex<Element>)
      -> [Vertex<Element>] {
    var queue = QueueStack<Vertex<Element>>()
    var enqueued: Set<Vertex<Element>> = []
    var visited: [Vertex<Element>] = []

    // more to come

    return visited
  }
}
```

Here, you've defined a method `breadthFirstSearch(from:)` that takes in a starting vertex. It uses three data structures:

1. `queue` keeps track of the neighboring vertices to visit next.
2. `enqueued` remembers which vertices have been enqueued before, so you don't enqueue the same vertex twice. You use a `Set` type here so that lookup is cheap and only takes $O(1)$.
3. `visited` is an array that stores the order in which the vertices were explored.

Next, complete the method by replacing the comment with:

```
queue.enqueue(source) // 1
enqueued.insert(source)

while let vertex = queue.dequeue() { // 2
  visited.append(vertex) // 3
  let neighborEdges = edges(from: vertex) // 4
  neighborEdges.forEach { edge in
    if !enqueued.contains(edge.destination) { // 5
      queue.enqueue(edge.destination)
      enqueued.insert(edge.destination)
    }
  }
}
```

Here's what's going on:

1. You initiate the BFS algorithm by first enqueuing the `source` vertex.
2. You continue to dequeue a vertex from the queue until the queue is empty.
3. Every time you dequeue a vertex from the queue, you add it to the list of visited vertices.
4. Then, you find all edges that start from the current vertex and iterate over them.
5. For each edge, you check to see if its destination vertex has been enqueued before, and, if not, you add it to the code.

That's all there is to implementing BFS! Let's give this algorithm a spin. Add the following code:

```
let vertices = graph.breadthFirstSearch(from: a)
vertices.forEach { vertex in
  print(vertex)
}
```

Take note of the order of the explored vertices using BFS:

```
0: A
1: B
2: C
3: D
4: E
5: F
6: G
7: H
```

One thing to keep in mind with neighboring vertices is that the order in which you visit them is determined by how you construct your graph. You could have added an edge between `A` and `C` before adding one between `A` and `B`. In this case, the output would list `C` before `B`.

Performance

When traversing a graph using BFS, each vertex is enqueued once. This process has a time complexity of $O(V)$. During this traversal, you also visit all the edges. The time it takes to visit all edges is $O(E)$. Adding the two together means that the overall time complexity for breadth-first search is $O(V + E)$.

The space complexity of BFS is $O(V)$ since you have to store the vertices in three separate structures: `queue`, `enqueued` and `visited`.

Key points

- Breadth-first search (BFS) is an algorithm for traversing or searching a graph.
- BFS explores all the current vertex's neighbors before traversing the next level of vertices.
- It's generally good to use this algorithm when your graph structure has many neighboring vertices or when you need to find out every possible outcome.
- The queue data structure is used to prioritize traversing a vertex's edges before diving down a level deeper.

Chapter 39: Breadth-First Search Challenges

By Vincent Ngo

Challenge 1: Maximum queue size

For the following undirected graph, list the **maximum** number of items ever in the queue. Assume that the starting vertex is **A**.

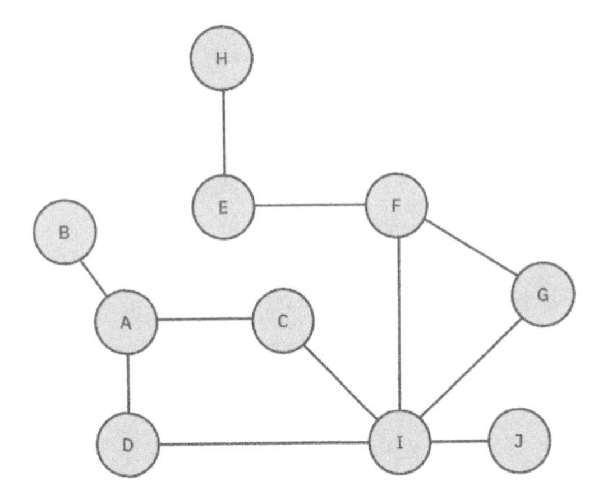

Challenge 2: Iterative BFS

In this chapter, you went over an iterative implementation of breadth-first search. Now write a recursive implementation.

Challenge 3: Disconnected Graph

Add a method to `Graph` to detect if a graph is disconnected. An example of a disconnected graph is shown below:

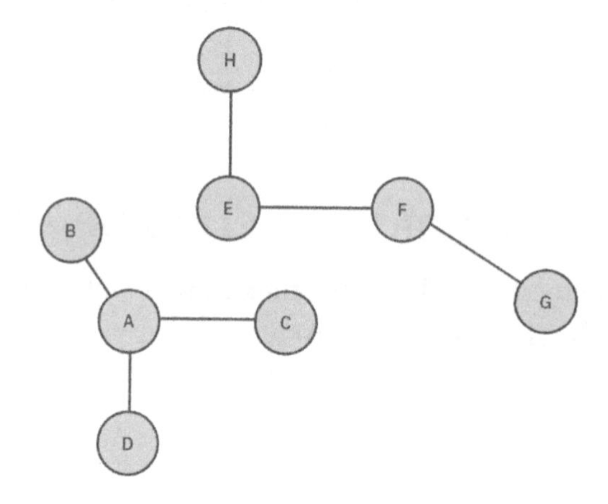

To help you solve this challenge, a property `allVertices` was added to the `Graph` protocol:

```
var allVertices: [Vertex<Element>] { get }
```

This property is already implemented by `AdjacencyMatrix` and `AdjacencyList`.

Solutions

Solution to Challenge 1

The maximum number of items ever in the queue is **3**.

Solution to Challenge 2

In the breadth-first search chapter, you learned how to implement the algorithm iteratively. Let's take a look at how you would implement it recursively.

```
extension Graph where Element: Hashable {

  func bfs(from source: Vertex<Element>) -> [Vertex<Element>] {
    var queue = QueueStack<Vertex<Element>>() // 1
    var enqueued: Set<Vertex<Element>> = [] // 2
    var visited: [Vertex<Element>] = [] // 3

    // 4
    queue.enqueue(source)
    enqueued.insert(source)
    // 5
    bfs(queue: &queue, enqueued: &enqueued, visited: &visited)
    // 6
    return visited
  }
}
```

`bfs` takes in the `source` vertex to start traversing from:

1. queue keeps track of the neighboring vertices to visit next.
2. enqueued remembers which vertices have been added to the queue. You can use a Set for $O(1)$ lookup. An array is $O(n)$.
3. `visited` is an array that stores the order in which the vertices were explored.
4. Initiate the algorithm by inserting the `source` vertex.
5. Perform `bfs` recursively on the graph by calling a helper function.
6. Return the vertices visited in order.

The helper function looks like this:

```
private func bfs(queue: inout QueueStack<Vertex<Element>>,
                 enqueued: inout Set<Vertex<Element>>,
                 visited: inout [Vertex<Element>]) {
  guard let vertex = queue.dequeue() else { // 1
    return
  }
  visited.append(vertex) // 2
  let neighborEdges = edges(from: vertex) // 3
  neighborEdges.forEach { edge in
    if !enqueued.contains(edge.destination) { // 4
      queue.enqueue(edge.destination)
```

```
            enqueued.insert(edge.destination)
          }
        }
        // 5
        bfs(queue: &queue, enqueued: &enqueued, visited: &visited)
      }
```

1. **Base case**, recursively continue to dequeue a vertex from the queue till it is empty.
2. Mark the vertex as visited.
3. For every neighboring edge from the current `vertex`.
4. Check to see if the adjacent vertices have been visited before inserting into the queue.
5. Recursively perform `bfs` till the queue is empty.

The overall time complexity for breadth-first search is $O(V + E)$.

Solution to Challenge 3

A graph is said to be disconnected if no path exists between two nodes.

```
extension Graph where Element: Hashable {

  func isDisconnected() -> Bool {
    guard let firstVertex = allVertices.first else { // 1
      return false
    }
    let visited = breadthFirstSearch(from: firstVertex) // 2
    for vertex in allVertices { // 3
      if !visited.contains(vertex) {
        return true
      }
    }
    return false
  }
}
```

1. If there are no vertices, treat the graph as connected.
2. Perform a breadth-first search starting from the first vertex. This process will return all the visited nodes.
3. Go through every vertex in the graph and check if it has been visited before.

The graph is disconnected if a vertex is missing in the `visited` set.

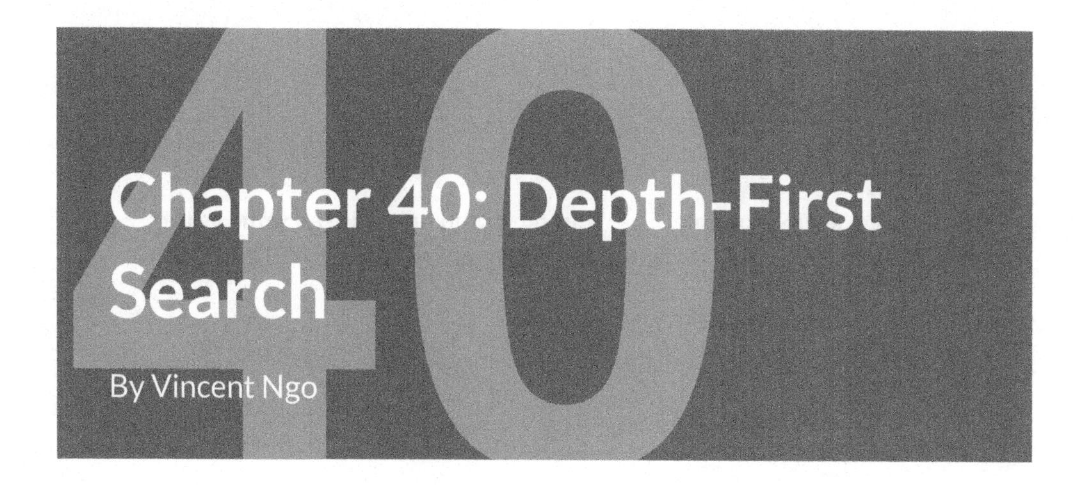

Chapter 40: Depth-First Search

By Vincent Ngo

In the previous chapter, you looked at breadth-first search (BFS), in which you had to explore every neighbor of a vertex before going to the next level. In this chapter, you will look at **depth-first search** (DFS), another algorithm for traversing or searching a graph.

There are a lot of applications for DFS:

- Topological sorting.
- Detecting a cycle.
- Pathfinding, such as in maze puzzles.
- Finding connected components in a sparse graph.

To perform a DFS, you start with a given source vertex and attempt to explore a branch as far as possible until you reach the end. At this point, you would **backtrack** (move a step back) and explore the next available branch until you find what you are looking for or until you've visited all the vertices.

Example

Let's go through a DFS example. The example graph below is the same as the previous chapter. This is so you can see the difference between BFS and DFS.

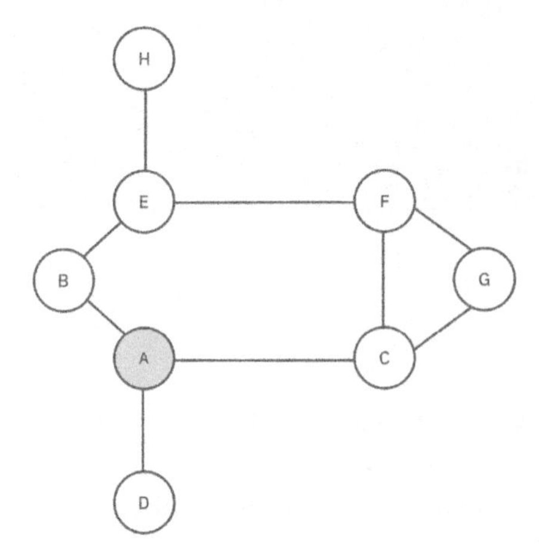

You will use a **stack** to keep track of the levels you move through. The stack's **last-in-first-out** approach helps with backtracking. Every **push** on the stack means that you move one level deeper. You can **pop** to return to a previous level if you reach a dead end.

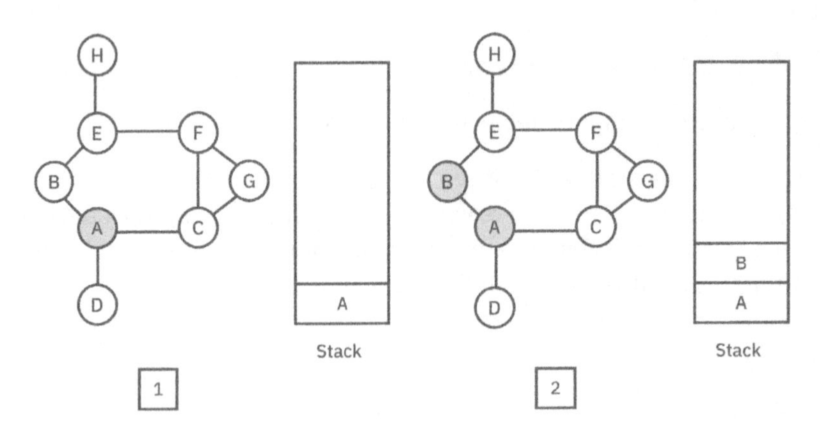

1. As in the previous chapter, you choose A as a starting vertex and add it to the stack.

2. As long as the stack is not empty, you visit the top vertex on the stack and push the first neighboring vertex that has yet to be visited. In this case, you visit A and push B.

Recall from the previous chapter that the order in which you add edges influences the result of a search. In this case, the first edge added to A was an edge to B, so B is pushed first.

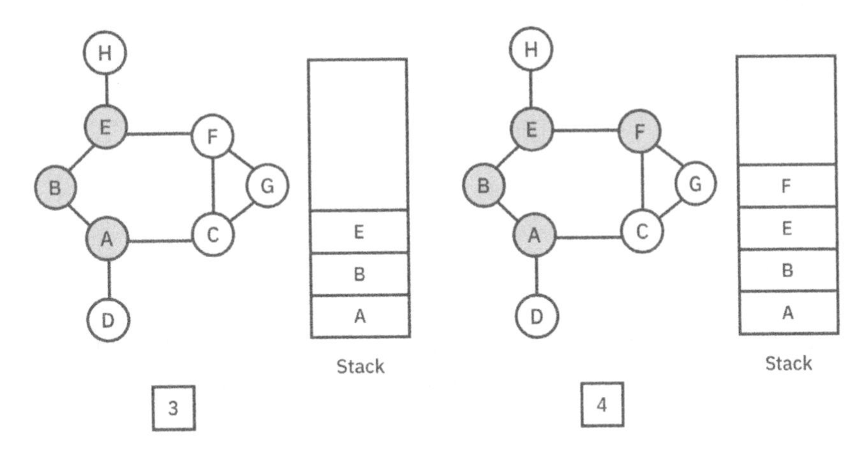

3. You visit B and push E because A is already visited.

4. You visit E and push F.

Note that every time you push on the stack, you advance farther down a branch. Instead of visiting every adjacent vertex, you continue down a path until you reach the end and then backtrack.

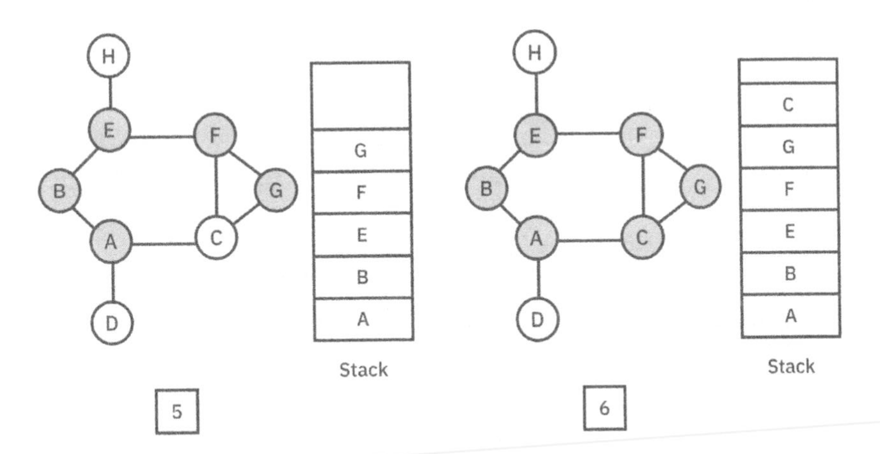

5. You visit F and push G.

6. You visit `G` and push `C`.

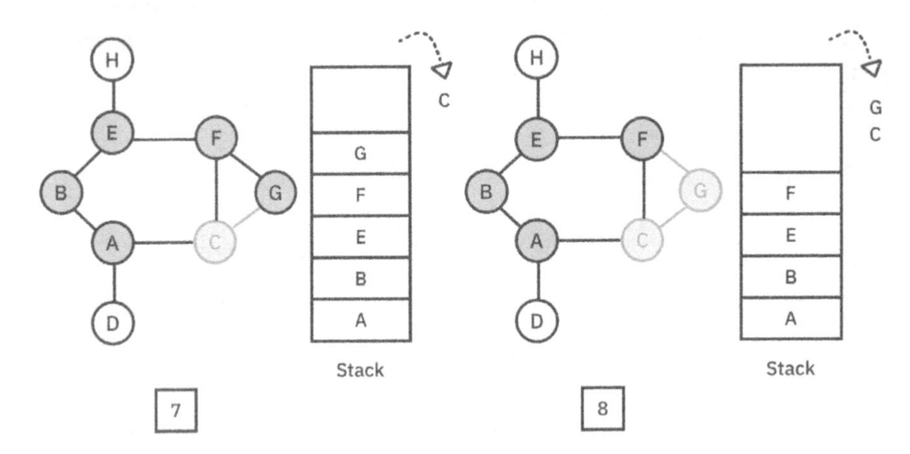

7. The next vertex to visit is `C`. It has neighbors `[A, F, G]`, but all of these have been visited. You have reached a dead end, so it's time to backtrack by popping `C` off the stack.

8. This brings you back to `G`. It has neighbors `[F, C]`, but all of these have been visited. Another dead end, pop `G`.

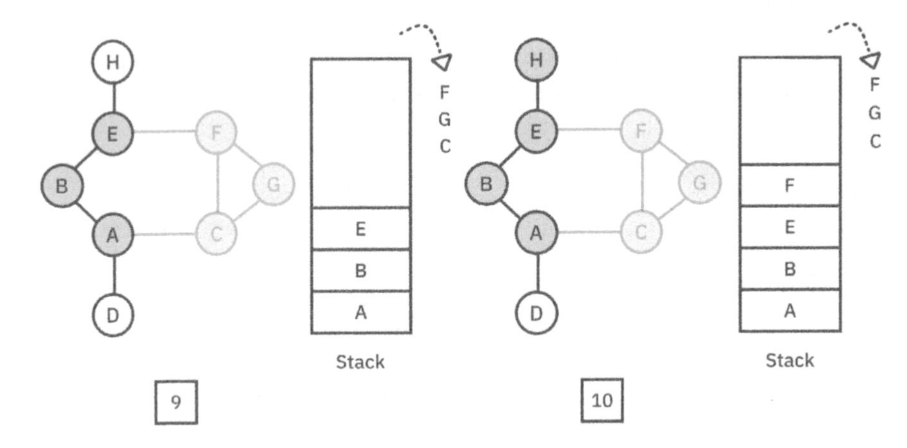

9. `F` also has no unvisited neighbors remaining, so pop `F`.

10. Now, you're back at E. Its neighbor H is still unvisited, so you push H on the stack.

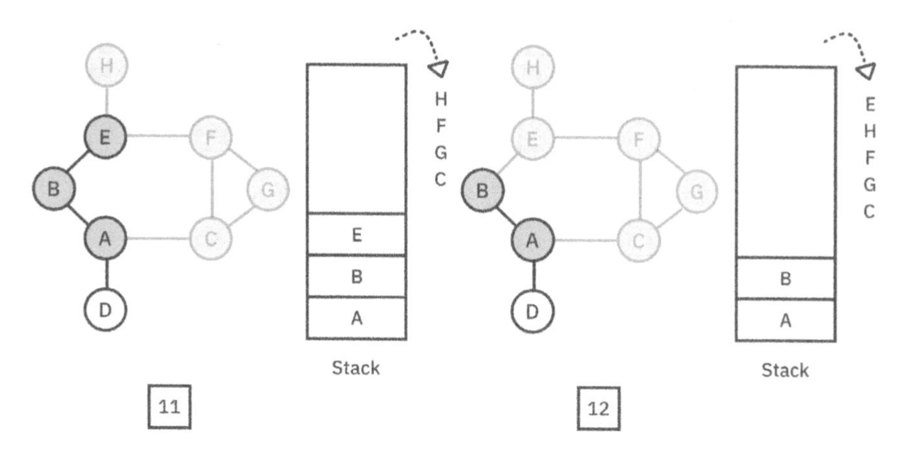

11. Visiting H results in another dead end, so pop H.

12. E also doesn't have any available neighbors, so pop it.

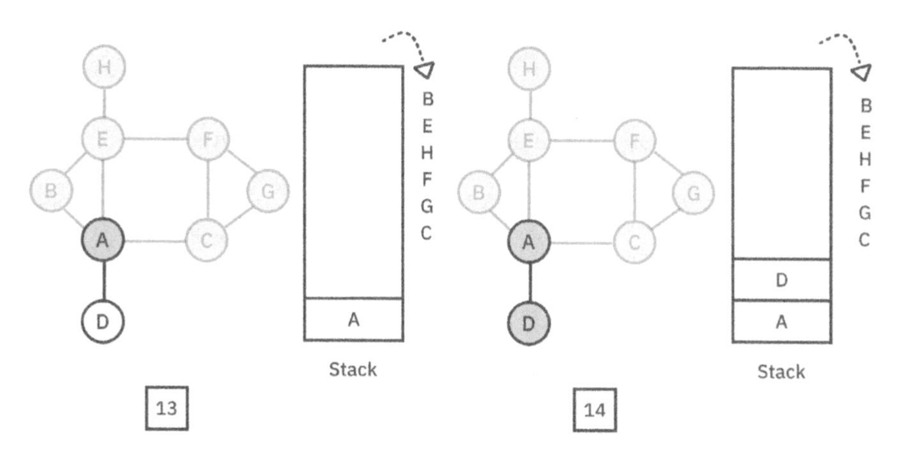

13. The same is true for B, so pop B.

14. This brings you all the way back to `A`, whose neighbor `D` still needs to be visited, so you push `D` on the stack.

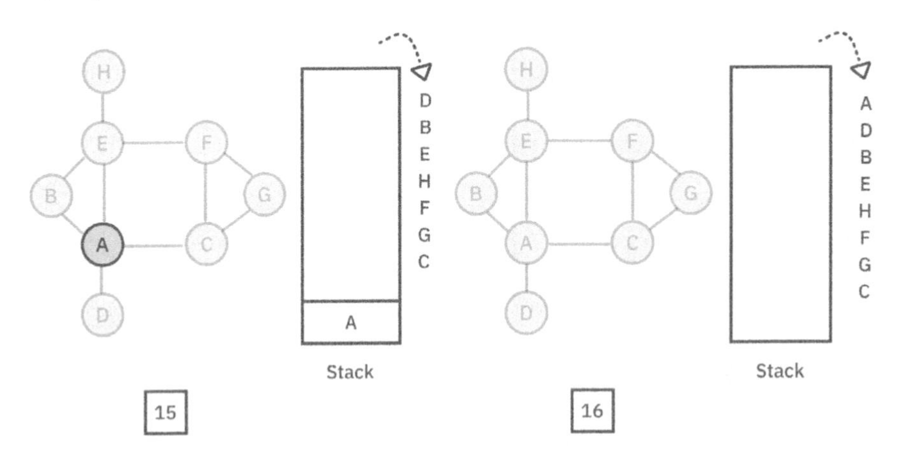

15. Visiting `D` results in another dead end, so pop `D`.

16. You're back at `A`, but this time, there are no available neighbors to push, so you pop `A`. The stack is now empty and the DFS is complete.

When exploring the vertices, you can construct a tree-like structure, showing the branches you've visited. You can see how deep DFS went compared to BFS.

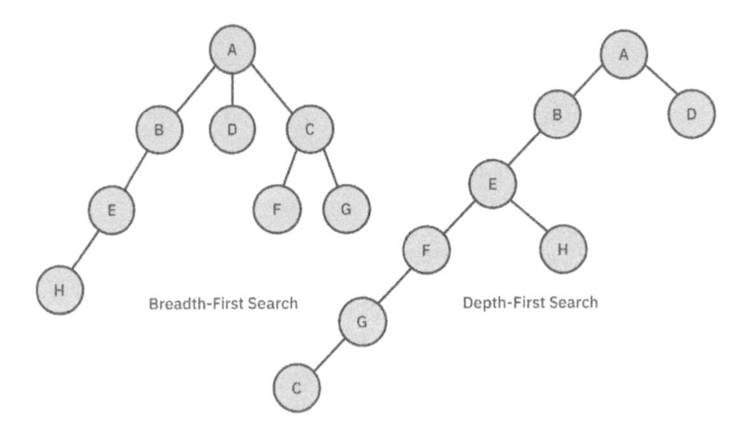

Implementation

Open up the starter playground for this chapter. This playground contains an implementation of a graph, as well as a stack, which you'll use to implement DFS.

In your main playground file, you will notice a pre-built sample graph. Add the following:

```
extension Graph where Element: Hashable {

  func depthFirstSearch(from source: Vertex<Element>)
      -> [Vertex<Element>] {
    var stack: Stack<Vertex<Element>> = []
    var pushed: Set<Vertex<Element>> = []
    var visited: [Vertex<Element>] = []

    stack.push(source)
    pushed.insert(source)
    visited.append(source)

    // more to come ...

    return visited
  }
}
```

Here, you've defined a method `depthFirstSearch(from:)`, which takes in a starting vertex and returns a list of vertices in the order they were visited. It uses three data structures:

1. `stack` is used to store your path through the graph.
2. `pushed` remembers which vertices have been pushed before so that you don't visit the same vertex twice. It is a `Set` to ensure fast $O(1)$ lookup.
3. `visited` is an array that stores the order in which the vertices were visited.

To start the algorithm, you add the `source` vertex to all three.

Next, complete the method by replacing the comment with:

```
outer: while let vertex = stack.peek() { // 1
  let neighbors = edges(from: vertex) // 2
  guard !neighbors.isEmpty else { // 3
    stack.pop()
    continue
  }
  for edge in neighbors { // 4
    if !pushed.contains(edge.destination) {
```

```
      stack.push(edge.destination)
      pushed.insert(edge.destination)
      visited.append(edge.destination)
      continue outer // 5
    }
  }
  stack.pop() // 6
}
```

Here's what's going on:

1. You continue to check the top of the stack for a vertex until the stack is empty. You have labeled this loop `outer` so that you have a way to continue to the next vertex, even within nested loops.
2. You find all the neighboring edges for the current vertex.
3. If there are no edges, you pop the vertex off the stack and continue to the next one.
4. Here, you loop through every edge connected to the current vertex and check if the neighboring vertex has been seen. If not, you push it onto the stack and add it to the `visited` array. It may seem a bit premature to mark this vertex as visited (you haven't peeked at it yet) but, since vertices are visited in the order in which they are added to the stack, it results in the correct order.
5. Now that you've found a neighbor to visit, you continue the `outer` loop and move to the newly pushed neighbor.
6. If the current vertex did not have any unvisited neighbors, you know you've reached a dead end and can pop it off the stack.

Once the stack is empty, the DFS algorithm is complete! All you have to do is return the visited vertices in the order you visited them.

To try out your code, add the following to the playground:

```
let vertices = graph.depthFirstSearch(from: a)
vertices.forEach { vertex in
  print(vertex)
}
```

Notice that the order of the visited nodes using a DFS:

```
0: A
1: B
4: E
5: F
6: G
2: C
7: H
3: D
```

Performance

DFS will visit every single vertex at least once. This process has a time complexity of $O(V)$.

When traversing a graph in DFS, you have to check all neighboring vertices to find one available to visit. The time complexity of this is $O(E)$ because you have to visit every edge in the graph in the worst case.

Overall, the time complexity for depth-first search is $O(V + E)$.

The space complexity of depth-first search is $O(V)$ since you have to store vertices in three separate data structures: `stack`, `pushed` and `visited`.

Key points

- Depth-first search (DFS) is another algorithm to traverse or search a graph.
- DFS explores a branch as far as possible until it reaches the end.
- Leverage a stack data structure to keep track of how deep you are in the graph. Only pop off the stack when you reach a dead end.

Chapter 41: Depth-First Search Challenges

By Vincent Ngo

Challenge 1: BFS or DFS

For each of the following two examples, which traversal (depth-first or breadth-first) is better for discovering if a path exists between the two nodes? Explain why.

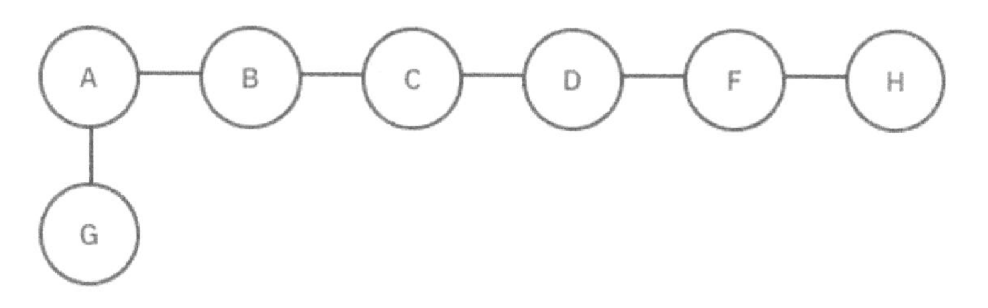

- Path from **A** to **F**.
- Path from **A** to **G**.

Challenge 2: Recursive DFS

In this chapter, you went over an iterative implementation of depth-first search. Now write a recursive implementation.

Challenge 3: Detect a cycle

Add a method to `Graph` to detect if a **directed** graph has a cycle.

Solutions

Solution to Challenge 1

- Path from **A** to **F**: Use depth-first because the path you are looking for is deeper in the graph.
- Path from **A** to **G**: Use breadth-first because the path you are looking for is near the root.

Solution to Challenge 2

In the depth-first search chapter, you learned how to implement the algorithm iteratively. Let's take a look at how you would implement it recursively.

```
extension Graph where Element: Hashable {

  func depthFirstSearch(from start: Vertex<Element>)
                         -> [Vertex<Element>] {
    var visited: [Vertex<Element>] = [] // 1
    var pushed: Set<Vertex<Element>> = [] // 2
    depthFirstSearch(from: start, // 3
                     visited: &visited,
                     pushed: &pushed)
    return visited
  }
}
```

1. `visited` keeps track of the vertices visited in order.
2. `pushed` keeps tracks of which vertices have been visited.
3. Perform depth-first search recursively by calling a helper function.

The helper function looks like this:

```
func depthFirstSearch(from source: Vertex<Element>,
                      visited: inout [Vertex<Element>],
                      pushed: inout Set<Vertex<Element>>) {
  pushed.insert(source) // 1
  visited.append(source)

  let neighbors = edges(from: source)
  for edge in neighbors { // 2
    if !pushed.contains(edge.destination) {
      depthFirstSearch(from: edge.destination, // 3
                       visited: &visited,
                       pushed: &pushed)
    }
  }
}
```

1. Insert the `source` vertex into the queue, and mark it as visited.
2. For every neighboring edge.
3. As long as the adjacent vertex has not been visited yet, continue to dive deeper down the branch recursively.

Overall the time complexity for depth-first search is $O(V + E)$.

Solution to Challenge 3

A graph has a cycle when a path of edges and vertices leads back to the same source.

```
extension Graph where Element: Hashable {

  func hasCycle(from source: Vertex<Element>) -> Bool  {
    var pushed: Set<Vertex<Element>> = [] // 1
    return hasCycle(from: source, pushed: &pushed) // 2
  }
}
```

1. pushed is used to keep track of all the vertices visited.
2. Recursively check to see if there is a cycle in the graph by calling a helper function.

The helper function looks like this:

```
func hasCycle(from source: Vertex<Element>,
              pushed: inout Set<Vertex<Element>>) -> Bool {
  pushed.insert(source) // 1

  let neighbors = edges(from: source) // 2
  for edge in neighbors {
    if !pushed.contains(edge.destination) &&
       hasCycle(from: edge.destination, pushed: &pushed) { // 3
      return true
    } else if pushed.contains(edge.destination) { // 4
      return true
    }
  }
  pushed.remove(source) // 5
  return false // 6
}
```

1. To initiate the algorithm, first insert the source vertex.
2. For every neighboring edge.
3. If the adjacent vertex has not been visited before, recursively dive deeper down a branch to check for a cycle.
4. If the adjacent vertex has been visited before, you have found a cycle.
5. Remove the `source` vertex so you can continue to find other paths with a potential cycle.
6. No cycle has been found.

You are essentially performing a depth-first graph traversal by recursively diving down one path till you find a cycle and back-tracking by popping off the stack to find another path. The time-complexity is $O(V + E)$.

Chapter 42: Dijkstra's Algorithm

By Vincent Ngo

Have you ever used the Google or Apple Maps app to find the shortest distance or fastest time from one place to another? **Dijkstra's algorithm** is particularly useful in GPS networks to help find the shortest path between two places.

Dijkstra's algorithm is a greedy algorithm. A **greedy** algorithm constructs a solution step-by-step, and it picks the most optimal path at every step in isolation. It misses solutions where some steps might cost more, but the overall cost is lower. Nevertheless, it usually arrives at a pretty good solution very quickly.

Dijkstra's algorithm finds the shortest paths between vertices in either directed or undirected graphs. Given a vertex in a graph, the algorithm will find all shortest paths from the starting vertex.

Some other applications of Dijkstra's algorithm include:

1. Communicable disease transmission: Discover where biological diseases are spreading the fastest.
2. Telephone networks: Routing calls to highest-bandwidth paths available in the network.
3. Mapping: Finding the shortest and fastest paths for travelers.

Example

All the graphs you have looked at thus far have been undirected. Let's change it up a little and work with a directed graph! Imagine the directed graph below represents a GPS network:

The vertices represent physical locations, and the edges represent one-way paths of a given cost between locations.

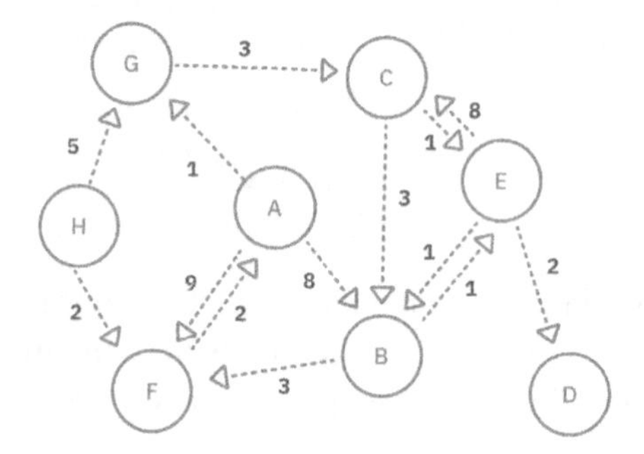

In Dijkstra's algorithm, you first choose a **starting vertex** since the algorithm needs a starting point to find a path to the rest of the nodes in the graph. Assume the starting vertex you pick is **vertex A**.

First pass

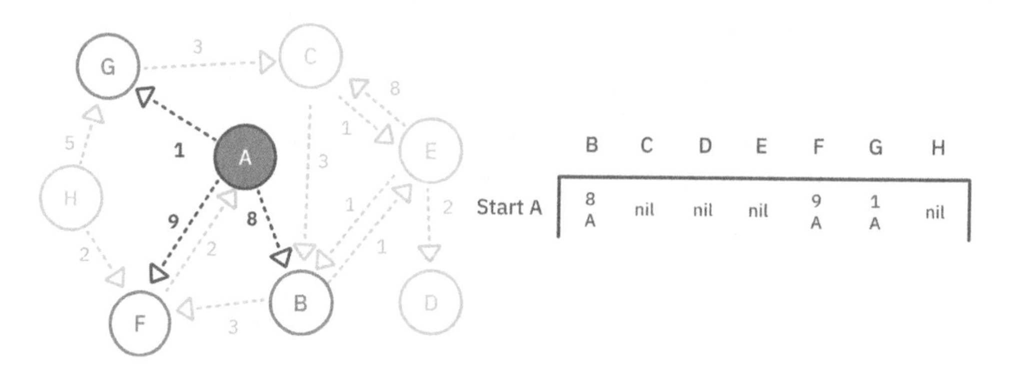

	B	C	D	E	F	G	H
Start A	8 A	nil	nil	nil	9 A	1 A	nil

From **vertex A**, look at all outgoing edges. In this case, you have three edges:

- **A** to **B** has a cost of **8**.
- **A** to **F** has a cost of **9**.
- **A** to **G** has a cost of **1**.

The remainder of the vertices will be marked as `nil` since there is no direct path to them from **A**.

As you work through this example, the table on the right of the graph will represent the history, or record, of Dijkstra's algorithm at each stage. Each pass of the algorithm will add a row to the table. The last row in the table will be the final output of the algorithm.

Second pass

	B	C	D	E	F	G	H
Start A	8 A	nil	nil	nil	9 A	1 A	nil

In the next cycle, Dijkstra's algorithm looks at the **lowest**-cost path you have thus far. **A** to **G** has the smallest cost of **1** and the shortest path to get to **G**. This path is marked with a dark fill in the output table.

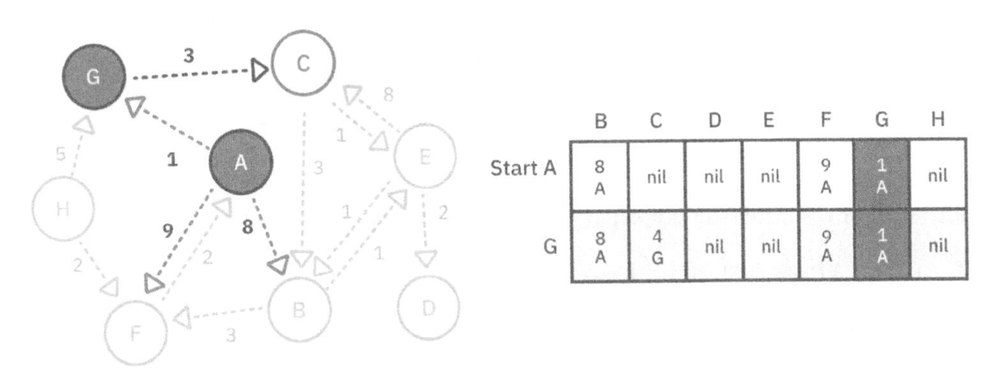

	B	C	D	E	F	G	H
Start A	8 A	nil	nil	nil	9 A	1 A	nil
G	8 A	4 G	nil	nil	9 A	1 A	nil

Now, from the lowest-cost path, **vertex G**, look at all the outgoing edges. There is only one edge from **G** to **C**, and its total cost is **4**. This is because the cost from **A** to **G** to **C** is **1** + **3** = **4**.

Every value in the output table has two parts: the total cost to reach that vertex and the last neighbor on the path to that vertex. For example, the value **4 G** in the column for vertex **C** means that the cost to reach **C** is 4, and the path to **C** goes through **G**. A value of `nil` indicates that no path has been discovered to that vertex.

Third pass

	B	C	D	E	F	G	H
Start A	8 A	nil	nil	nil	9 A	1 A	nil
G	8 A	4 G	nil	nil	9 A	1 A	nil

In the next cycle, you look at the next-lowest cost. According to the table, the path to **C** has the smallest cost, so that the search will continue from **C**. You fill column **C** because you've found the shortest path to get to **C**.

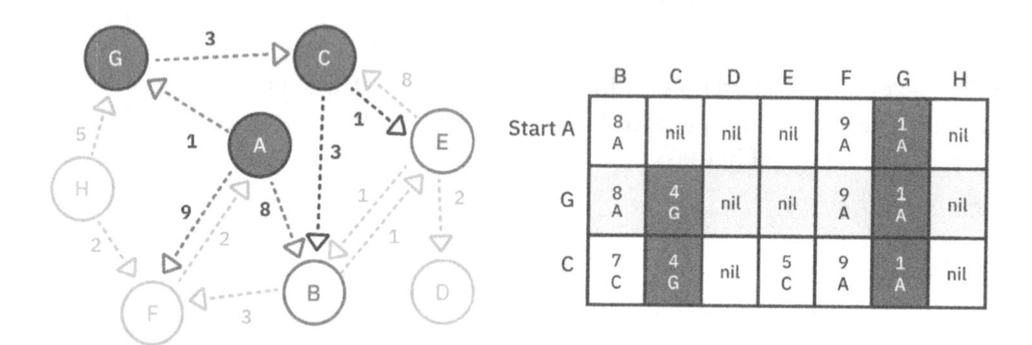

	B	C	D	E	F	G	H
Start A	8 A	nil	nil	nil	9 A	1 A	nil
G	8 A	4 G	nil	nil	9 A	1 A	nil
C	7 C	4 G	nil	5 C	9 A	1 A	nil

Look at all of **C**'s outgoing edges:

- **C** to **E** has a total cost of **4** + **1** = **5**.
- **C** to **B** has a total cost of **4** + **3** = **7**.

You've found a lower-cost path to **B**, so you replace the previous value for **B**.

Fourth pass

	B	C	D	E	F	G	H
Start A	8 A	nil	nil	nil	9 A	1 A	nil
G	8 A	4 G	nil	nil	9 A	1 A	nil
C	7 C	4 G	nil	5 C	9 A	1 A	nil

Now, in the next cycle, ask yourself what the next-lowest cost path is? According to the table, **C** to **E** has the smallest total cost of **5**, so the search will continue from **E**.

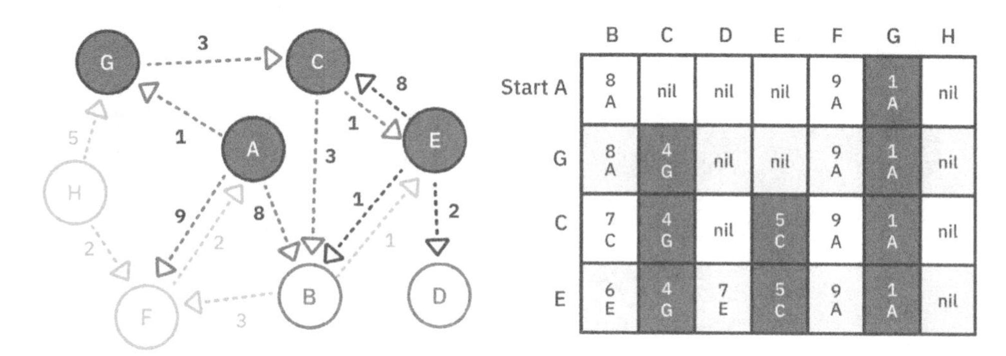

	B	C	D	E	F	G	H
Start A	8 A	nil	nil	nil	9 A	1 A	nil
G	8 A	4 G	nil	nil	9 A	1 A	nil
C	7 C	4 G	nil	5 C	9 A	1 A	nil
E	6 E	4 G	7 E	5 C	9 A	1 A	nil

You fill column **E** because you've found the shortest path. Vertex **E** has the following outgoing edges:

- **E** to **C** has a total cost of **5** + **8** = **13**. Since you have found the shortest path to **C** already, disregard this path.
- **E** to **D** has a total cost of **5** + **2** = **7**.
- **E** to **B** has a total cost of **5** + **1** = **6**. According to the table, the current shortest path to **B** has a total cost of **7**. You update the shortest path from **E** to **B** since it has a smaller cost of **6**.

Fifth pass

	B	C	D	E	F	G	H
Start A	8 A	nil	nil	nil	9 A	1 A	nil
G	8 A	4 G	nil	nil	9 A	1 A	nil
C	7 C	4 G	nil	5 C	9 A	1 A	nil
E	6 E	4 G	7 E	5 C	9 A	1 A	nil

Next, you continue the search from **B**.

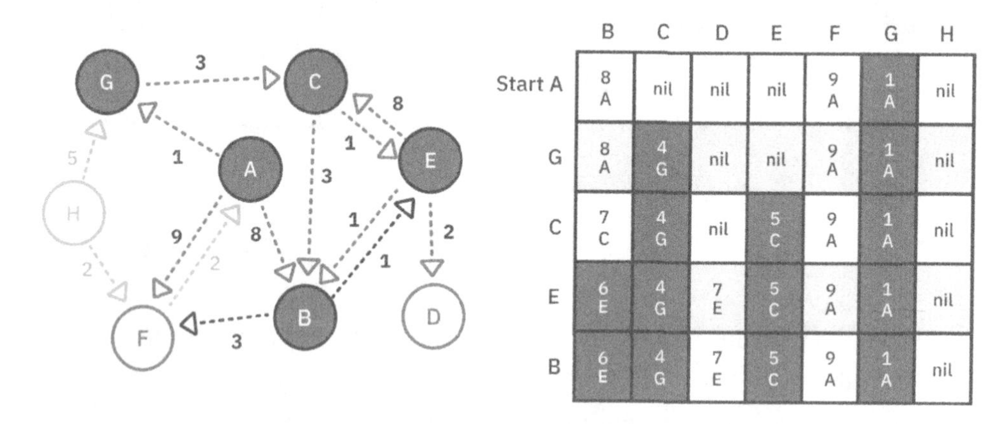

	B	C	D	E	F	G	H
Start A	8 A	nil	nil	nil	9 A	1 A	nil
G	8 A	4 G	nil	nil	9 A	1 A	nil
C	7 C	4 G	nil	5 C	9 A	1 A	nil
E	6 E	4 G	7 E	5 C	9 A	1 A	nil
B	6 E	4 G	7 E	5 C	9 A	1 A	nil

B has these outgoing edges:

- **B** to **E** has a total cost of **6 + 1 = 7**, but you've already found the shortest path to **E**, so disregard this path.
- **B** to **F** has a total cost of **6 + 3 = 9**. From the table, you can tell that the current path to **F** from **A** also costs **9**. You can disregard this path since it isn't any shorter.

Sixth pass

	B	C	D	E	F	G	H
Start A	8 A	nil	nil	nil	9 A	1 A	nil
G	8 A	4 G	nil	nil	9 A	1 A	nil
C	7 C	4 G	nil	5 C	9 A	1 A	nil
E	6 E	4 G	7 E	5 C	9 A	1 A	nil
B	6 E	4 G	7 E	5 C	9 A	1 A	nil

In the next cycle, you continue the search from **D**.

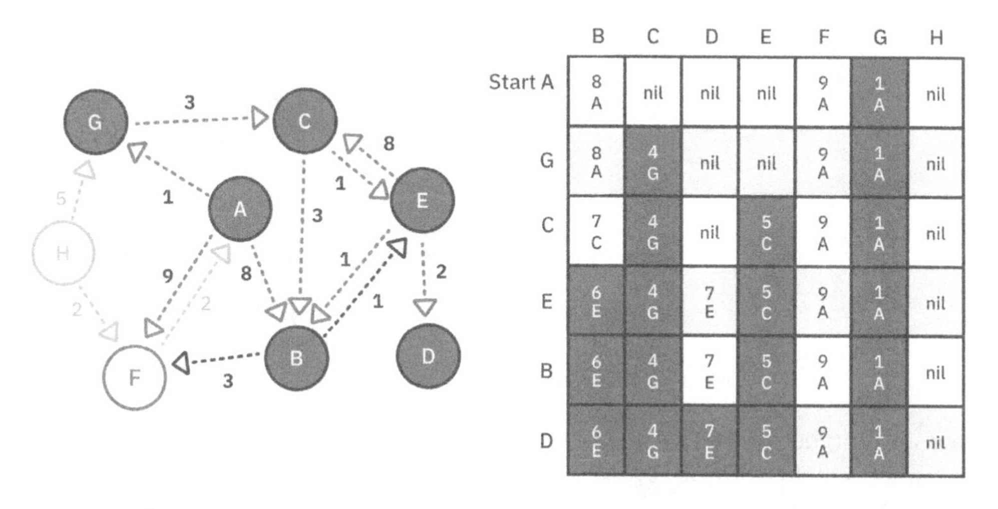

	B	C	D	E	F	G	H
Start A	8 A	nil	nil	nil	9 A	1 A	nil
G	8 A	4 G	nil	nil	9 A	1 A	nil
C	7 C	4 G	nil	5 C	9 A	1 A	nil
E	6 E	4 G	7 E	5 C	9 A	1 A	nil
B	6 E	4 G	7 E	5 C	9 A	1 A	nil
D	6 E	4 G	7 E	5 C	9 A	1 A	nil

However, **D** has no outgoing edges, so it's a dead end. You record that you've found the shortest path to **D** and move on.

Seventh pass

	B	C	D	E	F	G	H
Start A	8 A	nil	nil	nil	9 A	1 A	nil
G	8 A	4 G	nil	nil	9 A	1 A	nil
C	7 C	4 G	nil	5 C	9 A	1 A	nil
E	6 E	4 G	7 E	5 C	9 A	1 A	nil
B	6 E	4 G	7 E	5 C	9 A	1 A	nil
D	6 E	4 G	7 E	5 C	9 A	1 A	nil

F is next up.

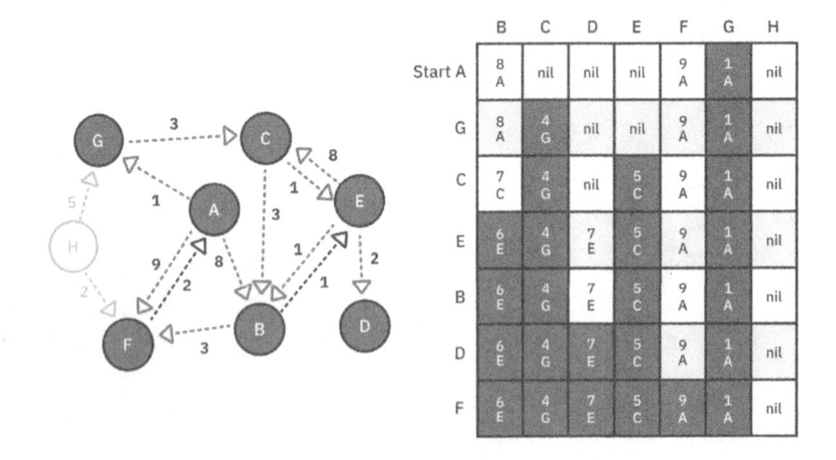

	B	C	D	E	F	G	H
Start A	8 A	nil	nil	nil	9 A	1 A	nil
G	8 A	4 G	nil	nil	9 A	1 A	nil
C	7 C	4 G	nil	5 C	9 A	1 A	nil
E	6 E	4 G	7 E	5 C	9 A	1 A	nil
B	6 E	4 G	7 E	5 C	9 A	1 A	nil
D	6 E	4 G	7 E	5 C	9 A	1 A	nil
F	6 E	4 G	7 E	5 C	9 A	1 A	nil

F has one outgoing edge to **A** with a total cost of **9 + 2 = 11**. You can disregard this edge since **A** is the starting vertex.

Eighth pass

You have covered every vertex except for **H**. **H** has two outgoing edges to **G** and **F**. However, there is no path from **A** to **H**. Because there is no path, the whole column for **H** is `nil`.

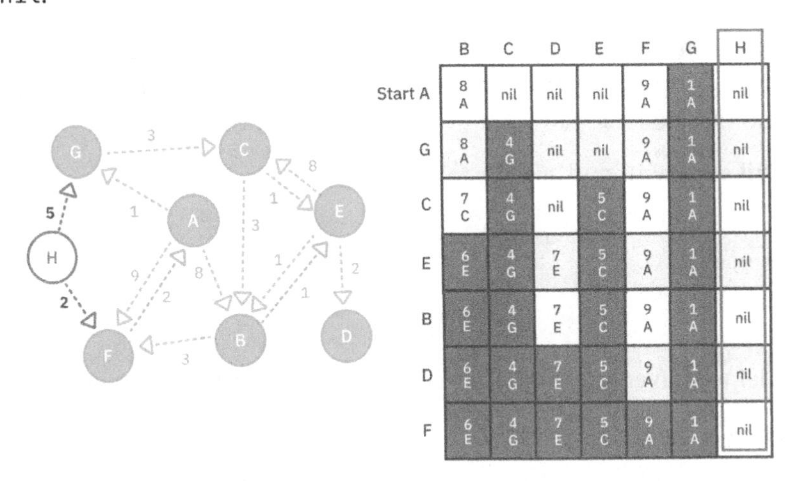

	B	C	D	E	F	G	H
Start A	8 A	nil	nil	nil	9 A	1 A	nil
G	8 A	4 G	nil	nil	9 A	1 A	nil
C	7 C	4 G	nil	5 C	9 A	1 A	nil
E	6 E	4 G	7 E	5 C	9 A	1 A	nil
B	6 E	4 G	7 E	5 C	9 A	1 A	nil
D	6 E	4 G	7 E	5 C	9 A	1 A	nil
F	6 E	4 G	7 E	5 C	9 A	1 A	nil

This step completes Dijkstra's algorithm since all the vertices have been visited!

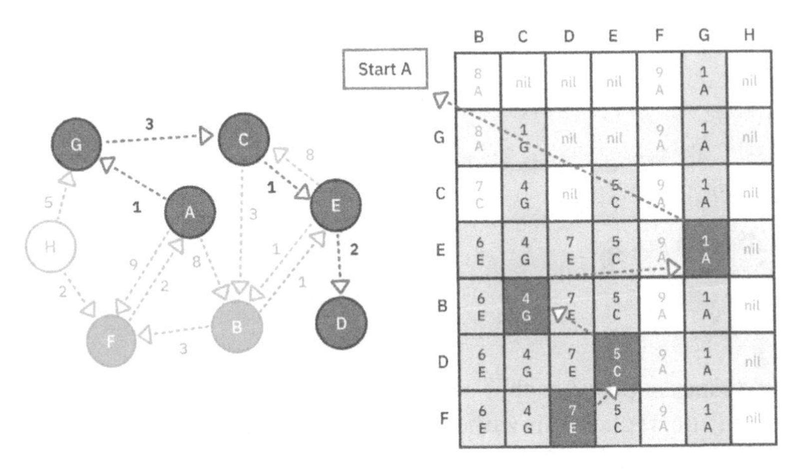

	B	C	D	E	F	G	H
Start A	8 A	nil	nil	nil	9 A	1 A	nil
G	8 A	1 G	nil	nil	9 A	1 A	nil
C	7 C	4 G	nil	5 C	9 A	1 A	nil
E	6 E	4 G	7 E	5 C	9 A	1 A	nil
B	6 E	4 G	7 E	5 C	9 A	1 A	nil
D	6 E	4 G	7 E	5 C	9 A	1 A	nil
F	6 E	4 G	7 E	5 C	9 A	1 A	nil

You can now check the final row for the shortest paths and their costs. For example, the output tells you the cost to get to **D** is **7**. To find the path, you backtrack. Each column records the previous vertex the current vertex is connected to. You should get from **D** to **E** to **C** to **G** and finally back to **A**. Let's look at how you can build this in code.

Implementation

Open up the starter playground for this chapter. This playground comes with an adjacency list graph and a priority queue, which you will use to implement Dijkstra's algorithm.

The priority queue is used to store vertices that have not been visited. It's a min-priority queue so that every time you dequeue a vertex, it gives you vertex with the current tentative shortest path.

Open up **Dijkstra.swift** and add the following:

```
public enum Visit<T: Hashable> {
  case start // 1
  case edge(Edge<T>) // 2
}
```

Here, you defined an enum named `Visit`. This type keeps track of two states:

1. The vertex is the starting vertex.
2. The vertex has an associated `edge` that leads to a path back to the starting vertex.

Now, define a class called `Dijkstra`. Add the following after the code you added above:

```
public class Dijkstra<T: Hashable> {

  public typealias Graph = AdjacencyList<T>
  let graph: Graph

  public init(graph: Graph) {
    self.graph = graph
  }
}
```

As in the previous chapter, `Graph` is defined as a type alias for `AdjacencyList`. You could, in the future, replace this with an adjacency matrix if needed.

Helper methods

Before building `Dijkstra`, let's create some helper methods that will help create the algorithm.

Tracing back to the start

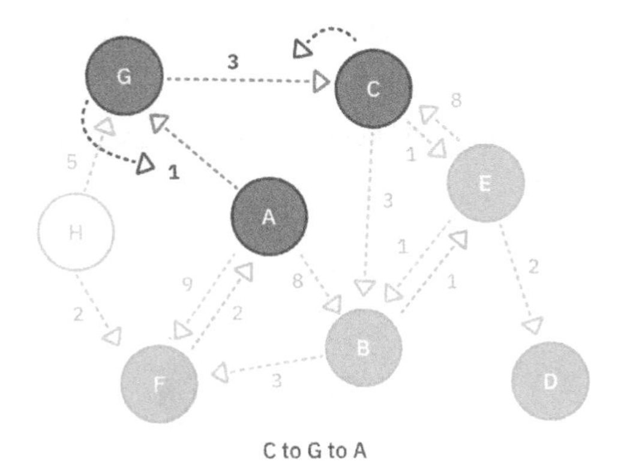

C to G to A

You need a mechanism to track the total weight from the current vertex back to the start vertex. To do this, you will keep track of a dictionary named `paths` that stores a `Visit` state for every vertex.

Add the following method to class `Dijkstra`:

```
private func route(to destination: Vertex<T>,
                   with paths: [Vertex<T> : Visit<T>]) ->
[Edge<T>] {
  var vertex = destination // 1
  var path: [Edge<T>] = [] // 2

  while let visit = paths[vertex], case .edge(let edge) = visit
{ // 3
    path = [edge] + path // 4
    vertex = edge.source // 5
  }
  return path // 6
}
```

This method takes in the `destination` vertex along with a dictionary of existing `paths`, and it constructs a path that leads to the `destination` vertex. Going over the code:

1. Start at the `destination` vertex.

2. Create an array of edges to store the path.

3. As long as you have not reached the `start` case, continue to extract the next edge.

4. Add this edge to the path.

5. Set the current vertex to the edge's `source` vertex. This assignment moves you closer to the start vertex.

6. Once the `while` loop reaches the `start` case, you have completed the path and return it.

Calculating total distance

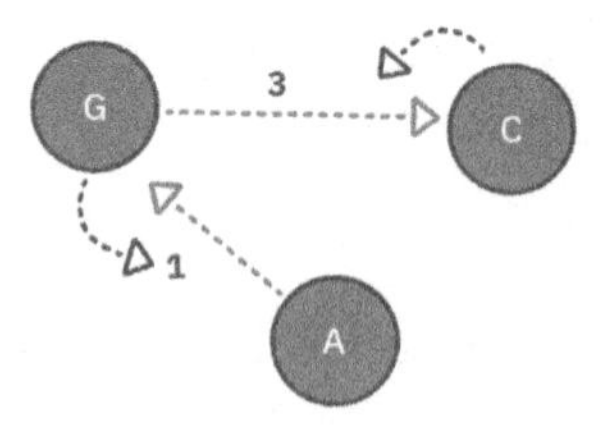

Total distance = 4

Once you have the ability to construct a path from the **destination** back to the **start** vertex, you need a way to calculate the total weight for that path. Add the following method to class `Dijkstra`:

```
private func distance(to destination: Vertex<T>,
                      with paths: [Vertex<T> : Visit<T>]) ->
Double {
  let path = route(to: destination, with: paths) // 1
  let distances = path.compactMap { $0.weight } // 2
  return distances.reduce(0.0, +) // 3
}
```

This method takes in the `destination` vertex and a dictionary of existing `paths` and returns the total weight. Going over the code:

1. Construct the path to the `destination` vertex.

2. `compactMap` removes all the `nil` weights values from the `paths`.

3. `reduce` sums the weights of all the edges.

Now that you have established the helper methods, you can implement Dijkstra's algorithm.

Generating the shortest paths

After the `distance` method, add the following:

```
public func shortestPath(from start: Vertex<T>) -> [Vertex<T> :
Visit<T>] {
  var paths: [Vertex<T> : Visit<T>] = [start: .start] // 1

  // 2
  var priorityQueue = PriorityQueue<Vertex<T>>(sort: {
    self.distance(to: $0, with: paths) <
    self.distance(to: $1, with: paths)
  })
  priorityQueue.enqueue(start) // 3

  // to be continued
}
```

This method takes in a `start` vertex and returns a dictionary of all the paths. Within the method you:

1. Define `paths` and initialize it with the `start` vertex.
2. Create a min-priority queue to store the vertices that must be visited. The `sort` closure uses the `distance` method you created to sort the vertices by their distance from the `start` vertex.
3. Enqueue the `start` vertex as the first vertex to visit.

Complete your implementation of `shortestPath` with:

```
while let vertex = priorityQueue.dequeue() { // 1
  for edge in graph.edges(from: vertex) { // 2
    guard let weight = edge.weight else { // 3
      continue
    }
    if paths[edge.destination] == nil ||
       distance(to: vertex, with: paths) + weight <
       distance(to: edge.destination, with: paths) { // 4
      paths[edge.destination] = .edge(edge)
      priorityQueue.enqueue(edge.destination)
    }
  }
}

return paths
```

Going over the code:

1. You continue Dijkstra's algorithm to find the shortest paths until all the vertices have been visited. You know you are complete when the priority queue is empty.
2. For the current `vertex`, you go through all its neighboring edges.
3. You make sure the edge has a weight. If not, you move on to the next edge.
4. If the `destination` vertex has not been visited before or you've found a cheaper path, you update the path and add the neighboring vertex to the priority queue.

Once all the vertices have been visited, and the priority queue is empty, you return the dictionary of shortest paths to the start vertex.

Finding a specific path

Add the following method to class `Dijkstra`:

```
public func shortestPath(to destination: Vertex<T>,
                         paths: [Vertex<T> : Visit<T>]) ->
[Edge<T>] {
  return route(to: destination, with: paths)
}
```

This method takes the `destination` vertex and the dictionary of shortest paths and returns the path to the `destination` vertex.

Trying out your code

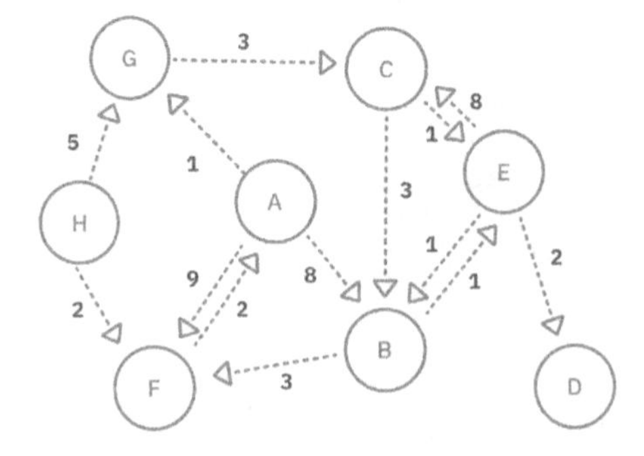

Navigate to the main playground, and you will notice the graph above has been already constructed using an adjacency list—time to see Dijkstra's algorithm in action.

Add the following code to the playground page:

```
let dijkstra = Dijkstra(graph: graph)
let pathsFromA = dijkstra.shortestPath(from: a) // 1
let path = dijkstra.shortestPath(to: d, paths: pathsFromA) // 2
for edge in path { // 3
  print("\(edge.source) --|\(edge.weight ?? 0.0)|--> \
(edge.destination)")
}
```

Here, you create an instance of `Dijkstra` by passing in the graph network and do the following:

1. Calculate the shortest paths to all the vertices from the start vertex **A**.
2. Get the shortest path to **D**.
3. Print this path.

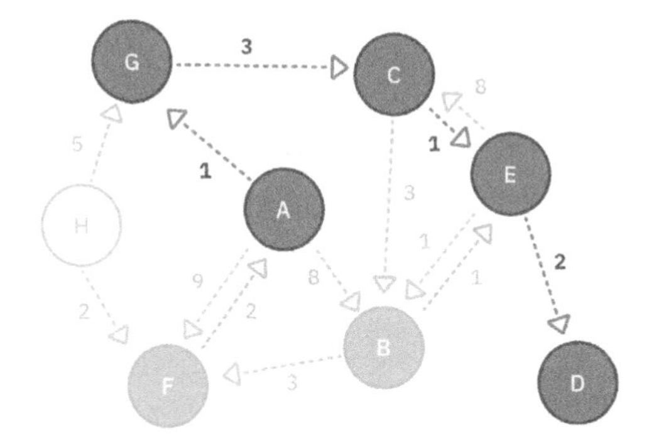

This outputs:

```
A --|1.0|--> G
G --|3.0|--> C
C --|1.0|--> E
E --|2.0|--> D
```

Performance

In Dijkstra's algorithm, you constructed your graph using an adjacency list. You used a min-priority queue to store vertices and extract the vertex with the minimum path. This process has an overall time complexity of $O(\log V)$. The heap operations of extracting the minimum element or inserting an element both take $O(\log V)$ respectively.

If you recall from the breadth-first search chapter, it takes $O(V + E)$ to traverse all the vertices and edges. Dijkstra's algorithm is somewhat similar to breadth-first search because you have to explore all neighboring edges. This time, instead of going down to the next level, you use a min-priority queue to select a single vertex with the shortest distance to traverse down. That means it is $O(1 + E)$ or simply $O(E)$. So, combining the traversal with operations on the min-priority queue, it takes $O(E \log V)$ to perform Dijkstra's algorithm.

Key points

- Dijkstra's algorithm finds a path to the rest of the nodes given a starting vertex.
- This algorithm is useful for finding the shortest paths between different endpoints.
- `Visit` state is used to track the edges back to the start vertex.
- The priority queue data structure ensures returning the vertex with the shortest path.
- Because it chooses the shortest path at each step, it is said to be greedy!

Chapter 43: Dijkstra's Algorithm Challenges

By Vincent Ngo

Challenge 1: Step-by-step diagram

Given the following graph, step through Dijkstra's algorithm to produce the shortest path to every other vertex starting from **vertex A**. Provide the final table of the paths as shown in the previous chapter.

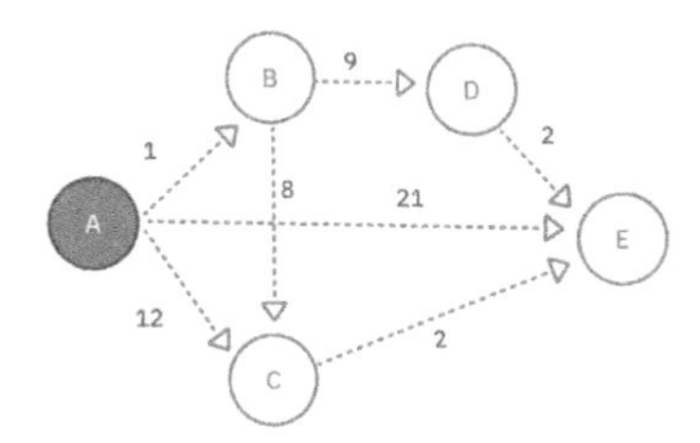

Challenge 2: Find all the shortest paths

Add a method to class `Dijkstra` that returns a dictionary of all the shortest paths to all vertices given a starting vertex. Here's the method signature to get you started:

```
public func getAllShortestPath(from source: Vertex<T>)
                              -> [Vertex<T> : [Edge<T>]] {
    var pathsDict = [Vertex<T> : [Edge<T>]]()

    // Implement Solution Here

    return pathsDict
}
```

Solutions

Solution to Challenge 1

	B	C	D	E
Start A	1 A	12 A	nil	21 A
B	1 A	9 B	10 B	21 A
C	1 A	9 B	10 B	11 C
D	1 A	9 B	10 B	11 C
E	1 A	9 B	10 B	11 C

- Path to B: **A** - (1) - **B**
- Path to C: **A** - (1) - **B** - (8) - **C**
- Path to D: **A** - (1) - **B** - (9) - **D**
- Path to E: **A** - (1) - **B** - (8) - **C** - (2) - **E**

Solution to Challenge 2

This function is part of **Dijkstra.swift**. To get the shortest paths from the `source` vertex to every other vertex in the graph, do the following:

```
public func getAllShortestPath(from source: Vertex<T>)
                              -> [Vertex<T> : [Edge<T>]] {
  var pathsDict = [Vertex<T> : [Edge<T>]]() // 1
  let pathsFromSource = shortestPath(from: source) // 2
  for vertex in graph.vertices { // 3
    let path = shortestPath(to: vertex, paths: pathsFromSource)
    pathsDict[vertex] = path
  }
  return pathsDict // 4
}
```

1. The dictionary stores the path to every vertex from the `source` vertex.
2. Perform Dijkstra's algorithm to find all the paths from the `source` vertex.
3. For every vertex in the graph, generate the list of edges between the `source` vertex to every vertex in the graph.
4. Return the dictionary of paths.

Chapter 44: Prim's Algorithm

By Vincent Ngo

In previous chapters, you've looked at depth-first and breadth-first search algorithms. These algorithms form **spanning trees**.

A **spanning-tree** is a subgraph of an undirected graph, containing all of the graph's vertices, connected with the fewest number of edges. A spanning tree cannot contain a cycle and cannot be disconnected.

Here's a graph G and all its possible spanning trees:

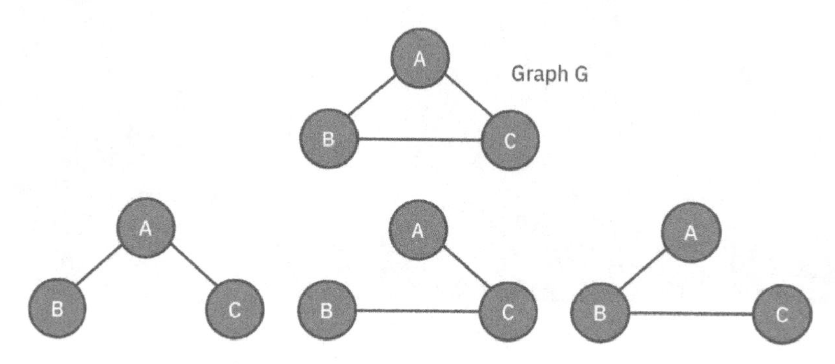

Spanning Trees, subgraph of G

From this undirected graph that forms a triangle, you can generate three different spanning trees in which you require only two edges to connect all vertices.

This chapter will look at **Prim's algorithm**, a greedy algorithm used to construct a **minimum spanning tree**. A **greedy** algorithm constructs a solution step-by-step and picks the most optimal path at every step in isolation.

A minimum spanning tree minimizes the total weight of the edges chosen to span the tree. It is helpful in a variety of situations. For example, you might want to find the cheapest way to layout a network of water pipes.

Here's an example of a minimum spanning tree for a weighted undirected graph:

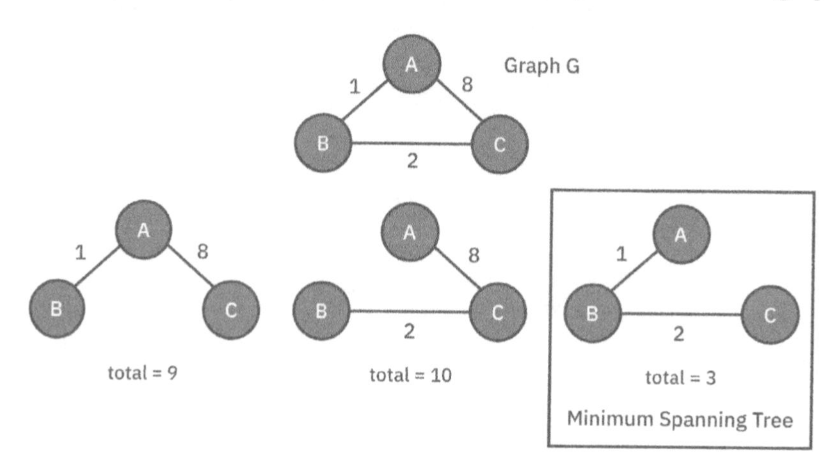

Notice that only the third subgraph forms a minimum spanning tree since its total cost is 3.

Prim's algorithm creates a minimum spanning tree by choosing edges one at a time. It's greedy because every time you pick an edge, you pick the smallest weighted edge that connects a pair of vertices.

There are six steps to finding a minimum spanning tree with Prim's algorithm:

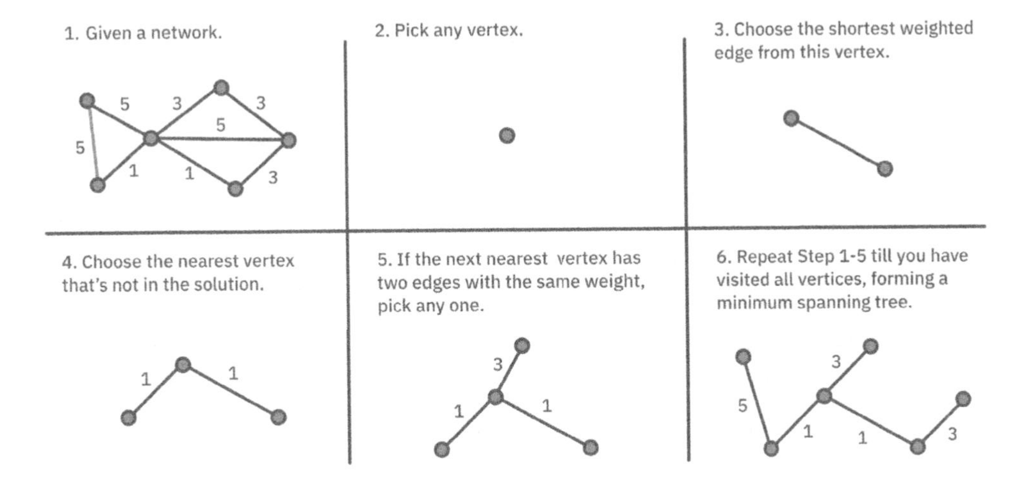

Example

Imagine the graph below represents a network of airports. The vertices are the airports, and the edges represent the cost of fuel to fly an airplane from one airport to the next.

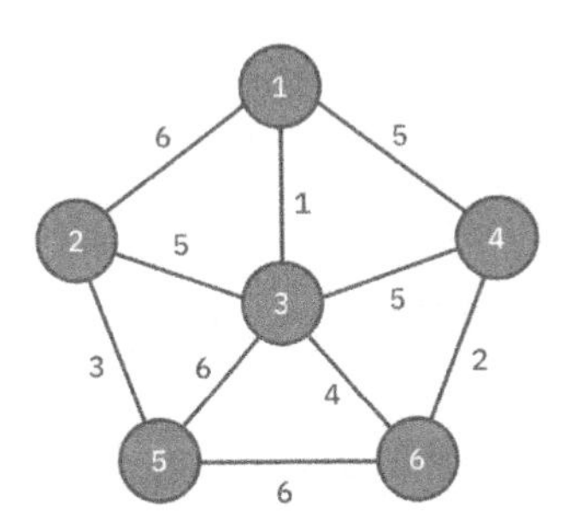

Let's start working through the example:

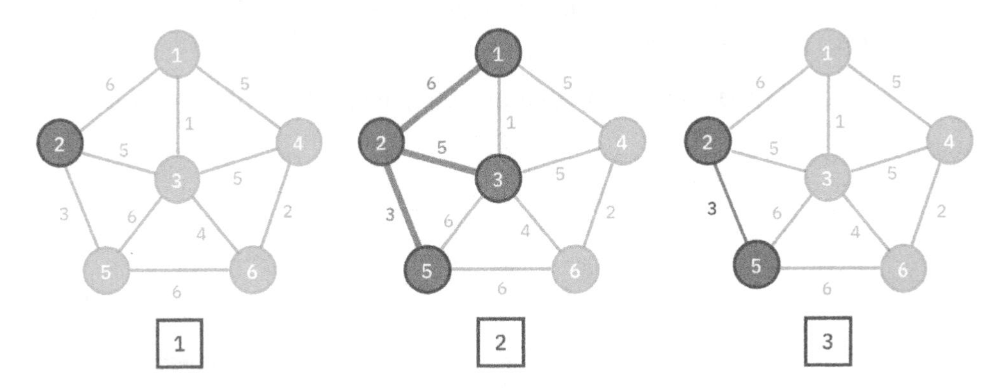

1. Choose any vertex in the graph. Let's assume you chose **vertex 2**.
2. This vertex has edges with weights **[6, 5, 3]**. A greedy algorithm chooses the smallest-weighted edge.
3. Choose the edge that has a weight of **3** and is connected to **vertex 5**.

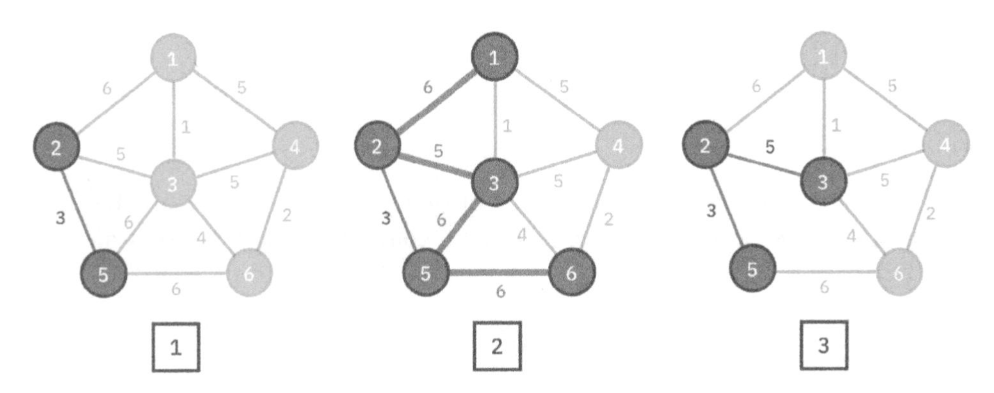

1. The explored vertices are **{2, 5}**.
2. Choose the next shortest edge from the explored vertices. The edges are **[6, 5, 6, 6]**. You choose the edge with weight **5**, which is connected to **vertex 3**.
3. Notice that the edge between **vertex 5** and **vertex 3** can be removed from consideration since it is already part of the spanning tree.

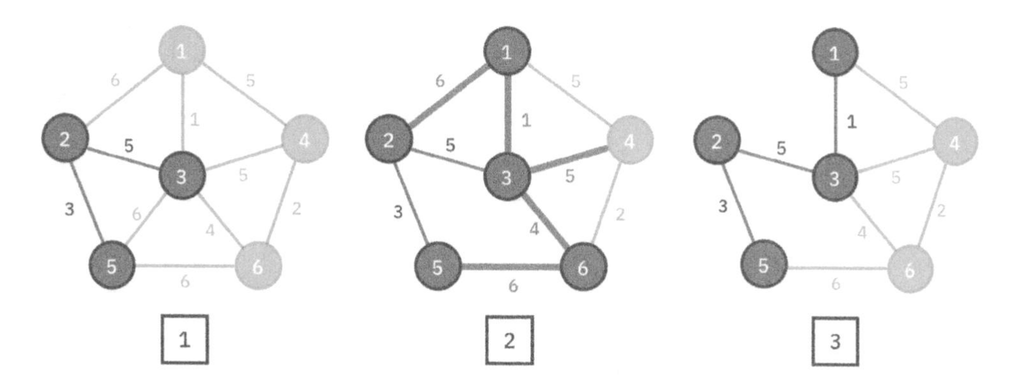

1. The explored vertices are **{2, 3, 5}**.
2. The next potential edges are **[6, 1, 5, 4, 6]**. You choose the edge with weight **1**, which is connected to **vertex 1**.
3. The edge between **vertex 2** and **vertex 1** can be removed.

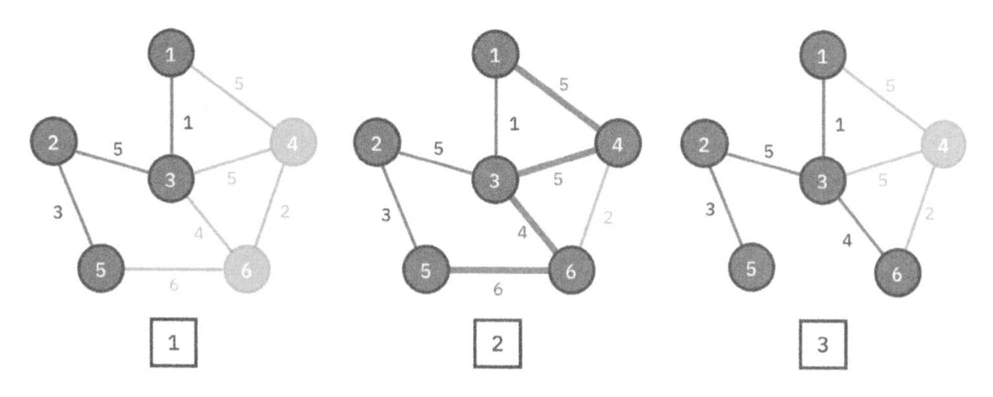

1. The explored vertices are **{2, 3, 5, 1}**.
2. Choose the next shortest edge from the explored vertices. The edges are **[5, 5, 4, 6]**. You choose the edge with weight **4**, which is connected to **vertex 6**.
3. The edge between **vertex 5** and **vertex 6** can be removed.

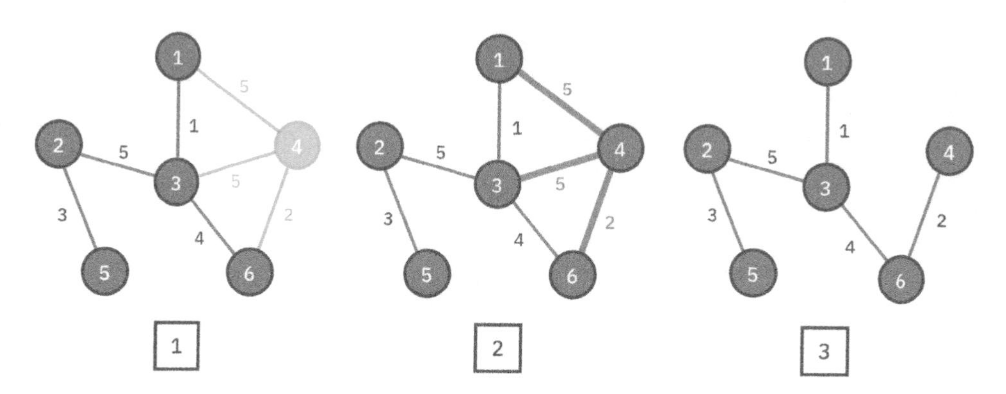

1. The explored vertices are **{2, 5, 3, 1, 6}**.
2. Choose the next shortest edge from the explored vertices. The edges are **[5, 5, 2]**. You choose the edge with weight **2**, which is connected to **vertex 4**.
3. The edges **[5, 5]** connected to **vertex 4** from **vertex 1** and **vertex 3** can be removed.

> **Note**: If all edges have the same weight, you can pick any one of them.

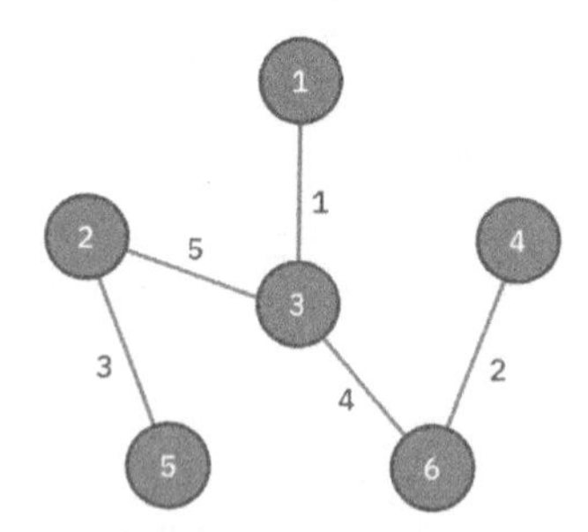

This final diagram is the minimum spanning tree from our example produced by Prim's algorithm.

Next, let's see how to build this in code.

Implementation

Open up the starter playground for this chapter. This playground comes with an adjacency list graph and a priority queue, which you will use to implement Prim's algorithm.

The priority queue is used to store the edges of the explored vertices. It's a min-priority queue so that every time you dequeue an edge, it gives you the edge with the smallest weight.

Start by defining a class `Prim`. Open up **Prim.swift** and add the following:

```
public class Prim<T: Hashable> {

  public typealias Graph = AdjacencyList<T>
  public init() {}
}
```

`Graph` is defined as a type alias for `AdjacencyList`. In the future, you could replace this with an adjacency matrix if needed.

Helper methods

Before building the algorithm, you'll create some helper methods to keep you organized and consolidate duplicate code.

Copying a graph

To create a minimum spanning tree, you must include all vertices from the original graph. Open up **AdjacencyList.swift** and add the following to class `AdjacencyList`:

```
public func copyVertices(from graph: AdjacencyList) {
  for vertex in graph.vertices {
    adjacencies[vertex] = []
  }
}
```

This copies all of a graph's vertices into a new graph.

Finding edges

Besides copying the graph's vertices, you also need to find and store the edges of every vertex you explore. Open up **Prim.swift** and add the following to class `Prim`:

```
internal func addAvailableEdges(
    for vertex: Vertex<T>,
    in graph: Graph,
    check visited: Set<Vertex<T>>,
    to priorityQueue: inout PriorityQueue<Edge<T>>) {
  for edge in graph.edges(from: vertex) { // 1
    if !visited.contains(edge.destination) { // 2
      priorityQueue.enqueue(edge) // 3
    }
  }
}
```

This method takes in four parameters:

1. The current `vertex`.
2. The `graph`, wherein the current `vertex` is stored.
3. The vertices that have already been visited.
4. The priority queue to add all potential edges.

Within the function, you do the following:

1. Look at every edge adjacent to the current `vertex`.
2. Check to see if the `destination` vertex has already been visited.
3. If it has not been visited, you add the edge to the priority queue.

Now that you've established the helper methods, you can implement Prim's algorithm.

Producing a minimum spanning tree

Add the following method to class `Prim`:

```
public func produceMinimumSpanningTree(for graph: Graph)
    -> (cost: Double, mst: Graph) { // 1
  var cost = 0.0 // 2
  let mst = Graph() // 3
  var visited: Set<Vertex<T>> = [] // 4
  var priorityQueue = PriorityQueue<Edge<T>>(sort: { // 5
    $0.weight ?? 0.0 < $1.weight ?? 0.0
```

```
  })
  // to be continued
}
```

Here's what you have so far:

1. `produceMinimumSpanningTree` takes an undirected graph and returns a minimum spanning tree and its cost.
2. `cost` keeps track of the total weight of the edges in the minimum spanning tree.
3. This is a graph that will become your minimum spanning tree.
4. `visited` stores all vertices that have already been visited.
5. This is a min-priority queue to store edges.

Next, continue implementing `produceMinimumSpanningTree` with the following:

```
mst.copyVertices(from: graph) // 1

guard let start = graph.vertices.first else { // 2
  return (cost: cost, mst: mst)
}

visited.insert(start) // 3
addAvailableEdges(for: start, // 4
                  in: graph,
               check: visited,
                  to: &priorityQueue)

// to be continued
```

This code initiates the algorithm:

1. Copy all the vertices from the original graph to the minimum spanning tree.
2. Get the starting vertex from the graph.
3. Mark the starting vertex as visited.
4. Add all potential edges from the `start` vertex into the priority queue.

Finally, complete `produceMinimumSpanningTree` with:

```
while let smallestEdge = priorityQueue.dequeue() { // 1
  let vertex = smallestEdge.destination // 2
  guard !visited.contains(vertex) else { // 3
    continue
  }
```

```
    visited.insert(vertex) // 4
    cost += smallestEdge.weight ?? 0.0 // 5

    mst.add(.undirected, // 6
            from: smallestEdge.source,
            to: smallestEdge.destination,
            weight: smallestEdge.weight)

    addAvailableEdges(for: vertex, // 7
                      in: graph,
                      check: visited,
                      to: &priorityQueue)
  }

  return (cost: cost, mst: mst) // 8
```

Going over the code:

1. Continue Prim's algorithm until the queue of edges is empty.
2. Get the `destination` vertex.
3. If this vertex has been visited, restart the loop and get the next smallest edge.
4. Mark the `destination` vertex as visited.
5. Add the edge's `weight` to the total `cost`.
6. Add the smallest edge into the minimum spanning tree you are constructing.
7. Add the available edges from the current vertex.
8. Once the `priorityQueue` is empty, return the minimum cost and minimum spanning tree.

Testing your code

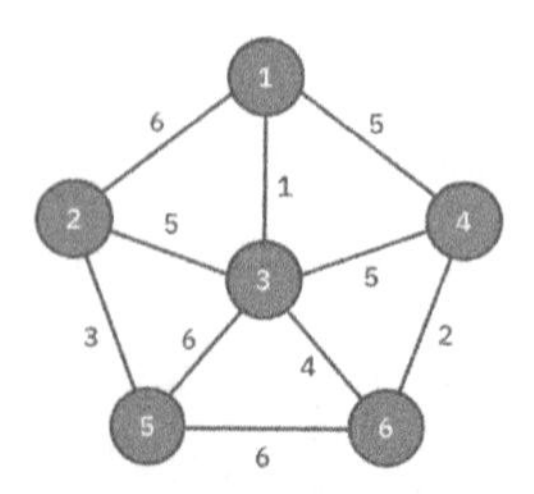

Navigate to the main playground, and you'll see the graph above has been already constructed using an adjacency list.

It's time to see Prim's algorithm in action. Add the following code:

```
let (cost,mst) = Prim().produceMinimumSpanningTree(for: graph)
print("cost: \(cost)")
print("mst:")
print(mst)
```

This code constructs a graph from the example section. You'll see the following output:

```
cost: 15.0
mst:
5 ---> [ 2 ]
6 ---> [ 3, 4 ]
3 ---> [ 2, 1, 6 ]
1 ---> [ 3 ]
2 ---> [ 5, 3 ]
4 ---> [ 6 ]
```

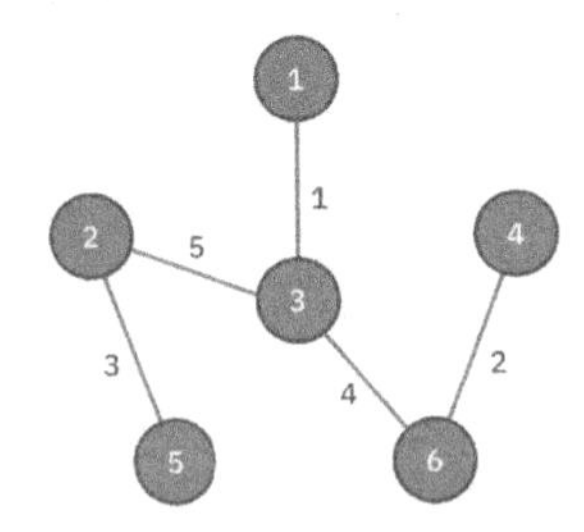

Performance

In the algorithm above, you maintain three data structures:

1. An adjacency list graph to build a minimum spanning tree. Adding vertices and edges to an adjacency list is $O(1)$.
2. A `Set` to store all vertices you have visited. Adding a vertex to the set and checking if the set contains a vertex also have a time complexity of $O(1)$.
3. A min-priority queue to store edges as you explore more vertices. The priority queue is built on a heap, and insertion takes $O(\log E)$.

The worst-case time complexity of Prim's algorithm is $O(E \log E)$. Each time you dequeue the smallest edge from the priority queue, you have to traverse all the edges of the `destination` vertex ($O(E)$) and insert the edge into the priority queue ($O(\log E)$).

Key points

- A spanning tree is a subgraph of an undirected graph containing all the vertices with the fewest edges.
- Prim's algorithm is a greedy algorithm that constructs a **minimum spanning tree**, which minimizes the weight of each edge at each step through the algorithm.
- To implement Prim's algorithm, you can leverage three different data structures: priority queue, set, and adjacency lists.

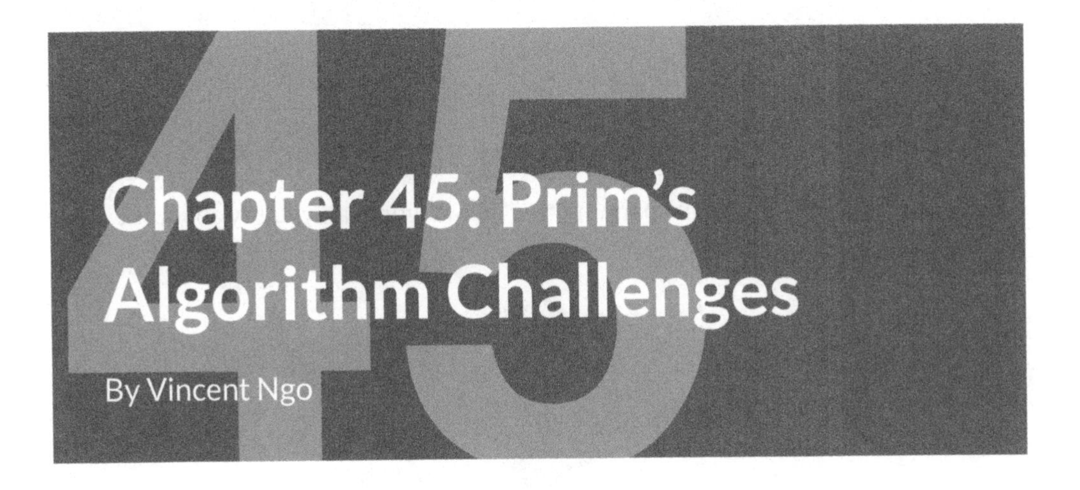

Chapter 45: Prim's Algorithm Challenges

By Vincent Ngo

Challenge 1: Minimum spanning tree of points

Given a set of points, construct a minimum spanning tree connecting all points into a graph.

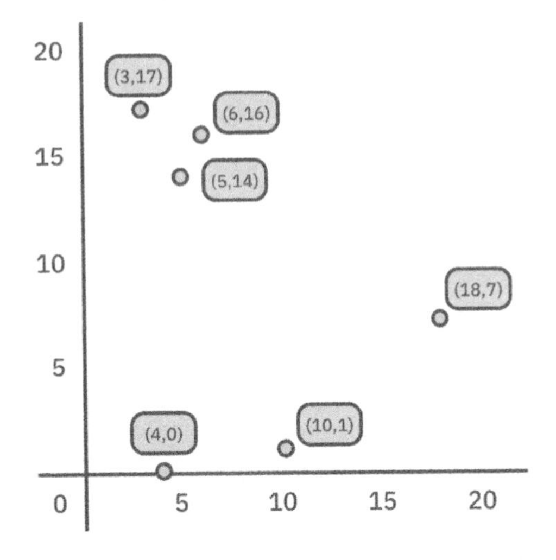


```
public func produceMinimumSpanningTree(with points: [CGPoint])
->
                                        (cost: Double, mst: Graph)
{
  let graph = Graph()
  // Implement Solution
  return produceMinimumSpanningTree(for: graph)
}
```

Challenge 2: What can you say about X?

Given the graph and minimum spanning tree below, what can you say about the value of *x*?

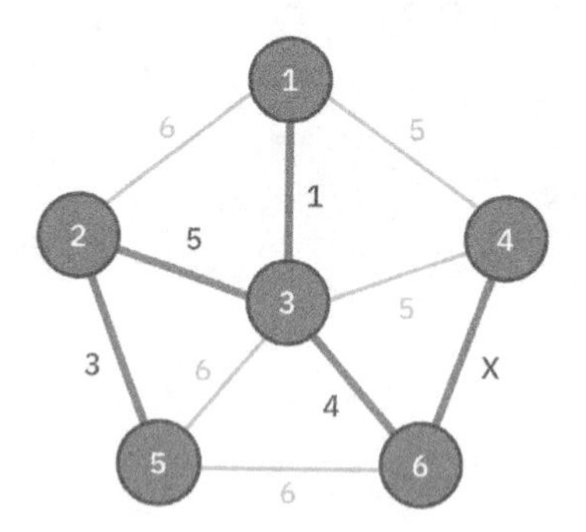

Challenge 3: Step-by-step Diagram

Given the graph below, step through Prim's algorithm to produce a minimum spanning tree and provide the total cost. Start at vertex **B**. If two edges share the same weight, prioritize them alphabetically.

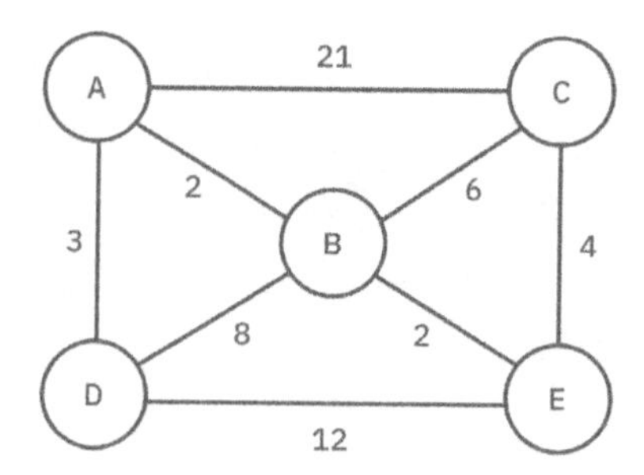

Solutions

Solution to Challenge 1

You can think of the points as vertices on a graph. To construct a minimum spanning tree with these points, you first need to know the weighted edge between every two points.

A `Vertex` requires its elements to be `Hashable`. The starter project provides an extension to `CGPoint`:

```
extension CGPoint: Hashable {
  public func hash(into hasher: inout Hasher) {
    hasher.combine(x)
    hasher.combine(y)
  }
}
```

Every vertex has an associated `CGPoint`. To form an edge to another vertex (`CGPoint`), you need to calculate the distance between points:

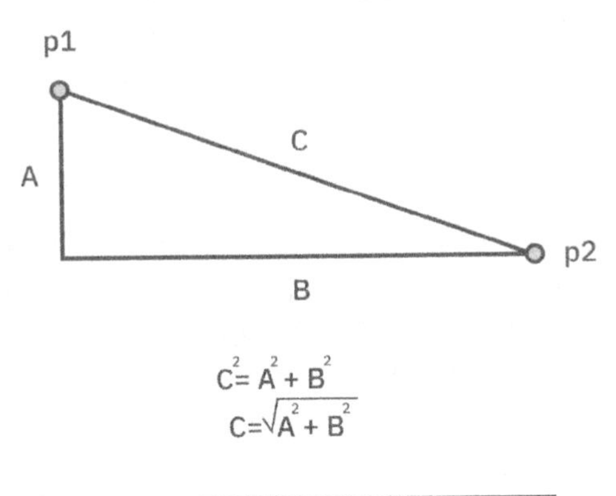

Add the following code below:

```
extension CGPoint {
  func distanceSquared(to point: CGPoint) -> CGFloat {
    let xDistance = (x - point.x)
    let yDistance = (y - point.y)
    return xDistance * xDistance + yDistance * yDistance
  }

  func distance(to point: CGPoint) -> CGFloat {
    distanceSquared(to: point).squareRoot()
  }
}
```

- `distanceSquared(_:)` calculates the hypotenuse's squared value by adding the squared distance of the opposite and adjacent sides.
- `distance(_:)` returns the hypotenuse by taking the square root of the distance squared.

Now that you've established a way to calculate the distance between two points, you have all the necessary information to form a minimum spanning tree!

> **Recall**: In the previous chapter, you learned how to construct a minimum spanning tree. You do this by picking an arbitrary vertex and greedily pick the cheapest edge to one of its neighboring vertices until an edge connects all the vertices.

To leverage Prim's algorithm, you must form a complete graph with the given set of points. A **complete graph** is an undirected graph where a unique edge connects all pairs of vertices. Imagine a five-sided pentagon with five vertices. Each vertex is connected to every other vertex to form a star!

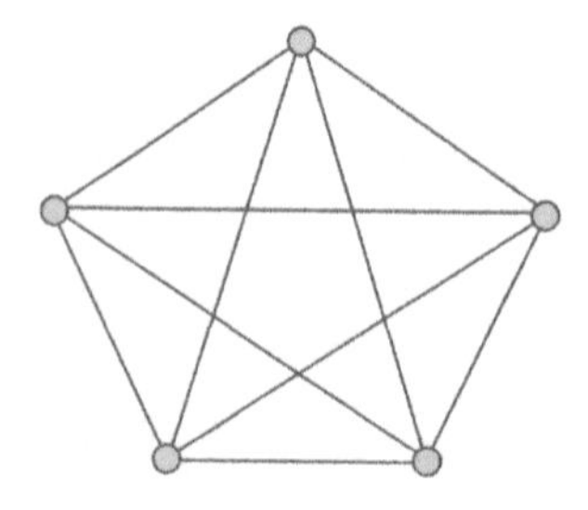

Add the following code:

```
extension Prim where T == CGPoint {

  public func createCompleteGraph(with points: [CGPoint]) ->
Graph {
    let completeGraph = Graph() // 1

    points.forEach { point in // 2
      completeGraph.createVertex(data: point)
    }

    // 3
    completeGraph.vertices.forEach { currentVertex in
      completeGraph.vertices.forEach { vertex in
        if currentVertex != vertex {
          let distance = Double(currentVertex.data.distance(to:
vertex.data)) // 4
          completeGraph.addDirectedEdge(from: currentVertex,
                                        to: vertex,
                                        weight: distance) // 5
        }
      }
    }

    return completeGraph // 6
  }
}
```

Here you create an extension as part of `Prim` and check if the element is of type `CGPoint`.

1. Create an empty new graph.
2. Go through each point and create a vertex.
3. Loop through each vertex and every other vertex as long as the two vertices are not the same.
4. Calculate the distance between the two vertices.
5. Add a directed edge between the two vertices.
6. Return the complete graph

You can now form a complete graph using the given points and leverage prim's algorithm to form a minimum spanning tree. Add the following after `createCompleteGraph(_:)`:

```
public func produceMinimumSpanningTree(with points: [CGPoint])
->
                                        (cost: Double, mst: Graph)
{
  let completeGraph = createCompleteGraph(with: points)
  return produceMinimumSpanningTree(for: completeGraph)
}
```

Below is a sample data set showing how the minimum spanning tree is formed:

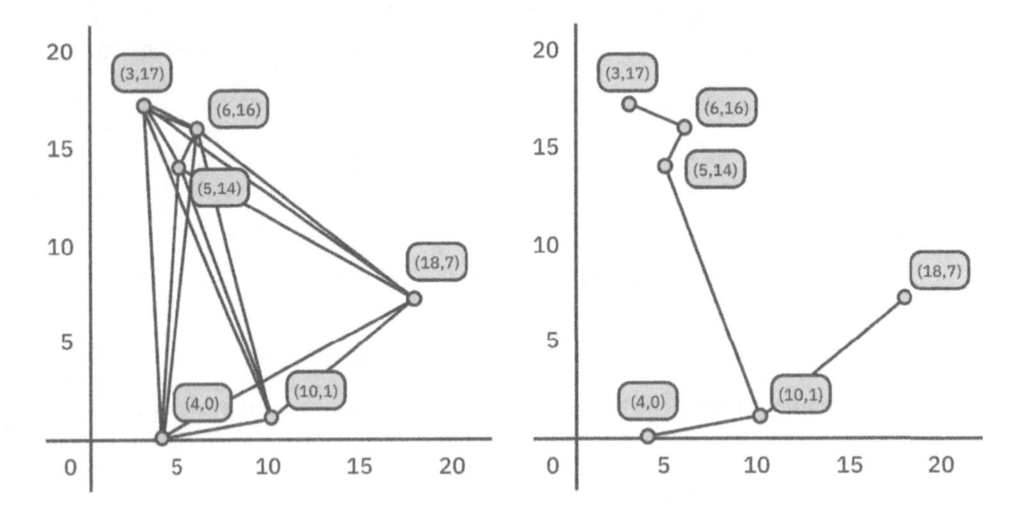

Solution to Challenge 2

The value of x is less than or equal to **5**.

Solution to Challenge 3

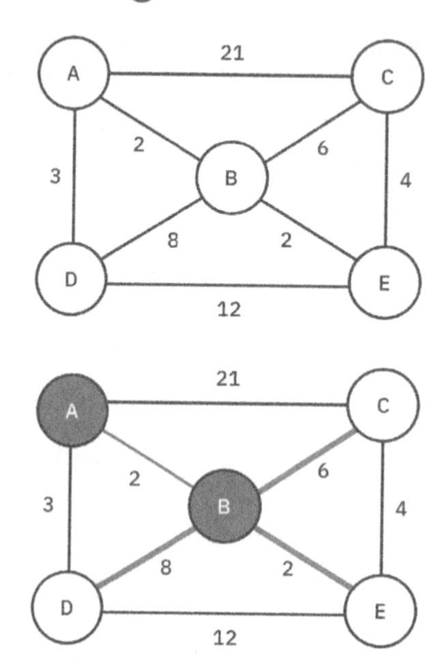


```
Edges [A:2, D:8, C:6, E:2]
Edges part of MST: [A:2]
Explored [A, B]
```

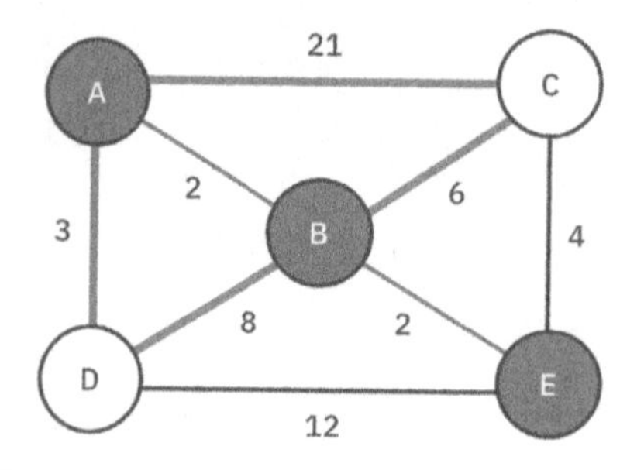


```
Edges [D:8, C:6, E:2, D:3, C:21]
Edges part of MST: [A:2, E:2]
Explored [A, B, E]
```

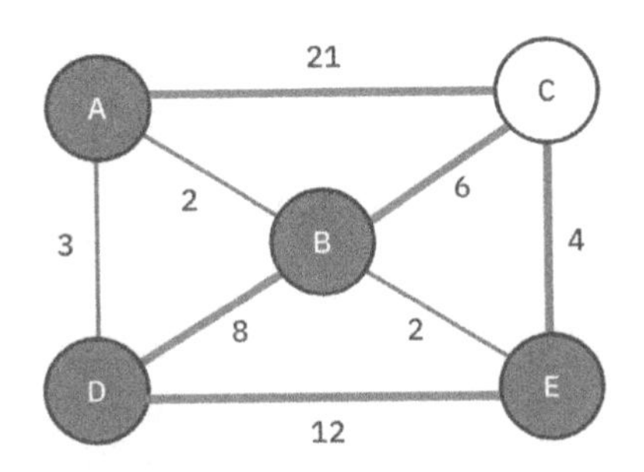


```
Edges [D:8, C:6, D:3, C:21, D:12, C:4]
Edges part of MST: [A:2, E:2, D:3]
Explored [A, B, E, D]
```

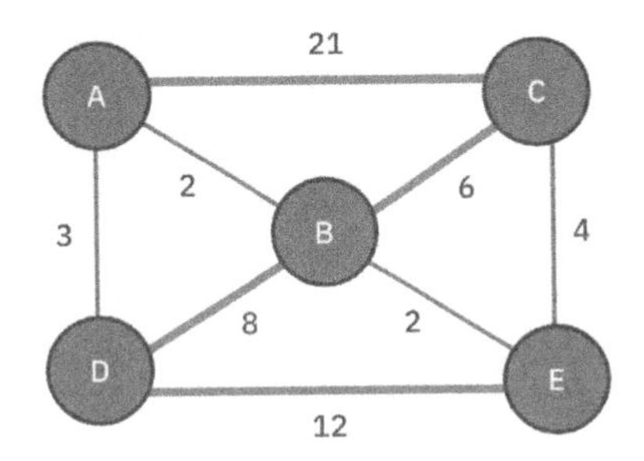


```
Edges [C:6, C:21, C:4]
Edges part of MST: [A:2, E:2, D:3, C:4]
Explored [A, B, E, D, C]
```

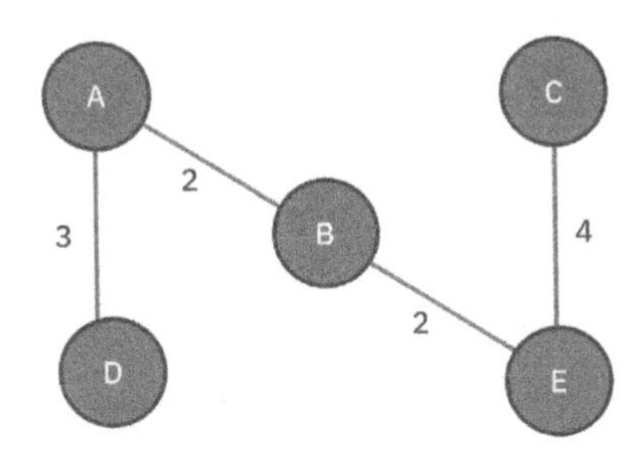


```
Edges [A:2, E:2, D:3, C:4]
Explored [A, B, E, D, C]
Total Cost: 11
```

46 Conclusion

We hope you learned a lot about data structures and algorithms in Swift as you read this book — and had some fun in the process! Knowing when and why to apply data structures and algorithms goes beyond just acing that whiteboard interview. With the knowledge you've gained here, you can quickly and efficiently solve pretty much any data manipulation or graph analysis issue put in front of you.

If you have questions or comments as you work through this book, please stop by our forums at https://forums.raywenderlich.com and look for the particular forum category for this book.

Thank you again for purchasing this book. Your continued support is what makes the tutorials, books, videos, conferences and other things we do at raywenderlich.com possible, and we truly appreciate it!

Wishing you all the best in your continued algorithmic adventures,

– Kelvin, Vincent, `Ray` and Steven

The *Data Structures & Algorithms in Swift* team

Made in the USA
Middletown, DE
17 February 2024